ROBBIE
A STRIKER'S STORY

by Paul Lennon

FOREWORD BY NIALL QUINN

Paperweight

First published in 2012 by Paperweight Publications, Level 4, Building 5,
Dundrum Townhouse Centre, Dublin 16, Ireland.

978-1-908813-02-2
Paul Lennon: Robbie: A Striker's Story

978-1-908813-03-9
Paul Lennon: Robbie: A Striker's Story - e-book

Printed and bound in the UK by
CPI Group (UK) Ltd, Croydon, CR0 4YY

Paperweight Publishing Group, Level 4, Building 5,
Dundrum Townhouse Centre, Dublin 16, Ireland.

www.paperweightpublications.ie

Dedication

For Peter, Ellen, Josephine, Kate and Margaret.

Paul Lennon
Born in Drogheda, County Louth in July, 1963, Paul Lennon is a lifelong football fan, having attended his first game as a seven-year-old when his home town club was defeated in the 1971 FAI Cup final by Limerick after a replay. He has worked as a journalist since 1983, initially with the Drogheda Local News before joining the Meath Weekender and then moving to the Sunday Tribune and Irish Daily Star, for whom he has worked as football correspondent since 1992. Paul is married to Josephine and they have a teenage daughter Kate.

Edited by Eoin Brannigan and Des Gibson
Designed by Rob Baker

Acknowledgements

I wish to sincerely thank each and every person who helped with the production and compilation of this book. Without their assistance it would not have been possible to complete the task.

Rob Baker, Lisa Bergin, John 'Bower' Bradley, Eoin Brannigan (sports editor Irish Daily Star), John Byrne, Peter Byrne, Ger Colleran (managing director Irish Daily Star), Eddie Corcoran, Eddie Cox, Glenn Crowe, Derek Daniels, Lynne D'Arcy, Cathal Dervan, Gavin Doyle, Kevin Fahy, John Fallon senior, John Fallon junior, Derek Foley, Larry Fox, Liam Gaskin, Des Gibson (deputy editor Irish Daily Star), Shay Given, John Givens, Ray Houghton, John Hudson, Greg Keane, Paul Kavanagh, Gary Kelly, Norman Kelly, Ger Keville, Derek Kinnevey, Jem Loughran, Martin Loughran, Jason McAteer, Mark McCadden, Mick McCarthy, Joe McGrath, Ronan O'Flaherty, Michael O'Kane (editor Irish Daily Star), James O'Reilly, John O'Shea, Niall Quinn, Philip Quinn, Robert Reid, Kathryn Rogers, Richard Sadlier, Peter Sherrard, Neil Silver, Manuela Spinelli, Charlie Stuart, Marco Tardelli, Giovanni Trapattoni, Declan Weldon, statistician Michael Hayes, all the staff at The Irish Daily Star, the printers at CPI Mackays, distributors Easons and you for buying the book.

Most of all, thanks to my wife Josephine and daughter Kate for their patience in recent months.

- **Paul Lennon,** May 2012

CONTENTS

Foreword
by Niall Quinn

WHAT a remarkable football career Robbie Keane has enjoyed in the past 15 years. And as somebody fortunate enough to play alongside Robbie for Ireland between 1998 and the 2002 World Cup finals in Japan and South Korea, I know at first-hand what an outstanding striker he is.

When Robbie first came into the Ireland squad, he couldn't sit still in training. Mick McCarthy would be trying to make a point and he'd have to say to Robbie, 'hey, calm down you'.

Then Mick would be talking again and Robbie would keep doing his own thing, his flicks and drills with the ball. Mick would have to pull him up and say 'do you mind?' In the end, Mick would take the ball off him and start again.

That cheekiness was there, as was the keenness. Robbie fitted in with the lads straight away. He didn't sit behind, cowering away from people. He loved it from the start, that was clear. In training, you could see he had an eye for goal and that was one of his strengths. He was always running non-stop, always busy and active. He slotted in well.

One of my most perceptive moments — although I didn't know it at the time — was after Robbie scored two goals against Malta in the 5-0 win at Lansdowne Road in 1998. They were his first international goals.

As I was walking from the pitch at the end of the match I was asked about Robbie's performance by RTE's Tony O'Donoghue, and I said: "Well I'm trying to get Frank Stapleton's Ireland goals record and this guy could double it — he could get 40 goals."

Tony laughed and I'm led to believe that when it went back to the studio, our good friends in there claimed Niall Quinn shouldn't be making reckless comments like that.

I can look back on that now with great pride. Robbie was

only playing first-team football with Wolves for just over a year at that time and has since gone on to become the greatest international goal-scorer in Ireland and the British Isles, which is a fantastic achievement.

After we qualified for the 2002 World Cup, I went to Mick McCarthy for a chat. My back was at me, I wasn't as fit as I could have been and I said to Mick that I could understand if he wanted to bring someone else to the tournament in Japan and South Korea. He said that we were light in terms of physicality.

We had David Connolly, Damien Duff, Robbie and Clinton Morrison so I thought to myself 'I've a job to do because I've been to a World Cup before'. I got myself prepared as best I could and then the whole hornets' nest stirred before the finals in Saipan. It was hard to work out whether I had made the right decision or not.

I didn't get a run in the first game against Cameroon and in the second game against Germany it didn't look great when we went behind. But I went on and felt comfortable. We got the goal late on when Robbie famously got on to one of my flicks. All I used to say to Robbie — and to Kevin Phillips when we were together at Sunderland — was that 'no matter where I am, I will head the ball inside, I will never head it straight towards goal'.

That's what happened in the Germany game. I turned so that I headed the ball inside, hoping that Robbie would be there. And he was. From my angle, I saw the goalkeeper, Oliver Kahn, get a touch and then the net bulged. It was a great moment.

Even though I was the old stager, I got caught up in the middle of the celebratory ruck. And when Richard Dunne, the last one to arrive, jumped on my back, that was my World Cup as good as gone. I barely got through the remaining two games.

To get the best out of Robbie, sometimes you have to play him at his own game. If he scored a goal, you'd tease him about the one he missed. You had to knock him to kid him along. In the early days, you'd say, 'when are you going to do some running', and he'd nearly always come back at you and say 'I am running, old man'.

That night at the World Cup against Spain, when we drew 1-1 with Robbie's last-minute penalty, he showed the world his burgeoning maturity. This may sound hard on Ian Harte, but if Robbie had taken the first penalty, things might have been a bit different.

I had a fairly good partnership with John Aldridge but it was a little bit easier to play up front alongside Robbie. I felt we worked well together and I always enjoyed playing with him. From the start, he was cheeky, he was like a firework, buzzing, lighting up the place. He was always on the move.

Even though players lose their pace as they get older, Robbie's always held that ability to sniff out a chance. Ahead of his 32nd birthday, he's not finished but I believe he hasn't got the credit for all he has done.

When I was growing up, I read about Bobby Charlton's 49 goals for England — every kid interested in football knew about it. It was said that nobody would ever touch it again.

There was an outcry when Gary Lineker tried to chip the keeper from the spot in his attempt to equal that record against Brazil before the Euro 92 finals. Graham Taylor only ever picked him for one more competitive match.

Then, all of a sudden, this lad from our country comes along and beats the record with 53 goals for Ireland at the time of writing. Sky Sports highlighted it after the game against Macedonia when he beat Charlton's record, but I think a much bigger deal should have been made out if it. It's absolutely phenomenal what he has done for Ireland as we're not a major power like England.

Ever since Steve Staunton handed him the captaincy in 2006 he has embraced the role very seriously and I feel that it has driven him on as a player. I like the way he's spoken about players who haven't turned up. It's put an onus on them to get themselves in order. Yet, I still see the cheekiness that has been his trademark during his career, that bit of panache.

Looking into the future, if Ireland qualify for Brazil 2014 should Ireland go to the finals without Robbie Keane? I don't think so.

Robbie reminds me a lot of Kevin Phillips who is still going strong at the age of 38. The hardest thing in football is to put the ball in the net. That's why those guys are paid the most and loved the most.

He could be a Ray Houghton-like figure at the European Championships but it's funny that he has to get another goal or two to receive the adulation which I feel he already deserves.

Paul McGrath was the probably the greatest player I played with for Ireland. Liam Brady, too, was amazing, but I wasn't with him at his best. They say John Giles was brilliant and Roy Keane obviously gets a shout. Robbie is right in there.

The title of Ireland's greatest player, in my eyes, should be a five-way tussle between Robbie, Paul, Roy, John and Liam.

If Robbie has a good tournament in Poland and Ukraine, if he gets a winning goal, he will move on to a new level with the public in terms of his place as one of Ireland's all-time greats. For me, he's already there.

Chapter 1
On top of the world

THE expensive timepiece on the wrist of referee Kim Milton Nielsen was ticking towards the third minute of stoppage time on a sultry night in Kashima Stadium. Within 90 seconds, Nielsen would sound three short, shrill blasts on his whistle to signal the end of this 2002 World Cup Group E match between Germany and Ireland.

Mathematically, if the 1-0 scoreline in Germany's favour remained, Mick McCarthy's side would still have a chance of qualifying for the last 16. But football reality dictated otherwise, and Miroslav Klose's 19th-minute goal had left the Boys In Green in a precarious situation.

Added to Ireland's opening day 1-1 draw with Cameroon, and with the African nation due to play group whipping boys Saudi Arabia 24 hours later, only the wildly optimistic would have suggested that the Irish could advance on the basis of taking one point from their first two games, even if they were playing the Saudis in their final encounter.

Four years earlier the Danish referee had controversially sent off David Beckham for England against Argentina in Saint-Etienne after Beckham flicked out with his boot at Diego Simeone. In the years that followed, the highly respected Nielsen would flash a red card at another Manchester United icon, Wayne Rooney, when he sarcastically clapped his hands in the official's face during a Champions League match.

On June 5, 2002, the eastern city of Kashima, located 80 miles northeast of Tokyo, looked like being the place where a turbulent three weeks for Irish football would end in disappointment. Ireland required a breakthrough of miraculous proportions in the shape of an injury time goal to keep alive the team's hopes of qualifying for the knockout phase of the tournament.

Step forward Robbie Keane, whose innate ability to read where Niall Quinn's headed flick would land proved crucial. The 21-year-old timed his run perfectly, controlled the ball with his midriff and then steered a right-foot shot high into the Germany net off the inside of the post. These few seconds of magic from the Ireland striker had transformed the side's championship and triggered wild celebrations.

"I knew the goal was coming," gushed Keane with a confidence that belied the fact that he had been brilliantly denied by Germany's fearsome keeper Oliver Kahn deep into the second half as the Irish began to turn the screw.

"It was like a film in my head. I said to Quinny that I knew he was going to come on and he'd flick one on to me. When I saw he was coming on, I knew that was it. When I scored, I realised that it had been in my head. Quinny could not have placed the header any better for me.

"When Quinny headed the ball down, it came off my stomach and fell well for me. Kahn was on fire and it looked like nothing would go past him. I'd had an overhead shot before that and missed it when I should have scored.

"I saw Kahn coming out this time, he comes out very fast and he looks huge. So I kept coming and I just hit it. He even got a hand to it. Sometimes you need a bit of luck, it hit the post and went in."

Keane made the most of the split-second he had to shoot before the covering Thomas Linke or Christoph Metzelder could close him down. He joked of the big duo: "If they had caught me, they would have killed me!"

With Kahn on his knees in shock, Keane raced to the corner flag and celebrated with his trademark cartwheel of delight. Ireland manager Mick McCarthy punched the air with a mixture of relief and ecstasy while the estimated 20,000 Irish fans in the attendance of 35,854 erupted. Back home, with the time creeping towards 2.30 in the afternoon, millions decided to drop tools and salute the Boys In Green. It was an equaliser that the Irish thoroughly deserved, even if they were outplayed in the opening 25 minutes and had been fortunate not to concede a second goal when, as Ireland left gaps at the back, towering striker Carsten Jancker bore down on Shay Given's goal only to send his shot wide.

Manager McCarthy recalled: "For 15 minutes they were really strong, over-ran us and scored the goal with Miroslav Klose's header. They were the better side. But from the minute they scored, we settled down and played really well.

"We deserved our draw and were the superior team for most of the game. Before half time we were playing great stuff. And then Robbie equalised. It was one of those that a striker just touches, and he has got such technical ability. In training we used to applaud him. Some of the stuff he did was outstandingly good, scarily good. He was and still is such a talent."

From being on the verge of putting one foot on the KLM jumbo jet for home, Keane had instructed the Ireland squad, management and the fans to prepare for a longer sojourn at the tournament. And the post-match party back in the squad's New Otani Hotel base in Makuhari Messe — halfway between the metropolis of Tokyo and industrial city of Chiba on the north-eastern curve of Tokyo Bay — reflected the fact that this World Cup was now all about football.

The simmering Saipan row between McCarthy and Roy Keane had been consigned to the background. It was little surprise that players, management, backroom staff, FAI officials and staff, family members, friends, supporters and some members of the media managed to guzzle their way through around €20,000 worth of drink!

With Cameroon only beating Saudi Arabia 1-0 the following day thanks to Samuel Eto'o's goal, Ireland knew that a two-goal winning margin against the gulf power in the final group game in Yokohama would guarantee their passage to the second round, no matter what happened between Germany and Cameroon in Shizuoka. As it transpired, Germany's comfortable 2-0 success meant that a victory by any margin against Saudi Arabia was enough for the Irish, who would leave no room for error with a 3-0 success.

Ireland had again reached the second phase of the World Cup finals to emulate their predecessors' achievements at Italia 90 and USA 94. And the pivotal figure was Robbie Keane, whose late intervention against the Germans would be followed up by his classy volleyed strike against the Saudis in the seventh minute to lay the foundations for Ireland's biggest ever margin of victory at a major tournament.

For a footballer still a few weeks shy of his 22nd birthday, it was a truly remarkable feat, but one that had been built on four years of sustained development in McCarthy's team. Germany had Klose, England boasted Beckham, Brazil featured a certain Ronaldo and Sweden could name-check Henrik Larsson. But Ireland fans could proudly proclaim the name of Keane less than a month after a player of the same name had split the country following his exit from the squad in a seismic Saipan episode.

Robbie Keane was arguably not even Ireland's best player in the four games in Japan and South Korea during that gripping, pulsating month. Many awarded that accolade to Damien Duff.

In the wake of Roy Keane's dismissal by McCarthy, and then the failure of subsequent efforts to reconcile the skipper and manager in the week leading up to the opening match, the players were mentally shattered. McCarthy and his coaching staff were equally drained. It showed on their faces in the 48 hours prior to the 1-1 draw with Cameroon in Niigata.

The first half of that game didn't go well, and the Irish went in trailing at the interval to Patrick Mboma's 39th-minute finish. During the break, Irish fans — who had paid thousands of euro to travel to the finals — sat glumly in their seats.

Fortunately, below them in the Irish dressing-room, McCarthy and Matt Holland were issuing rallying cries that inspired a second-half resurgence. Holland equalised in the 52nd minute, Keane struck the post and substitute Steven Reid forced keeper Alioum Boukar into a stunning late save to keep out his fiercely-hit drive.

If Duff's wizardry on the ball was mesmerising, Niall Quinn's impact from the bench crucial, Shay Given's saves impressive and the workrate of midfielders Holland and Mark Kinsella indispensable, it was Keane's goals that became the understandable focal point of the team's journey from Niigata to their exit in Suwon.

In the 2002 World Cup finals, Keane was the poster boy of the Ireland team with the performances and goals to go with it. It was a campaign that began in the Amsterdam Arena in early September, 2000 when Ireland took on a Dutch side depleted by retirements and injuries. The Dutch were also trying to overcome the shock of their Euro 2000 semi-final exit at the hands of Italy nine weeks earlier in the same stadium.

In the absence of Edgar Davids, Dennis Bergkamp, Jaap Stam, Ruud van Nistelrooy, Marc Overmars and Keane's new Inter Milan teammate Clarence Seedorf, Ireland took a 2-0 lead through Keane's 21st-minute header and Jason McAteer's brilliantly taken 65th-minute shot.

However, the hosts hit back with late goals from Jeffrey Talan and Giovanni van Bronckhorst. And it would take a stunning piece of defensive work in the dying seconds by Richard Dunne to prevent Patrick Kluivert from nicking an undeserved winner. In the aftermath of the draw, skipper Roy Keane accused McCarthy of asking his side to retreat during the second half and inviting on the Dutch to claim a point they didn't appear capable of winning.

It was a public glimpse of the fissure developing between the pair that would erupt on a remote Pacific island 20 months later. The foundations for the successful 2002 World Cup qualifying campaign were laid during the US Cup trip in June, 2000 to Chicago (2-2 draw with Mexico), Boston (1-1 draw with USA) and New York (2-1 win against South Africa) when McCarthy used a squad comprising experienced internationals that numbered Quinn, Terry Phelan, McAteer, Mark Kennedy, Alan Kelly, Given and Phil Babb. Also on that trip were relative rookies and uncapped players like Robbie Keane, Kevin Kilbane, Dean Kiely, Stephen Carr, Richard Dunne, Barry Quinn, Dominic Foley, Gary Breen, Gareth Farrelly, Stephen McPhail, Gary Doherty and Alan Mahon.

The performances against average opposition may have been mixed but the team-bonding in the three cities was memorable, aided by the fact that the squad was based in Fitzpatrick's Grand Central Hotel in downtown Manhattan during the final leg of the 10-day trek. McAteer, 29 going into those World Cup qualifiers, recalls that his initial exchanges with Robbie Keane were feisty. However, the pair quickly developed a strong relationship that later became a key factor in the team's strong displays in a group that also included Portugal.

"My first real recollection of Robbie was that the youths and Under-20 teams were making noises in the late 1990s and that there was a lot of talk of a lot of good young players coming through, like Robbie and Damien," says McAteer.

"Gary Kelly, Phil Babb and myself were brought in as young blood in 1994 but it was a really hard job finding young players at that stage. Then there was talk of this golden team coming through and we thought that was brilliant as we could then be the senior lads with these boys coming through.

"Being at Liverpool at the time, I was probably a big hitter in the squad when Robbie came into the squad. We went to America and he was cheeky with the real arrogance of a young kid who, instead of showing respect, showed none. He went the other way. There are people who show you a lot of respect when they come into the squad, but he was the opposite and showed none at all.

"It was something that I didn't really like and I didn't really hit it off with him. We had words. But it cleared the air and we both knew where each other stood.

"I was at Liverpool when he came into the squad and had played in big games. I was also with Ireland for a number of years and you have this cheeky kid who is calling me all kinds of things and taking the piss out of me," adds McAteer, whose patience finally snapped during an evening of sightseeing in the Big Apple.

"So he needed putting in his place and we had words. Once that happened, we started again and I would like to think now that we are very good friends and very close."

Keane had made a strong impact in the Euro 2000 qualifiers and McAteer is in no doubt that the Dubliner's emergence facilitated McCarthy's preference to develop a style of play that no longer relied mainly on the presence of a towering centre forward in the mould of Quinn or Tony Cascarino.

He added: "Robbie was good from day one and you could tell that he had bags of talent. His movement was unbelievable and he was something different from what I was used to playing beside with Ireland, when you were playing with Quinny, Cas, John Aldridge and Tommy Coyne up front.

"He was different and he liked getting the ball into feet, always wanted to be on the ball and offering himself for a pass. And that went against the way that Jack Charlton had decided to play. If you ever played the ball into the strikers' feet under Jack you could find yourself being dragged off. So it never really happened.

"I really enjoyed playing alongside Robbie because we had been quite one-dimensional with Jack. Jack had the players to play quite an expansive game and players like Roy Keane, Andy Townsend and Denis Irwin were great footballers.

"Quinny up front could play and I was on the wing and could play with decent feet. Under Jack we played a certain way, even though he had players who could play a different game. But the system worked, we played to it and got on with it.

"With Mick, I think he believed he had the players available to play a different way and let us express ourselves a bit more. And certainly when Robbie and Duffer came into the team, Mick said 'right, go and play'.

"That then released me to go and play on the wing and put more crosses in and maybe play one-twos on the edge of the box and not worry about giving the ball away.

"You knew you were going to get it back off Robbie and Duffer. Roy was also very supportive of that way of playing. Roy knew there was quality in the team, so why not play to it?

"So Robbie was in the right place at the right time in the sense of having the right international manager. I don't think he would have played under Jack as he was completely different from the type of striker that Jack liked.

"Robbie gradually gained the confidence of the lads. If you got the ball into him, he would do something with it and make something happen. That made him popular with the players as well as the fans."

On that opening night in Amsterdam on Saturday, September 2, 2000, McAteer hugged the line in his favoured right-wing role and set up Keane's headed opener with a measured cross from the endline.

McAteer continued: "Robbie really flourished in that campaign. He had come through his bedding-in period and had made a name for himself in the squad. He and Duffer were big players in that campaign. They were not kids anymore and there was a lot of expectation on them to do well.

"Going into the campaign nobody really gave us a chance but among the lads we knew we had enough quality to get results against Portugal and Holland. The first game was away to Holland and we were at peak fitness as it was September, a time when we were all doing well at club level.

"So we were always going to give the Dutch a game and then Robbie got the first goal. I put a ball in and he met it with a great header. Then myself and Robbie linked up for my goal. There were good little passages of play and we outplayed the Dutch that night. It was the sign of things to come in that campaign that we were not going to be one-dimensional.

"We played some nice football in that group and got great results, so we deservedly ended up qualifying."

As can often happen in sport, Keane's well-taken header against the Dutch would be his last goal in the green shirt for

14 months as he endured a hugely-frustrating spell that saw him fail to find the net in six competitive and two friendly games.

Significantly, Keane's two goals were crucial as he netted in the 2-2 draw away to the Dutch and also scored in the 2-0 play-off home success against Iran. That win provided a sufficient cushion for the 1-0 away defeat in the Tehran second leg not to derail Ireland's path to the finals.

"Robbie's amazing goal record for Ireland did not surprise, he was always a goal scorer, always one who sniffed out chances," adds McAteer.

"The best goal scorers that I have played with — the Fowlers, the Aldridges, the Rushies — have got the knack of being in the right place at the right time. And Robbie has got that, he knows where to be.

"And he's a very, very clever player and if you are on his wave-length you strike up a good partnership. I always felt that me and Robbie had a great partnership and I created a lot of goals for Robbie because I would put the ball into certain areas and he would be on the end of it.

"Against Holland away, I crossed for him and then in the home play-off against Iran he scored from the free kick I sent in that Gary Breen knocked down."

Keane and Quinn started that World Cup qualifying group as the first-choice Ireland strikeforce, although Duff partnered Keane against Holland at Lansdowne Road, in an indication of things to come in the finals. On that memorable day, McAteer's coolly-taken goal secured Ireland all three points and ensured that the side would at least finish second in the group and clinch a play-off spot.

"It was the big man, little man combination and when you have the brains that Robbie has, he was able to read where Quinny was going to put the ball," adds McAteer.

"Quinny was a very clever player, he knew where Robbie liked to run. They hit it off and became a good partnership. I would hit balls in from the right, Ian Harte from the left with

Robbie getting on the end of Quinny's knockdowns. It was a system that worked but not in the way that Jack had it."

McCarthy had thrown Keane into the opening Euro 2000 qualifier against Croatia in September, 1998 and watched the teenager mature for both club and country. Now, with Keane playing for Inter Milan, McCarthy was looking to him to score goals but to also harness the now 20-year-old's youthful enthusiasm.

"Robbie was not the big player or the 30-year-old superstar of the team," says McCarthy. "He came in when he was 17 and was only 21 when he played at the World Cup finals. He was so young and fresh and he just wanted to play football.

"It's a cliché but he did play as if he was playing in the park on a Sunday. In training, he did things with the ball that had us applauding. He was vital for me because it was Robbie or Quinny up front, or Robbie and somebody else. Him and Duffer were a really good partnership in the World Cup and it probably suited playing that way at the tournament."

While Keane suffered his longest goal drought at international level, Ireland made steady progress through a testing group. A month after the draw in Amsterdam, Matt Holland's 25-yard drive secured an equaliser and a share of the spoils with Portugal in the old Stadium of Light in Lisbon. A 2-0 home win over dogged Estonia was followed by a flattering 4-0 away success over Cyprus in Nicosia. It was a night when Roy Keane's inspirational presence allowed the visitors to overcome a very patchy 90 minutes, with two goals by the Corkman and one each from uncle and nephew, Gary Kelly and Ian Harte.

The squad then flew to Barcelona for the following Wednesday's 3-0 victory over Andorra, with Roy Keane's understandable fury over the steerage class conditions for the players on the initial flight from Dublin to Larnaca made public in a Sunday newspaper interview the morning after the Cyprus match.

Unfortunately for all concerned, the cramped conditions on the plane to the Catalan capital were even worse. The fuse for Saipan was now burning brightly. In June, Roy Keane once again put aside his reservations about the squad's logistical preparations and arrangements by capping a classy personal display in the 1-1 home draw with Portugal by scoring the opening goal, only for Luis Figo to level with a header. Four days later, Richard Dunne and Matt Holland were on target on a dreadful pitch in the Estonian capital of Tallinn to clinch a 2-0 win — the perfect professional 90 minutes from the Irish, although Robbie Keane did not start and was an unused substitute.

He had ended the 1999-2000 club season at Coventry City suffering from several niggling injuries and had been hauled ashore on the hour mark during the Portugal game. Estonia was the only time that Keane did not start for McCarthy when available, although the manager insists that it was down to a lack of fitness rather than any dip in form by the forward.

"We played well on a tip of a pitch and beat them 2-0," says McCarthy. "I would not be leaving Robbie Keane out, he was such a good player. There would have been something wrong with him or something not right to make a decision like that."

McAteer's unforgettable winner against the Dutch in Dublin the following September meant that Ireland were now playing for automatic qualification for the finals against the Portuguese, with Louis van Gaal's men holed under the waterline by their defeat in Dublin and their surprise earlier 2-0 home reversal by Portugal. But Ireland's 5-0 success over the visiting Cypriots in the final group game could not prevent Portugal from topping the group on goal difference, to condemn the Irish to a tricky two-legged showdown with Iran in November.

Fortunately, Keane got back among the goals at Lansdowne Road in the 2-0 first-leg victory — Harte netting the first from the penalty spot — and Ireland duly booked their passage to the Orient after losing by the only goal in the return in Tehran.

Moving into 2002, McCarthy used the spring and early summer Lansdowne Road friendlies against Russia (2-0), Denmark (3-0), USA (2-1), Nigeria (1-2) and Niall Quinn's end-of-season charity testimonial against Sunderland at the Stadium of Light to mix and match his team.

With the manager unsure if Quinn — by now 35 — would be able to last 60 or 70 minutes in the heat and humidity of Japan, he was now deploying Duff as Keane's partner up front. And when Ireland strode on to the pitch to take on Cameroon in their opening fixture in Niigata on Saturday, June 1, it was Duff and Keane in attack with the versatile Kilbane on the left wing in a midfield that saw McAteer on the other flank and Holland paired with Kinsella in the centre.

"They were both fantastic players," outlines McCarthy about his front men. "Robbie had proved himself with such good movement and Duffer could drop and pick it up and damage them. And Robbie was able to do the same thing by stretching the opposition.

"We were not reliant on putting a ball up to a big man. We had fabulous midfield cover in Kevin Kilbane, Mark Kinsella and Mattie Holland. Either Gary Kelly, Steve Finnan or Jason McAteer could play on the right.

"We were really solid and we had two really great strikers, both could get goals and get away from defenders. They could also keep possession and run the channels. It was only me who thought that they could be a good pairing. They could both play up front, although it was a surprise to a lot of people. There was a lot of discussion about it but we had such a tough midfield four that we could play these two fantastic strikers."

And before the first ball was kicked, McCarthy had told the media during a press conference in the city of Izumo — where the Irish had been based after Saipan and prior to moving to Niigata — that he believed sacrificing Duff on the wing would work.

"I don't know anybody who has watched our games who would be happy to play against Robbie and Damien," declared McCarthy five days before the Cameroon game.

"They'll cause problems for every team and those two boys

could be the stars of the World Cup. If not injured, they are a real threat to any defence. Robbie and Damien both enjoy an excellent first touch, can explode with pace and are never afraid to take players on. That's a great sign because there are loads of strikers who are good on the ball but lack that extra bit of spark to go past people. On top of all this, Damien and Robbie enjoy a great understanding and that's vital in any pairing in attack."

Against Cameroon, Keane missed a good chance with a first-half header but would later strike the post as the Irish gathered momentum in the final quarter and finished the stronger of the two sides.

If Saipan had provided Irish sport's greatest nightmare, then the island's climate and the squad's dietary details and training sessions had left McCarthy's players in excellent physical shape — a condition that would be borne out in all four games at the finals.

Keane went into the tournament with 10 senior international goals from 33 appearances but with just two goals in the previous two years of competitive action. While there was no external pressure on the now Leeds United forward to rediscover his knack of hitting the net, Duff's role as a creator rather than a taker of opportunities meant that Ireland would require Keane to be on form during the tournament.

Not for the first time, Keane delivered with his equaliser against Germany. In an interview after that match he confirmed that his palpable inner belief in his talent at scoring was never far from his mind.

"If you miss a chance then you cannot be thinking about it or speculating that you will miss the next opportunity that comes your way," Keane stated before the Saudi Arabia game in Yokohama.

"I always feel that it's up to you to believe that you'll put away the next one, and thankfully that's what happened. It was great to score that goal but first and foremost drawing with Germany was a great result for the team. We showed the true character and spirit of the squad with the way we battled back from being a goal down.

"The game might have been in injury time but we never stopped believing and we got our reward in the 92nd minute. The goal is definitely up there as one of my favourites and to score in the World Cup finals is a dream come true.

"Growing up as a kid you always dreamed of playing in the finals, so the next big thing is to score in the tournament. Please God there is another goal or two out there but I'm not too bothered as long we get the result that sends us into the next round.

"I've had a great time since I arrived over here and I feel quite sharp in training. Before the Cameroon match, Niall Quinn said that you must enjoy moments like these because they don't come around too often. I took that into account and now I hope that we can get the right result against Saudi Arabia and advance to the next round."

For one man in particular, Keane's goal against the Germans struck a deep chord. That was Noel Byrne, who had first managed Keane for Fettercairn United and who watched the late drama in Molly Heffernan's pub.

"My wife Patricia and Anne, Robbie's mam, were crying their eyes out when he scored — what a moment," said Byrne, who would have further reasons to acclaim his former star before the month was out.

Within seven minutes of the start of the final group match against Saudi Arabia, Keane was on target with the goal that sent Ireland on their way to a 3-0 victory.

"When Gary Kelly sent in the cross I could see Mattie Holland coming in," said Keane. "I shouted 'leave it' to Mattie and he did, which gave me the chance to connect well with it."

Gary Breen's angled strike and Duff's late shot through the hands of goalkeeper Mohamed Al-Deayea rounded off a clear-cut victory on the scoreboard that was anything but in reality, given the largely subdued Irish display.

The move leading up to Keane's goal against the Saudis had been started by Steve Staunton's superb inch-perfect cross-field pass from the left to the raiding Gary Kelly, who then hooked his cross into the penalty area where Keane met it with a right-foot volley.

"I played the ball in from the right endline and Robbie caught it on the volley," says Kelly. "That settled us because it was the first goal on the night and we needed to win that game by two goals to make sure we went through.

"You would rather play against the bigger teams as you are on a no-loser, but against the likes of Saudi Arabia they can go out on a given day and beat one of the bigger teams, such as us."

It was also the night when Keane's bow-and-arrow celebration routine replaced his usual cartwheel.

"I did that for a friend back in England who I spoke to on the phone before the match," revealed Keane. "He asked me to do the bow-and-arrow celebration if I scored. I don't know why he asked me but I was happy to do it."

Back in Tallaght, Keane's family, friends and neighbours joined the celebrations with gusto, as Kevin Farrell of the Irish Daily Star confirmed from Robbie's estate, Glenshane Grove. Robbie's aunt Vivienne and uncle, Noel Byrne, beamed their delight for the photographer.

"Thank God for today, thank God for Robbie Keane," said locally-based Holy Union nun Sister Geraldine, who had taught Keane at St Brigid's Junior School and St Aidan's Primary School.

"Today Tallaght is making the national news for all the right reasons. It could not have happened to a nicer chap or a nicer family. He was just a thin little lad. I remember he'd be out with a ball from the age of four. But when you were passing by, he would stop. He was always so mannerly."

Keane's dad, Robert, echoed those sentiments, stating: "We're delighted for Tallaght and for Rob — it was marvellous."

His mother was almost bursting with pride as she declared: "He has now scored two goals in two games. We are so, so proud of him. He's a great lad."

Keane's family and friends raised a glass in celebration. The striker, himself, found it impossible to do so. For the second consecutive game, Keane had been drawn at random to undergo a FIFA drugs test that required him to provide a urine sample immediately after the game.

Three hours later, Keane finally managed to produce the 75 millilitres just as his teammates — apart from Kevin Kilbane, who was also selected — were quenching their thirsts on pints of Asahi, Kirin and Suntory.

"I was called over straight after the final whistle and I didn't even get time to go into the dressing room," revealed Keane.

"My name came out of the hat and it was unfortunate that it did two games in-a-row. I was in bits after the game and I drank about eight bottles of water to try and produce a sample. In the end it worked but it didn't help me too well in bed last night!" added Keane two days later.

"It took me almost three hours to produce a specimen, while I was also held back for two and a half hours after the Germany match. I didn't get back to the hotel until three in the morning along with Kevin Kilbane. It's a complete joke because people are asking me what it was like in the dressing room after the match and I haven't got a clue.

"To be honest, it's ridiculous and stupid from FIFA's point of view. They have got to sort something out about the way they do these tests. There must be another way of conducting the tests, because after the game is the wrong time.

"Maybe they should even do away with the urine sample and just take the blood sample, which is the same way as the other system. I don't mind being asked to do a second test, even if I've had one a few days earlier.

"All that concerns me is that the tests are carried out at the right time instead of being denied the chance to enjoy the craic and the banter with the lads after the match."

However, as the Ireland squad prepared to fly to Seoul ahead of their second-round game against Spain in Suwon, Keane gave an upbeat assessment of the tournament to that point.

"There's no doubt that this is the best part of my career because we are playing on the biggest stage. I'm enjoying every minute of it. And the fact that the team is doing well is great — and when you score a few goals it makes it even better."

McCarthy had built a squad that was competitive on the pitch and happy off it, with the manager giving his players a reasonable amount of flexibility when it came to relaxing between games.

Gary Kelly recalls how the players enjoyed the lengthy trip to the east and how Keane's new-found status as a World Cup star helped a number of the panel out of a sticky situation one night.

"We had the craic and we were kids who were lucky to be playing international football," recalls Kelly. "We were at a World Cup but we nearly forgot that we were at one!

"The Roy Keane situation was mental but we just really got on with it when it was over. Any team would have benefited from Roy but everybody else probably talked about it more than the players. At the time we did pull together, the banter in the camp was great and Robbie was always the life and soul of it. Then, Robbie and Duffer took that World Cup by the scruff of the neck.

"Scoring the equaliser against Germany was just fairytale stuff for Robbie. But it didn't change him one bit. He never got big-headed and he never became flash. In those finals, you just knew that if Robbie got half a chance then he could score. And that's what happened. As a result, we said to ourselves 'we have a chance of going on here'. "We all knew that Robbie was the star among the local fans. We could see it in the hotel and when people were asking for autographs. But it was an incident one night that really showed us how popular he was.

"Steve Staunton and his wife at the time, Joanne, organised a trip to Disney World near Tokyo. So most of the squad went except my wife Jules, me, Robbie, Richard Dunne, Richard's dad and uncle and the chef.

"We went on the razz and later in the evening 'Stan' Staunton organised a karaoke night. So we met up with the rest of them in this particular karaoke bar where you had to give the owners your passport to get in.

"We thought we were rock and roll stars and were really getting into the spirit of the event. Unfortunately, the owner did not understand our loud humour, panicked and called the cops. So these two policemen arrived. Joanne was panicking but Niall Quinn was crying with the laughter.

"Richard and myself thought we were done for but when the two cops saw Robbie they shrieked 'Raawbie Keeeane'. So Robbie had to get his picture taken with the two of them.

"Poor Stan flipped and said that Mick was going to kill us. But we got away with it because the two cops idolised Robbie."

The buoyant Ireland squad now flew to Seoul, where the success of the co-hosts in reaching the knockout stages had turned the South Korean capital into a party town.

When Guus Hiddink's side played, the main square of the city was packed with orderly, mainly young, flag-waving Koreans who would gather three and four hours before kick-off to watch the games on massive TV screens. The FAI hotel was just a two-minute walk from the square but any worries about late-night revelry by locals upsetting the sleeping habits of the Irish players were quickly dismissed as the centre of town shut down shortly after midnight.

Even on the night of Friday, June 14 — 48 hours before Ireland would play Spain — South Korea's 1-0 group win over Portugal in Incheon was celebrated with true fervour, but without the alcohol-fuelled sessions associated with most European fans. Within 45 minutes of the final whistle, the city centre was eerily quiet.

On Sunday, the Ireland party made the 90-minute trip south to Suwon for that evening's showdown against Jose Antonio Camacho's Spain, who had topped the relatively weak group of Paraguay, South Africa and Slovenia with maximum points.

It was not a side brimming with the individual talents of the Spanish team that would emerge by the end of the decade, but it still boasted keeper Iker Casillas, defenders Ivan Helguera, Carles Puyol and skipper Fernando Hierro, and the feared strikeforce of Raul and Fernando Morientes.

But there was real optimism in the Ireland camp that Mc-Carthy's men had the ability to progress to the last eight and so match the exploits of Charlton's side of 12 years previously.

It was a viewpoint that would be endorsed as the match wore on, only to be dashed in the penalty shoot-out. For the third consecutive match in these finals, McCarthy would name an unchanged side. And in a repeat of the games against Cameroon and Germany, Ireland started worryingly slowly and found themselves a goal down to Morientes' eighth-minute header which caught the Irish defence and midfield cold.

Ireland faced a massive task to turn around this game. Once more, Keane would be to the fore in this endeavour. Even before Spain's goal, Keane and Kevin Kilbane had knitted a neat one-two on the edge of the Spanish penalty area for Keane to curl a right-foot shot only narrowly wide with Casillas beaten.

Before the break, Keane's overhead kick just cleared the crossbar while in the opening minutes of the second period, Casillas dropped KIlbane's cross with Hierro forced to make a hurried clearance.

The Irish were pressing strongly for a goal and the 55th-minute introduction of Quinn for Kelly would prove once again to be pivotal. Duff now dropped to the right wing, where he began to give Juanfran a torrid time, leading to his concession of a 62nd-minute penalty when he made a mistimed challenge on Duff inside the area. However, Ian Harte chose the wrong moment to strike one of his rare poorly-hit spot kicks and Casillas parried, with Kilbane blasting the rebound well wide when it seemed easier to score.

Every Irishman, woman and child in the Suwon Stadium was crestfallen. Had Ireland's chance of taking the tie to extra time evaporated in the oppressive weather conditions that — as ever — had dark underarm patches of sweat on Camacho's light blue shirt?

The Irish regrouped, with Duff firing narrowly wide and David Connolly was sent on for Harte with nine minutes remaining. McCarthy was now playing 4-3-3 with Connolly and Keane flanking Quinn up front and the midfield of Duff, Kinsella and Holland pushed high up the pitch to pressurise the tiring Spaniards.

But for all the Irish possession, an equaliser did not look like materialising until an orthodox set-piece and a brave moment of refereeing by Anders Frisk combined to secure a second penalty of the night for Ireland.

Finnan's 89th-minute angled free kick from the right wing was drifting just beyond the penalty spot, where Quinn was the target. However, the veteran of Euro 88 and Italia 90 — who had been cruelly robbed of a role at USA 94 by a cruciate ligament injury — was never going to connect as Hierro had taken a vice-like grip of his shirt.

Most of these types of fouls go unseen by referees. Frisk had already awarded one cast-iron penalty so he would have received little or no flak from neutrals had he decided that Quinn may have been leaning into the vastly-experienced Hierro.

Frisk's career had included the Euro 2000 final between Italy and France in Rotterdam and he would go on to take charge of the semi-final of the 2004 tournament between Holland and Portugal before two disgraceful events in the 2004-05 season prompted the 42-year-old Swedish insurance official to retire early.

In September, 2004, Frisk was forced to abandon the Roma-Dynamo Kiev Champions League group game in Rome's Olympic Stadium when struck by a coin thrown by a home fan as the players and officials walked from the pitch at half-time.

UEFA awarded Dynamo a 3-0 victory and ordered the Italian club to play its remaining two home group games in an empty ground. By the following March, Frisk had quit the game following death threats made to him and his family by Chelsea supporters following a Champions League game against Barcelona. Frisk had sent off Chelsea striker Didier Drogba while Blues boss Jose Mourinho had made the false allegation that Frisk had invited Barcelona coach Frank Rijkaard into his room for a half-time chat. Mourinho received a touchline ban from UEFA for the quarter-final tie with Bayern Munich.

In Suwon, Frisk correctly pointed to the penalty spot and, with Harte now in the dugout, Keane readily took possession of the ball and coolly slotted his effort to Casillas's right, with the keeper diving to his left.

The tie would enter extra-time. The levelling goal flummoxed the Spaniards and Ireland continued to press forward as the additional 30 minutes ticked by. And the Irish cause was aided when David Albelda — only on the pitch since the 71st minute — was forced to retire at the midway point of extra time with an injury, leaving the Irish with an extra man.

However, McCarthy and the Irish bench did not appear to notice their numerical superiority as Duff later acknowledged. "We only found out a couple of days later," said Duff. "We were bossing them anyway. I don't think any of us knew they were down to 10."

Keane fired his left-foot volley from just outside the box narrowly wide while Connolly's low shot from similar range trickled agonisingly past the upright. Had either effort gone in, Ireland were through to the last eight by virtue of the same golden goal rule that would see South Korea controversially defeat Giovanni Trapattoni's Italy two days later.

So the tie went to spot kicks, with Keane putting Ireland one goal up with the first penalty. Hierro equalised before Holland hit the crossbar with the first of Ireland's three unconverted efforts. Ruben Baraja put Spain 2-1 up before Connolly, Juan-fran, Kilbane and Juan Carlos Valeron all failed to find the net. Finnan finally stopped the rot with a right-footed penalty that flew high into the net. Yet it would count for nothing if Gaizka Mendieta beat Shay Given with the last of the regulation 10 kicks. And the Lazio star calmly struck his low effort down the middle past Given to send Ireland out of the tournament on a 3-2 shoot-out verdict.

Many Irish fans and some Ireland players maintained that Mendieta miskicked his penalty, but he says otherwise.

"I did not miskick, I used to look at the goalkeepers and they usually moved earlier than you kick," explained Mendieta. "I saw Given going to his right. If you have more time to hit it, you can go closer or wider but because he was so close, he went too close.

"Even for myself, when I saw the ball I thought it was too close. But it was a bit in the air, it went over his boots and went in. It was the way I normally took penalties."

So the adventure in the Orient was over. As night gave way to dawn on Monday morning back in Seoul, the Irish players headed to bed trying to come to terms with their dramatic month and two days spent on international duty.

The judgment of the media on the side's performance against Spain was positive, yet critical of the failure to realise that the opposition had only 10 men when those in the press box had noticed it.

Around Ireland, the fans saluted the players who had dealt with the mental scars of Saipan to once again deliver a series of displays that bore the test of close scrutiny. Ireland may have drawn three of their four matches but they had avoided defeat and gone so, so close to making the last eight.

What's more, the same steely determination to battle for a

common cause and to forego personal glory — the foundation of the success at Euro 88 and the 1990 and 1994 World Cups — was again evident in bundles.

Roy Keane may have been absent but the squad had tapped into that same work ethic so beloved of the former skipper.

In Molly Heffernan's in Fettercairn, Robert Keane senior reflected on the pictures from Suwon.

He said: "We're gutted with the result but we're delighted with Robbie's performance. We're worn out. We just want to have a few drinks together and let it all sink in."

And mother Anne turned her thoughts to the heroes' return that would take place on Tuesday evening at Dublin's Phoenix Park.

"He did brilliantly, we are so proud of him," said Anne. "We are just dying to see him when he gets home."

As the family prepared to welcome home Keane, his 74-year-old granduncle, Roger, paraded his banner that declared: 'There's Only One Keano says Roger — Robbie!'

At the Phoenix Park — where the welcome home for the 1994 panel had been more muted — close to 100,000 fans thronged the famous 15 acres close to the Papal monument.

As the players and McCarthy were introduced to the crowd by RTE presenter Peter Collins, Keane grasped the microphone and said: "You are simply the best fans in the world."

Jet-lagged and exhausted, there was only one place where the players wanted to retreat to — Lillie's Bordello at the bottom of Grafton Street.

The party would last well into the early hours of Wednesday with Niall Quinn, Kevin Kilbane, Steve Staunton, Robbie Keane, Jason McAteer, Richard Dunne, Alan Kelly and Kenny Cunningham entertained by former Eurovision Song Contest winner Paul Harrington.

But it was Keane who stole the show with his rendition of David Gray's 'This Year's Love'. Even with the greatest show on earth now over for Ireland, Keane was still centre stage.

Chapter 2
Skinny little fella from Tallaght

IN the early summer of 1990 there was only one story in town as Jack Charlton and his Ireland football team took Italia 90 by storm.

If the unbridled joy of the nation's breakthrough at Euro 88 had been special, then the epic drama of the 1990 World Cup tournament topped it.

Never before had a single sporting event managed to secure such a mesmeric grip on the attention of so many Irish people. Until Euro 88, Ireland's international sporting success was largely achieved in individual codes, although the rugby team had achieved occasional glory in the Five Nations, albeit with limited world impact.

Athlete Eamonn Coghlan's success on the track, the elite standing of Sean Kelly and Stephen Roche in the pounding world of professional cycling, Dennis Taylor and Alex Higgins's exploits in snooker and Barry McGuigan's world featherweight boxing title had all helped lift the nation psychologically during the austere eighties. The continued success of Irish jockeys, horses and trainers in national hunt and flat racing was another source of pride.

However, none of these outstanding achievements competed with the World Cup, where the 24 best teams in the most popular game on the planet gathered in Italy — the country with three crowns and recognised as the leading European nation in the sport at that time.

A tournament that never really ignited and that produced too many dour matches appropriately ended with Andreas Brehme's well-taken penalty-kick winning the final for West Germany against an Argentina side ravaged by injury and suspension in Rome's Olympic Stadium.

Eight days earlier in the same arena, Ireland had been

squeezed out at the quarter-final stage by the hosts, thanks to Salvatore 'Toto' Schillaci's predatory strike after Packie Bonner failed to hold Roberto Donadoni's pile-driver.

More than two decades later, Jack Charlton and the Ireland players still maintain that the game against Italy was an encounter they could have won, or at least taken into extra time. But for a country that had never graced such a stage before, it was still an achievement to savour.

England and Holland had been held to 1-1 group draws and while the scoreless clash with Egypt in Palermo was horrendous to watch, the gripping outcome of the second round penalty shoot-out victory over Romania in Genoa temporarily halted an EU summit being held in Dublin and served up one of Irish sport's all-time iconic images, with Bonner's spot-kick save from Daniel Timofte. Seconds later, David O'Leary — banished from the squad by Charlton for two and a half years until a defensive and midfield injury crisis triggered a call-up in November, 1988 — stepped up to net the kick that meant Ireland were among the top eight international football teams.

No other sporting event had ever seduced the country's population in this manner and when the squad arrived back into Dublin the day after the defeat to Italy, close to 500,000 people thronged the streets of the capital to welcome them back.

In the Dublin suburb of Tallaght, the unfolding events in Italy had a deep impact on the population, just as it had throughout the land. This area of the capital — seven miles southwest from O'Connell Street at the foot of the Dublin Mountains — had been transformed from a sleepy, almost rural village of the 1960s into a sprawling but largely unplanned satellite town.

Houses — largely in the form of council estates — were built by the thousand but primary services such as schools, sporting amenities, proper transport links, shops, pubs, libraries and medical centres were often added as an afterthought. A few facts and figures starkly illustrate how quickly Tallaght had changed.

In the 1966 census, Tallaght's population stood at 2,476 but

15 years later it was a staggering 55,100, with the population growing by no less than 792 per cent in the 10 years from 1971 to 1981.

Tallaght was spared the high-rise tower blocks but was still poorly planned, with row after row of houses constructed on either side of the winding road to Blessington in county Wicklow. It was here, on newly-built Glenshane Grove, that Robert and Anne Keane raised their family from the early eighties when Robbie was still in a cot.

In common with the majority of Tallaght's citizens, the Keanes flourished as a family unit and as individuals despite the obstacles placed in their way by those in authority who should have known better. And Robbie — with older siblings Graham and Natasha and younger sister Amy — would enjoy his childhood where money was scarce but parental love, family security and a supportive community were present in abundance.

Robbie attended St Brigid's and St Aidan's primary schools in nearby Brookfield, an area that would experience the horrific trauma in February, 2012 of learning that 16-year-old Melanie McCarthy-McNamara's young life had been ended by a shooting.

Pretending that this part of Tallaght does not have its share of problems centring on crime, drugs and general delinquency would be to ignore the truth. Yet, the overwhelming majority of the people in the area have always been law-abiding. During the suburb's early years, most parents had grown up elsewhere in the city before relocating there. They would become proud of Tallaght while their children's roots were firmly embedded.

From primary school, Keane made the short journey to St Aidan's Community School in 1993, where he would make the acquaintance of teacher and vice-principal Kevin Fahy, who would share the emotions of his future underage success with Ireland in his role as a football official. Fahy had long been involved in the organisation of schools football in the Football Association of Irish Schools (FAIS), the FAI Youths Committee and, subsequently, the FAI Senior Council where he would ultimately serve as the FAI's hugely-respected honorary secretary in the early part of this century.

And when Brian Kerr's Under-16 and Under-18 sides conquered Europe in 1998 and competed in the FIFA Under-20 World Cup the following year in Nigeria, Fahy was chairman of the FAI Youths Committee and head of delegation.

"Robbie was a very quiet lad and he came from a very good family," says Fahy, who did not teach Keane but had his brother Graham and sister Natasha in class.

"There was never any problem with Robbie, he was always very well behaved at school. His parents would not have had it any other way. That's the kind of upbringing he had.

"I remember there was a Fettercairn youth team that was winning all around them and some players were then signed by other clubs. That was the first that I heard of Robbie and then I saw him playing. I was not involved in managing any of his teams but I could see that he looked the part. He was a small, very slight little fella and he was mates with Jason Gavin — whom I taught — who was also in the school.

"Jason and Robbie went off to England at the same time with Jason going to Middlesbrough. Jason was a big lad and when you looked at the contrast in their physiques, you would have thought that of the two, it was Jason who had the better chance of making it long-term in the professional game.

"Jason did get into the Middlesbrough first team and was very unfortunate with injuries, which blighted his career in England. Robbie had told us well before the Junior Cert that he was going off to Wolves so we were always wondering how he was getting on. Then somebody brought in 'Shoot!' magazine one day and there was a big article on Wolves with him being very central to it.

"The coach was talking about this young Irish guy he had and for whom they had very high hopes. Not too long after that he made his debut for Wolves against Norwich City and scored those two famous goals. It was onwards and upwards after that."

In a part of Dublin usually starved of good publicity, Keane's emergence as a potential star in the making was big news. Fahy clearly remembers the positive impact that Keane's progress at Wolves and with Ireland had inside and outside the school gates.

"It was a great boost for the school and for the area. We were delighted as Brookfield, Glenshane and Fettercairn are all our catchment area. It would be considered a tough neighbour-hood but with a lot of great people there, the vast majority of them. The area and the people did not always get the best publicity but it only takes a few to create a negative impression. So Robbie's success was really positive.

"When Robbie came home on holidays he would call down to the school before he became too famous! I remember after he made his Wolves debut that he visited us. He was not that long gone and the kids would have known him and greeted him with a 'Hi, Robbie'. He would also come into the staff room.

"Not too long afterwards, when he had moved to Coven-try City, Robbie called down at the end of the season to the school. He was strolling down to the staff room when there was a change of class. Suddenly, the school corridors were full of screams by the girls. We had to go and rescue him by bring-ing him into the staff room! However, that didn't stop him from coming back to the school."

Fahy pinpoints a trait that had already been noticed by Keane's school team mentors and that would become a recur-ring theme for all those who came into contact with him.

"What impressed me most about Robbie, apart from his goal scoring and pace, was his absolute self-belief and confidence. When he got a sniff of goal there was no hesitation. For a lad of 13 or 14 years of age, that was special."

Keane admits that academic qualifications did not rank too high in his list of life goals during his early teenage years.

"I wasn't interested in school, I was there for the football and the Gaelic football," says Keane.

"I played everything just to get half days. I never concentrated in school and I could never concentrate. I was always getting other people to help me out. I would come home and then I would be out playing football on the street. I would play until I was called for my dinner. Then it was straight back out again until it was time to go to bed. That's how I grew up."

Having completed his Junior Certificate examination, Keane moved to Wolves in the summer of 1996. However, apart from his hugely welcome visits to his alma mater, Keane and Fahy would enjoy several further reunions on foreign fields.

"When Ireland won the European Under-18 championships in 1998 in Cyprus, by happy coincidence I was chairman of the FAI Youths Committee and was head of delegation. And two past-pupils, Robbie and Jason Gavin, were on the team while Richard Dunne was also from the area. That was fantastic and the fact that we won the tournament was absolutely wonderful.

"I remember FAI commercial manager Eddie Cox got posters printed up with the Under-16 and 18 teams on it. I also asked photographer David Maher to take a snap of Jason, Robbie and I together at the end of the final. I got the poster and photo framed and presented them to the school."

As the most famous past pupil of St Aidan's, Keane's continued exploits for club and country remain a source of much pride for staff and pupils, current and past, alike.

"We would all be very proud of him, why would we not be!" says Fahy, who suggests that the striker is a role model for those enrolled at the school now.

"I agree, there's no doubt about it that he's a role model. The fact that he has achieved what he has achieved, particularly when he was appointed captain of Ireland, that was a very proud day for him, his family and also for the school as well. We were proud for him and it was a great honour."

When Ireland kicked off their World Cup finals campaign against Bobby Robson's England in Cagliari's Sant'Elia Stadium on June 11, 1990, Keane had not yet hit double figures in birthdays.

When he did celebrate his 10th year on July 8, he had been captivated by the television pictures, radio images and newspaper words transmitted back to Ireland of the historic events in Italy.

There were few boys across the land who were any different while a whole new generation of female fans were attracted to football for the first time. Men of a certain vintage shook their heads at the wonder of finally witnessing a team in green — and not from Northern Ireland — playing in the finals of the World Cup, while those women for whom football was a TV irritant happily signed up as fans for the month of June.

By 1990, Ireland had emerged from the worst of the 1980s recession but money remained scarce for most of the population. The majority of the hundreds of thousands who had quit the country in the previous decade had yet to venture back home to seek employment. Unemployment across the land in 1990 stood at 13.9 per cent according to the Central Statistics Office — a total that was down from the peak of that era of 17.3 per cent in 1985 but that would climb again to 15.7 per cent in 1993 before the steady and welcome decline to single digit figures recorded in 1998.

Finding a job in Tallaght in the late eighties and early nineties was an even tougher proposition in a part of the city where manual, skilled and unskilled trades traditionally offered work to the male population but had suffered badly in the recession.

So the percentage of those unable to find work in the area fluctuated from between 20 and 50 per cent from one area to another, as it did in many other working class areas of cities and towns. The Keanes were no different to many families in Ireland, where the basics of life were the priority ahead of luxuries that included sports gear.

"There were times when my parents could not afford to buy me football boots, that was the reality," explained Keane later as he discussed the incredible lifestyle that his football career had given him. Yet to suggest that financial hardship was a burden that sucked the life from the people of Tallaght would be well wide of the mark.

As was the case throughout Ireland, people knuckled down, made the most of what they had and prayed, worked and scrimped in the hope that matters would improve. And although it could not provide a remedy to Tallaght's problems, the opening of the massive Square Shopping Centre in October, 1990 acted as a lightning rod for local pride and a sense that the area was finally on an upward curve.

The area's development accelerated after Keane left to ply his trade in England, with the arrival in 2009 of Shamrock Rovers to the newly-built South Dublin County Council Tallaght Stadium offering a major boost. This, along with the Luas tramline from Dublin city centre, was hailed as a significant addition to a community that was no longer being overlooked by those in power.

Suggesting that the success of the Ireland football team was the catalyst for the Celtic Tiger has become fashionable in certain quarters, even if the truth is somewhat different. However, it cannot be denied that the Jack Charlton era gave millions of Irish people incredible joy and memories that would last a lifetime.

By the end of the last century, Tallaght would become the country's richest breeding ground of professional and semi-professional footballers, overtaking Dublin's traditional hotbeds such as Ringsend, Cabra and Finglas.

By 2000, several dozen were plying their trade in the League of Ireland while another 11 were on the books of clubs in England. Jason Gavin was with Middlesbrough, Stephen Bradley and Graham Barrett were on the books of Arsenal, Millwall had signed Mark Mulraney, Niall Byrne was recruited by Liverpool, Graham Gartland had opted for Barnsley, Richard Dunne was blossoming at Everton, Nottingham Forest snapped up Keith Foy, Conor Kenna had joined Coventry City along with Daire Doyle while Kenna's brother Ciaran had plumped for Doncaster Rovers. And then there was Keane at

Wolves and subsequently Coventry City.

As a kid, Robbie had spent every waking hour when not at school kicking a ball in the garden of the family's Glenshane Grove house, in the street, on the nearby green and at the rough-and-ready strip of ground that served as the home pitch for Fettercairn Youth Football Club.

Keane's mam, Anne, recalls the euphoria of Italia 90 among her own children and the neighbours' offspring.

"There wasn't anything for him to do growing up except play football," said Anne. "The area was nothing but fields and that's what he and his friends did all day, they kicked a ball around.

"He went football-mad around the time of the World Cup. He collected the stickers and everything. My dad was a brilliant footballer and when Robbie was only one he was kicking a ball. I remember my father saying to me 'If God spares me, that young fella is going to be a brilliant footballer'. I asked him why and he said 'he kicks with both feet'.

"Ever since Robbie could walk he's played with a ball. He was always mad about football. My dad went to see all of Robbie's matches and he used to cycle to them. But my father died when Robbie was 14 so he never got to see him playing in England."

In his early teens, Keane dabbled for a few weeks with kick-boxing at the local Black Panther club in Brookfield, where his good friend Derek Howe would go on to become a national champion. Founded by local man Norman Kelly in 1993, the Black Panther club offered local kids of all ages an opportunity to develop themselves in a well-run, disciplined and friendly environment.

Although Howe continued to progress in the tough sport with the club that now caters for more than 80 members, Keane — who also played Gaelic football for Naomh Eanna and Crumlin as a child — decided that football was where his own sporting vocation lay. And he didn't have to look far to find a home for his talent. The local Fettercairn YFC offered Keane the platform to harness the talent he had already shown in his garden, on the street and in the nearby park although there were others on the Under-11 side who were equally promising.

Fettercairn were managed by Noel Byrne, an uncle of Keane through marriage having wed Robbie's mother's sister, Patricia. Byrne's own son, Jason, was taking his own first steps in what would prove to be an outstanding career spent mainly in the League of Ireland, one that would see him become the country's secondmost prolific scorer of all-time in domestic football and win two senior Ireland caps.

Anne Keane's father, Thomas Nolan — who had played Gaelic football for St Agnes in Crumlin — sadly passed away before either Keane or his other gifted grandson Jason Byrne began their careers, but he was surely smiling down as the pair went on to score hundreds of goals in the senior game from the late nineties.

Byrne — two and a half years older than Keane — would also move from Fettercairn YFC to Crumlin United and then join St Colmcilles back in Tallaght. Shrewd Bray Wanderers manager Pat Devlin signed him for the League of Ireland club in the summer of 1998. And in a career which included an injury-ravaged stint at Cardiff City, he went on to play for Shelbourne, Bohemians and Dundalk, before returning to Bray in 2012.

Byrne clocked up his 183rd League of Ireland goal on April 13, 2012 while playing for the club that gave him his big break, establishing him as the second highest marksman of all time to Brendan Bradley on 235.

Keane thrived at Fettercairn YFC and scored freely as he got his first taste of the game on an organised basis. It was a period of his life that he did not forget, and he financially backed the re-establishment of the club in 2007 after it had ceased to operate for a number of years.

Today, the Los Angeles-based star still contributes to the ambitious club's funding of its nine schoolboy teams and one Leinster Senior League Major One side and also attends the annual trophy presentation. And in keeping with the family tradition, his cousin Jason and uncle Noel are part of the coaching set-up that caters for hundreds of children.

Keane's exploits with Fettercairn were noticed by two men who had been handed the responsibility of co-managing the Crumlin United Under-12 team for the 1991-92 season in the Dublin and District Schoolboys League that had established its own place in the football lore of these islands by producing hundreds of Ireland internationals.

Larry Fox and Jimmy Loughran had both played for Crumlin United in their day and were excited by the prospect of building a side that they hoped would compete with established clubs Home Farm, Cherry Orchard, St Kevin's Boys, Lourdes Celtic and Belvedere Boys. Founded in 1967, Crumlin United steadily grew from humble schoolboy origins to become, by 2012, one of the leading intermediate and underage clubs in the country with a total of 22 teams at all age levels (including girls) and a further 30 youngsters between the ages of four and seven attending their weekly academy. Among its notable ex-players is former St Patrick's Athletic and Ireland manager Brian Kerr, who also cut his coaching teeth at Crumlin as a teenager.

Fox and Loughran had promised each other that they would build a side that no longer acted as a feeder outfit for other clubs and within a year of Keane's arrival, Jason Gavin was signed to play alongside his Tallaght neighbour at Under-13 level.

Loughran recalls: "I went to school with Robbie's da, the late Robert, from Stanaway Road and I knew his mother Anne and all his uncles, so that gave us a little bit of help to get him down to Crumlin.

"After he signed for us, his da never missed a match but would not get involved in it. He would not be roaring and shouting from the sideline so there was no pressure on Robbie. His da didn't play football but he played in a band and was brilliant on the guitar. His favourite song was 'Hey Jude'. He was always there for Robbie.

"So Robbie signed and he played for us in the Under-12 Premier Division. We wanted to get into the top division. We knew of Jason Gavin, Robbie Keane and a few other lads so we chased them. They were in lower divisions again and we had a system where we went to those leagues and got a few good players and tried to get them to sign."

Within a few weeks of opting to join Crumlin, Keane was banging in the goals. He might have been up to a year younger than some of his teammates and opponents but that did not bother him in the slightest.

"He always loved scoring, he would miss chance after chance but we always knew that he was going to score a goal for us or win a game for us," adds Loughran. "Missing never fazed him and even now when you see him on television and he misses a chance, he just continues.

"From the very start he wanted to be a professional footballer. When he played against Richard Dunne and Home Farm, the physical difference was huge but the bit of pace took over. People think he is slow but I don't think so.

"And when he got a kick, he would just get up and get on with the game. I don't think he has ever retaliated and I don't think he was ever booked with us. Robbie took the penalties, nobody else, and he seldom missed them. And he's still the way now as he was then, if he misses one then he'll still take the next one.

"At Under-14, he got a hat-trick against Home Farm at Mobhi Road and they were considered the top team at that level, with Richard Dunne at centre-half and Stephen McPhail in central midfield. He was scoring for fun."

Larry Fox looks back with equal fondness and pride on those first few months when Keane decided to return to his family's Crumlin roots in order to progress a career that was already suggesting that it had only one trajectory. And that was upwards.

"The Belvederes, Home Farms, St Kevin's used to come and

rob our players," smiles Fox. "Robbie was invited down to the World Cup five-a-side mini league that took place over a week at Pearse Park. I was lucky enough to manage him in those games and I knew at the end of the first of those games how good he was.

"And that continued from the first training session. There was this raw talent — he was a raw diamond but he knew how to score. He had the knack of getting in between players. We sold ourselves and we sold the club to Robbie because we were young and enthusiastic in the job.

"Robbie played Under-12 as a very, very young Under-11 due to the deadline for birth dates. He was very thin, there was not a pick on him. We had to teach him to be patient about when to run across the line and time it. At Under-13, it just took off and we won the Liam Brady Cup and at Under-14 we won everything."

Keane's dedication to his new team continued even after he had signed a contract to join Wolves in July, 1996. It made a lasting impression on Fox and Loughran.

"In the last season Robbie played for us, where six months before kids go to England they don't really perform, Robbie scored 59 goals for us and he was busting a gut in the last match against Rivermount in Finglas to get 60," points out Fox.

"That paints a picture of Robbie and his attitude and temperament. But it's more than that again, you have to have that bit extra to be a professional footballer."

And Loughran feels that the good habits — largely self-taught — that Keane had at that age gave him the foundation for future success at the highest level.

"None of the players gave us lip because we wouldn't take it off them. We trained and there was no messing but afterwards we would have a bit of craic.

"We trained 10 hours per week, which was a bit longer than most teams. When Robbie saw a trick on the telly he would not stop practising it until he got it. We would come back early in the summer and train twice a week, maybe on Sunday morning and Sunday afternoon.

"But we would also bring them to a pitch at Blackrock and then take them to the beach for a swim. When Jason and Robbie went to England, the two clubs could not believe how fit they were."

So was Robbie the main reason why Crumlin swept all before them as the team progressed through the various age groups?

"You could say yes and no," believes Loughran. "It was a very good side and they all got on together. You cannot say that he was the one who made the team tick."

Fox and Loughran's determination to create a top-class schoolboy side was not confined to matches and training sessions. Regular bag-packing expeditions to supermarkets in the local suburbs were an essential aspect of fund-raising.

"We funded the team and trips ourselves, while all the players had tracksuits," says Loughran, who recalls another amusing episode from Keane's youth. "While we were packing bags one day in Tallaght, the singer Daniel O'Donnell arrived at the checkout.

"Robbie was cheeky and he said 'mister, are you Daniel O'Donnell? Our club needs money so will you do a gig for us?' Unfortunately, Daniel referred us to his manager."

Around the same time, Keane made a real impact on the pitch while playing in an exhibition match at Tolka Park prior to a Shelbourne-Spurs friendly.

"Shels were playing Spurs at Tolka so I wrote to Shels asking if we could play a game against Tolka Rovers before the main match," says Fox. "Shels agreed and we beat Tolka 4-1 with Robbie scoring a hat-trick.

"After our match and before the friendly kicked-off, one of the Spurs players came up to me and a few other of our lads and told me that he and a few of his teammates had watched part of our game and were all raving about the 'skinny little fella up front'!"

It wasn't the only impact that Keane made that day, adds Fox.

"When our match was finished, we got changed and were in a room where there were sandwiches and tea. We assumed that the spread was for us so we scoffed the lot.

"Then one of the Shels officials walked in and shouted 'what the hell are you doing?'. The food and drink was for the Shels and Spurs players but it was a bit too late!"

The progressive work by Fox and Loughran on and off the pitch saw Keane and his teammates make several trips to England to play in tournaments. And on Easter Saturday, 1993 Keane was at Old Trafford when two late Steve Bruce goals helped Manchester United to a crucial 2-1 league win over Sheffield Wednesday that sent Alex Ferguson's side to the top of the table and on the way to the club's first title in 26 years.

And while the then 12-year-old Keane may have been dreaming about emulating the stars he had watched that afternoon, including Denis Irwin, could he have really believed that he would be playing at the famous ground six years later?

"Robbie was a Liverpool fanatic but we have photographs of him in a United hat and scarf!" laughs Fox. "And we would threaten to show them to others! But we also brought them to see Liverpool play Norwich City at Anfield a year later when The Kop was used for the last time as terracing."

It was during the first of these excursions across the Irish Sea that Fox and Loughran became bemused by Keane's dietary habits. If steak and chips was the staple diet of the professional when asked to divulge his favourite meal in a magazine, then Keane had more basic tastes.

"We went to Pontins in Blackpool beside Pleasure Beach and played two games against local teams," recalls Loughran. "We had full-board in Pontins and there was the choice of about 10 different meals at breakfast, lunch and dinner. But all that Robbie was interested in was Corn Flakes or Rice Crispies.

"He would have six or seven bowls of Rice Crispies or Corn Flakes and he also loved ice cream. We would say to him 'Robbie, you would want to start eating to put a bit of weight on'. He would reply 'Ah, I'll be alright.'"

On match day in Crumlin, it was a similar story.

"On Saturday morning he would play for us and after that he would go to either Jimmy's ma's house, my mother's house or Beatty's house next door," says Fox.

"They were all beside each other in Windmill Park. He liked Beatty's stew on a Saturday or in my house he'd have sandwiches and Tayto and then he'd have biscuits or something like that in Jimmy's. Then he would go off and play a Gaelic football match for Crumlin."

Even when Keane had settled into life in England with Wolves, he would yearn for his favourite meal at home. "His favourite food was still potatoes and brown sauce!" says Fox.

If the youngster's calorie intake was somewhat lopsided, Keane was thriving at Crumlin and had easily adapted to life in the higher division where both teammates and opponents were of a higher quality. And it was fuelling his thirst to turn his abiding passion into a career.

"I would call to the house before training and ask his mother Anne where he was," says Fox. "Anne would say 'Jaysus, Larry, he's out there kicking a ball for the last two hours'. And that was before training.

"Robbie and Jason Gavin lived on the same road and Robbie would be telling us about a fella who lived beside him who was six foot high and a centre-half but who was not playing football. We used to leave Robbie home and one night I saw Jason.

"I was asking Jason, asking Robbie and asking Jason's mother and father if Jason would play. One evening, I saw him and asked him to get his boots so he came down to us. They were great pals but the whole team were great pals. And what gave the team that success was the bond the players had. Jimmy and I also got on so well too."

Now Gavin was on the same route to a successful professional football career — with a little help from his friend.

Chapter 3
Cross-channel choices

'HE wouldn't lace his brother's boots', 'he was only trotting after his oul' fella', 'they missed the real star when they ignored the left-winger'.

If pub talk replaced the reality of professional football, then the world's most popular game would be populated by clubs scarcely able to field a team every Saturday afternoon.

Instead of fearless centre-halves, we would laugh at impotent imposters unable to jump, raiding wingers would be replaced by overweight plodders while priceless poachers would make way for disinterested sporting shrinking violets.

According to this football language, no manager ever signed the right player and few clubs were ever capable of selecting the real protégé from the ranks of the schoolboy, junior or lower-league grades. As is often the case in sport, the truth is somewhat different. Thousands of fine prospects in football have wilted between the ages of 16 and 20 having joined the world's biggest clubs, with a considerable percentage of them never earning even an average living from the game having been released or sold on.

Separate the genuine hard luck stories — usually related to a serious injury or a succession of such problems — from those who had exited football by their mid-twenties and it's reasonably easy to pinpoint why the major stars thrived in such circumstances, as they sought to settle into a sometimes brutal man's world before they had any need to shave.

In short, they usually managed to marry their talents to hard work and stubborn persistence, which helped them succeed. If they then got the breaks — absence from injury and with good coaching at a well-run, stable club — then they were well on their way to success at some level of the professional game. Ask any experienced Premier League manager what is often their

41

players' best asset and they will point to a positive attitude. From his early teens, it was clear that Robbie Keane possessed deep-rooted perseverance that would allow him to climb the hurdles that seemed to pop up regularly in front of him.

Almost two decades on, Larry Fox — joint manager with Jim Loughran of Keane's Crumlin United team from Under-13 to Under-16 — believes that Keane was only just into his teens when he knew that he would soon be leaving home for a life in the professional game.

"On reflection, I felt that Robbie knew when he was 13 because he constantly told us," states Fox. But before he committed himself to Wolves at the age of 15 and then signed his first professional contract at 16, Keane had to deal with the first of a series of blows that would test his resolve to succeed.

Keane had played for the DDSL's Under-12 team as a 12-year-old in August 1992 in a 3-2 win against their Manchester United equivalents. The match took place prior to a friendly between Alex Ferguson's United and a loosely-titled Ireland XI at Lansdowne Road to raise funds for the Athletic Union League's Clonshaugh football complex.

Yet, as he made steady progress with Crumlin, he discovered that further representative recognition was harder to secure.

"He was overlooked for the Kennedy Cup even though he made the preliminary panel," explains Fox about Keane's exclusion from the prestigious annual Under-14 inter-league competition.

"The training session was at St Patrick's Athletic and when the squad was announced, he started bawling crying. He never made it although he was the highest goalscorer in the league. They took a guy from Home Farm who was big and strong, that's what they tend to do."

In the knowledge that they had a real gem in their midst, Fox and Loughran started to write letters to the top clubs in England. But their efforts were in vain.

"I have copies of nine or ten letters that I wrote to the clubs in England and Jimmy has the same telling them about Robbie.

And none of them would sign him."

Even a chance meeting with then Liverpool manager Roy Evans during the 1994-95 season, when Keane was 14, didn't smooth the youngster's path to an English club.

"Richard Dunne, Robbie and Stephen McPhail were going over on trial to Everton so it was my job to bring them down to the boarding gate at Dublin Airport," remembers Fox. "The Liverpool squad was in the departures lounge on their way home after playing a friendly in Dublin. The three lads were in awe of the Liverpool players, especially Robbie, who was Liverpool-mad.

"So I went over to Ronnie Moran and Roy Evans and explained to them that the lads were going over on trial to Everton. They joked to me about not mentioning Everton! I told them that the three of them were well worth taking a look at and, in particular, Robbie.

"Ronnie replied that I should speak to Noel McCabe, who was then the Liverpool scout here. I told him that unfortunately Noel didn't really rate Robbie. But I reckon that Robbie has always been motivated by these disappointments. They drive him on."

Fox's belief is given further credence by the fact that while Keane was now firmly established as one of the brightest stars in the DDSL, he was not called up to the Ireland Under-15 squad for their fixtures in 1994 or 1995, and he was again overlooked for the tri-nations European Under-16 Championships qualifying group against Iceland and Norway in Dublin in late September, 1995.

As the final months of the Jack Charlton era lumbered towards the 2-0 defeat by Holland in the Euro 96 qualifying play-off at Anfield in December of 1995, Joe McGrath — the manager of the Under-15 and 16 teams — was continuing to work off the panel he had successfully used in the previous 20 months at both ages towards preparing a panel for the UEFA Under-16 qualifiers. With refreshing honesty, McGrath — who was central to the establishment to the first ever FAI/FAS

League of Ireland trainee scheme in 1989-90 that featured Roy Keane — now says that he was well aware of Robbie Keane's credentials but felt he had better options in attack.

"Robbie probably should have been in the Under-15 squad but we had an outstanding group of lads," says McGrath. "At Under-15 with the panel that then became the Under-16 side, Jason Gavin played against England at Tolka Park and scored two goals in the 2-0 win. Richard Dunne was also in the squad but Robbie was not.

"I didn't pick Robbie for the qualifiers because I probably felt that he wasn't good enough. We had some very good players and, bear in mind, I would be watching seven or eight matches every weekend.

"The Wolves scout, Eddie Corcoran, used to slag me, saying 'why is Robbie not in?'," says McGrath, who can point to victories over Northern Ireland, Wales, Switzerland, Cameroon, Israel (twice), England and a draw with Spain by the Under-15 side in 1995 as evidence that his team was producing.

Another hugely experienced scout, John Fallon senior from Dublin, was working for Tottenham Hotspur at the time and has similar memories of watching Keane.

"I first came across Robbie when he was Under-14 or 15 and I remember him scoring a hat-trick in the All-Ireland final," says Fallon.

"To be honest, I wasn't pulling up trees about him although you would say to yourself that he was scoring loads of goals. I watched him but probably not enough. But I think the deal had already been done with Wolves and he was happy and he loved Wolves. All the bigger clubs in England looked at him but once he got to Wolves his progression was rapid.

"Wolves pushed the boat out for him — not in financial terms — but they made him feel wanted. A club like Wolves has got to make the lad feel that much better when he is with them so they can beat the bigger club to sign him. And Eddie Corcoran kept in constant touch with him when he went over first.

"But nobody thought that Robbie would do as well as he did. It was like Roy Keane. I laugh when people come out when an Irish player has done well in England and say 'I knew he was going to do well'. They don't know, no more than they know about the current crop."

As Keane moved closer to signing for Wolves, McGrath's Under-16 side defeated Iceland 3-0 and Norway 2-1 in September, 1995 to book its place in the following spring's UEFA Under-16 finals in Austria.

David Freeman of Nottingham Forest and exciting Wexford forward Paddy Fitzpatrick of Taghmon — who would sign for Celtic within months — formed McGrath's attack in a side that also boasted Stephen McPhail of Leeds United, Home Farm's Richard Dunne and Keane's Crumlin United colleagues Gavin (centre-half) and Sean Mannion (midfield).

With Liverpool youth striker Niall Byrne making waves at The Reds' youth academy and pushing for a place in the attack, and Fitzpatrick grabbing both goals against the Norwegians, it was clear that Keane had work to do if he was to force his way into McGrath's plans before the finals.

Then, in early 1996, McGrath quit his job with the FAI to take up the post as New Zealand senior national team manager.

"I wanted to postpone taking up the New Zealand job so that I could go to the Under-16 finals in Austria that April. I went to see the FAI officers and told them this. The New Zealand FA had agreed to the idea but the FAI would not let me.

"The FAI appointed Liam O'Brien from Midleton in Cork and Con Flanagan as manager and assistant, and they had done work during the previous years. Con had worked on the FAS course in Stewarts Hospital in Dublin with me and when I would be away with the Under-16 squad, he would take charge of the Under-15s along with Liam, with Maurice Price also involved."

Just prior to the finals in Austria, Paddy Fitzpatrick suffered a serious injury and O'Brien called up Keane to join the squad. The Dubliner would score on his Ireland debut and continue what he had been doing all season for his schoolboy club.

On the back of Wolves' persistence in signing him, this latest twist suggested that the Dubliner's fortunes had changed for good.

Sixteen years later and, with Keane now one of the world's leading international goalscorers, McGrath sees the same strengths that made Keane a standout teenager and believes Giovanni Trapattoni is using these traits for the benefit of Ireland.

"Back then, Robbie was never in the one place, would not stay up front and was always dropping into midfield which is his natural game. If I was doing it again tomorrow then I would use him in a different way.

"And that's why I think people misunderstand Giovanni Trapattoni. He is no fool and he knows he is getting the best out of Robbie. If Robbie stayed up front I think we would get slaughtered in midfield.

"He gives the defence an awful lot of relief when he gets the ball and gets into the old inside-right or inside-left positions, the vacant space between the full-backs and midfield. He does a lot of good work there and unsettles the other team as they have no-one to mark him.

"Centre-halves hate having no-one to mark and they hate roaming out of position so I can see why Trapattoni is using him like that. It probably suits Robbie, too, as he doesn't have to make 70-yard runs and is working in that small area.

"Robbie has brilliant football intelligence because if you are a centre-half and come out to mark him, then he runs in behind you. You don't know what to do. I think his greatest asset and attribute is when he's in the box, when he seems to always make time for himself."

Keane's fortunes had started to turn on the club front in the autumn of 1995, with Wolves and Liverpool emerging as the two most serious suitors for his signature.

"Robbie was going over to Wolves regularly when he was 15 in that Under-16 season in 1995-96, while he also had trials at

Everton and Leeds," recalls Fox.

"Liverpool kept ringing the house and ringing the house in Tallaght. I think Liverpool handled it wrong, they pestered him to the point where he said 'ah, no'."

Fox also feels that Keane's acute streetwise nature helped him arrive at the decision to join the then First Division Wolves.

"Robbie would have gone over to Liverpool — and you don't see this in many kids — eight months before he signed for Wolves, gone to the training ground and trained with the lads in the academy.

"He would have looked ahead into the youth team to see what chance he had of progressing through the youths and reserves. Instead, he joined Wolves and the following year he was making his debut for the first team. That showed how intelligent he was football-wise."

Persuading Keane to join Wolves was the job of Dubliner Eddie Corcoran, whose involvement in the game stretched back to the 1950s as a player and manager and, since the 1960s, as a widely-respected scout for a series of clubs that had included Liverpool.

"I first became aware of Robbie when he was 13-years-old and playing for Crumlin United when my old friend Jack Bermingham saw him," explains Corcoran. "We were looking at another player at Crumlin and Jack rang me up and said 'there's a lad playing for Crumlin United called Robbie Keane' and I said that I had never heard of him. "Jack said 'you might not notice him because of his size but he has a great knack of scoring goals'. I told Jack that we'd keep an eye on him and look at him again.

"So we went to look at him a few times, but at 13 you cannot as a scout go near a lad. We kept watching Robbie and when he was 14 he started to improve. But he didn't get much stronger and he was never that big as a kid. When he reached 15, he started to blossom. He enjoyed playing for Crumlin United and got on well there."

Keane's relentless quest for goals saw him register week after week in the DDSL and he would always unleash a gem when needed.

"I remember Robbie got an unbelievable goal against Home Farm at Under-14 level one Saturday afternoon. How he scored it, I don't know, he beat five players and stuck it in the back of the net. And he's still capable of doing that today," says Corcoran.

"He always had an eye for goal, although he was never the quickest and is still not so today. But Robbie had this priceless knack of being able to read the game and that was really important."

As has so often been the case when it comes to recruiting the golden prospect, others in the game felt that Keane's Crumlin teammate Sean Mannion was the one who would move to the big club in England.

"They were all amazed that I went for Robbie instead of Mannion and when I went to Crumlin games, they thought I was watching Mannion. But I never told them that it was Robbie I was there to see when I was going up there Saturday after Saturday," says Corcoran.

Liverpool and their academy director Steve Heighway — a former Ireland winger from the seventies — were intent on capturing Keane, with the battle to sign the 15-year-old intensifying in the summer and autumn of 1995.

"Liverpool came in for him at the time but I persuaded him to go to Wolves because I believed he would have a better chance of making a career in the game," adds Corcoran.

"I had scouted for Liverpool when Bill Shankly was the manager but I was able now to persuade Robbie not to sign for Liverpool. I told the people at Anfield that Robbie had no chance at Liverpool and that he was better off going to a lower division club or a club that was not quite as big as Liverpool.

"A lot of other English clubs looked at him but only Liverpool and Wolves tried to sign him as the others were put off by his lack of pace.

"I went to see his parents, Anne and the late Robert, who

were lovely people, real Dubs, with a lovely family, quite a few times. It took a lot of persuading by me for Robbie to opt for Wolves as Liverpool were naturally a bigger club and offering a lot more money than we could.

"But as I said to him and his mother and father, 'at the end of the day, it's not about money now at your age, it's about going to a club where you are going to have a chance of progressing'. I said it to the father, who was an intelligent man, what I felt was best for Robbie.

"One night I brought Jack Bermingham with me and Robbie's father said to me 'I can see where you are coming from'. But it was the people at Wolves who sold Wolves to Robbie and the parents. Liverpool also did a great job and Steve was brilliant. We never fell out over it as I knew him for years and continue to do so. And joining Wolves was the best move for Robbie, as his career has proved.

"It was the case then and is still the same today that kids go to these big clubs like Manchester United and Liverpool and they don't come through the system, or very few of them do."

A weekend visit to Wolves to view the ground and the club's training academy also proved pivotal, according to Corcoran.

"I went with his ma and da over to Wolves before he signed when he was playing in a friendly match for the youths. His parents were very impressed with the way they were treated by Wolves as they were put up in a nice hotel and the club ensured they were made feel welcome.

"Graham Taylor was the manager and he is a true gentleman. He made Robbie feel very welcome, as did his assistant Bobby Downes — they both really looked after him and his parents.

"I dealt directly with Graham on the deal, although he didn't last long afterwards at Wolves. It didn't take much to persuade Graham to sign Robbie as the coaching staff at the club liked him, including Chris Evans and other youth team coaches.

"Bobby thought he was exceptional in terms of scoring goals. And he was right. And although Robbie got a good financial deal at the beginning, the club continued to look after his parents in the following years.

"Once he went to Wolves, he developed quickly. I think he got the breaks, but all good players need breaks. Remember, Roy Keane got the breaks. Robbie was a quiet individual and never caused any trouble and he got on well at Wolves. They liked him, he did well and his career snowballed from there.

"Robbie became very friendly with Wolves' youth coach Chris Evans and he made rapid strides in that side and then with the reserves. I never saw Robbie playing for the Wolves first team as my back was giving me some trouble and I was very busy with work and with the Ireland senior side.

"Crumlin were very, very helpful in completing the transfer and they were and still are a good club. And they never had any problems getting looked after by Wolves."

Corcoran would be able to track Keane's international progress at close hand in his role as FAI logistical officer to the senior squad. His background in the hotel and catering industry made him an ideal candidate to assist Jack Charlton and Mick McCarthy's planning for away matches.

"Robbie never lacked confidence and he was always full of his own importance. He was never afraid to talk and once he went out to train he would be very upbeat. Quickly, he became very friendly with Richard Dunne in the senior squad and they are still great mates. They always roomed together."

However, he admits that he would have never forecast such a phenomenal career for his Molineux recruit.

"I never thought that he would be as successful as he has become. I always believed he would make a good career for himself but not to end up where he has. That's a credit to him as he has worked bloody hard. He has never been afraid of work and never afraid to train and in the early years looked after himself.

"I kept saying to him 'behave yourself and don't be going out with this, that and the other fella'. He listened to that advice when he was younger but when he got older they all go the same way, don't they? Full marks to him — he deserves the success that he gets.

Robert senior made a huge impact on Robbie; (*below*) Communion day; (*right*) nailing his colours to the mast

It's been said that Robbie Keane was always at his happiest with a ball at his feet — but he was just as content to have one balancing on his neck

Representing his country has been an enormous source of pride for Keane

Robbie and Damien Duff sport a pair of questionable hairstyles in the early days

Keane made a major impact during his time with the Ireland underage teams

Robbie with his former underage teammates (*from left*) Jason Gavin and
Alan Mahon; (*below*) Keane relaxes in the pool with Alan Quinn, Gavin and
Barry Quinn during a trip abroad in their days with the Under-18 side

Robbie Keane (*front row, right*) and Richard Dunne (*back row, third from right*) line out at underage level and (*below*) Robbie with his parents and Wolves manager Graham Taylor after signing for the Molineux club

Robbie puts pen to paper on a professional contract for Wolves as his proud parents look on and (*below*) he takes to the field behind Don Goodman at a sold-out Molineux — Keane would go on to make 87 appearances for the club

Robbie has always been known for his cheeky charm and sense of humour. He's also fond of a bit of devilment, as his former teammates are only too happy to point out. So it was no surprise that when the snow fell during this international trip, Keane was first to fire the snowballs

Senior Ireland recognition and big-money moves brought Keane's fame to a higher level and, even though he made a few dodgy calls when it came to fashion accessories, he has been an outstanding role model since day one

"Spotting the chance to score and having that knack to do so is still the basis of his game. Look at him over the last five years and you see him scoring goals out of nothing."

As coincidence would have it, Corcoran had moved on to become Coventry City's eyes in Ireland when Gordon Strachan decided to sign Keane in August, 1999.

"Their chief scout Trevor Gould, Bobby's brother, rang me to ask me what I thought of Robbie. I said 'go and get him, he has what it takes'.

"Coventry did very well out of him by selling him on to Inter Milan a year later. A £7m profit was a massive amount of money then."

Keane may have left Crumlin United behind but he certainly had not forgotten the club that had helped to mould his future career.

"When Robbie and Jason went to England, every summer two weeks before they went back to their clubs they would ring me," says Loughran. "We would go down to the pitch to do a bit of training and running. They would have great craic with Robbie saying 'come on Jason, take the ball off me' but he never could."

Fox was present for Keane's home debut for Wolves in August, 1997 when an expectant Molineux was abuzz following the 17-year-old's two goals in the opening day 2-0 win at Norwich City.

"They were playing against Sheffield United and Paul McGrath. I went to Paul before the match and said 'there is a young lad playing against you today who played for me — will you take it easy against him — it's Robbie Keane'. "Paul said 'I've heard a lot about him and a lot of people are talking about him'. I replied 'you would want to be on your game today!'"

The game ended scoreless. In the years that followed, Keane's former club teammates or mentors would receive the same warm welcome that his family and friends received when they travelled over to England for a game.

"Robbie would often ring us or text us so he still keeps in touch. And he always offered to look after us if we went over to a game," says Loughran. "We were over for the FA Cup semi-final against Arsenal during his first season when we went to his house in Telford that he had just bought off Dougie Freedman. It was a detached three bedroom house. Dougie must have been big into the bright colours because everything was white and cream! Robbie asked us did we mind if we took our shoes off."

Initially, Crumlin received only £10,000 for Keane — the standard fee for a schoolboy moving to a British club at the time — but were paid additional cash for add-on clauses in the transfer deal.

"Crumlin got between £5,000 and £10,000 plus extra money for playing first team games and Ireland internationals. It was about £30,000 in total but there was no sell-on clause."

Crumlin United cannot but have regretted the absence of such a clause in the deal — although very few Irish clubs, schoolboy or League of Ireland, included them at that time — as they watched open-mouthed as Wolves sold Keane for £6m to Coventry City in 1999.

Within a year, the Sky Blues agreed a £13m deal with Inter Milan for the Dubliner. Leeds United then splashed out £11m to bring him back to English football, bringing the total transfer fees involved in Keane's career by July 2001 to a staggering £30m.

While any sell-on clause would only have been triggered by Keane's first move from Molineux to Highfield Road, a 10 per cent cut would have been worth £600,000 to Crumlin United.

However, FIFA would come to Crumlin's rescue in September, 2001 when it introduced a new scheme of solidarity payments for clubs whose schoolboy and youth team players went on to change hands for transfer fees as full-time professionals.

FIFA decreed that five per cent of the transfer fee raised when a player transferred between professional clubs would be paid to the clubs at which he spent his career with between the ages of 12 and 21. So when Keane joined Spurs from Leeds in August, 2002, for £7m, Crumlin United found themselves firmly in the money as they qualified as his schoolboy club for the four years between his 12th and 16th birthdays.

Crumlin were due €151,000 which translated to the four years Keane spent at their club and was in accordance with their cut of the five per cent ruling. However, there was an initial reluctance to hand over the cash — a stance that is repeated to this day by many British clubs who somehow feel that such FIFA rules and statutes don't apply to them.

So in the autumn of 2002, FAI careers officer Eoin Hand began the painstaking process of proving that Crumlin United was fully entitled to five per cent of the £7m that Tottenham had paid for the striker. Hand spent many hours logging the exact details of Keane's career from the age of 12 to when he moved to Wolves and presented a case that irrefutably proved that Crumlin were entitled to the solidarity payment.

FIFA received the documents from Hand and the FAI and the global body immediately instructed Leeds United and the FA to pay up.

"This is probably the best feeling I've had since I was manager of the Irish team and we beat France 3-2," mused Hand when FIFA issued its edict. "It's a landmark decision that will have huge implications for Irish clubs at every level of the game."

And so it did, with Damien Duff's then Irish record transfer of £17.7m from Blackburn Rovers to Chelsea in the summer of 2003 instantly earning his three Dublin schoolboy clubs massive and welcome windfalls. Leicester Celtic received €64,000, Lourdes Celtic got €192,000 and St Kevin's Boys were €128,000 better off. Incredibly, a decade later and Hand still finds himself chasing British clubs for money that is the automatic entitlement of clubs in this country.

Now, once a British club signs an Irish teenager, they must pay up an amount determined by a system devised by FIFA that takes into account the relative sizes of the two clubs involved in the deal. This happens before any future transfer to another club happens.

"It's amazing that some British clubs seem to think that FIFA's rules don't apply to them," says Hand. "So I spend a lot of time assisting clubs of all shapes and sizes to ensure they get the money they are due."

Since FIFA introduced its new solidarity payment regime in September, 2001, a figure of close to €6m has been paid to Irish clubs by British clubs — and Hand is still battling on Irish clubs' behalf.

In one almost comical episode in 2009 and 2010, Hand finally forced the world's richest club, Manchester City, to cough up €20,000 to Galway schoolboy club Cregmore Claregalway for Greg Cunningham following the defender's move to City from Mervue United in 2008.

Meanwhile, the cash injection could not have come at a more appropriate time for Crumlin, who were then planning to upgrade their Pearse Park facilities to incorporate a full size all-weather pitch. On hearing the news from back home, Keane texted then club chairman Sean Wall 'Fair play, delighted for yis'.

Two decades after Fox and Loughran first set eyes on the whippet-like figure of Keane in Fettercairn, his former mentors still shake their heads in awe of what he has achieved in the game.

"We will never — and I scout for Ipswich Town and spend my time looking for another Robbie Keane — see his likes again," smiles Fox.

Chapter 4
The company of Wolves

FROM the moment that Robbie Keane set foot at Wolverhampton Wanderers Football Club in July, 1996, he established an immediate bond with the west midlands sporting institution and, equally importantly, with the professional game.

Since the 1950s when a small trickle of Irish youngsters first sought to carve out a career in the English Football League by signing up as poorly paid club apprentices, it's estimated that at least 10,000 boys have crossed the Irish Sea to follow that career path.

To this day, the vast majority's quest ends in disappointment although many of this number go on to enjoy satisfying careers in the League of Ireland or in the junior echelons, so ensuring that their experiences are still harnessed by the game. Pinpointing the reasons for failing to make the cut produces almost as many reasons as there are youngsters who make that trek. Homesickness, injury, a club's poor form, a change in manager, financial restrictions, job cuts, fecklessness on the part of some, sheer bad luck and a lack of the required quality all enter the equation.

But in Keane's case, the possibility that the raw 16-year-old from Tallaght would end up lamenting his time in England appeared to be slim right from day one. He arrived at Molineux alongside fellow Dubliners Keith Andrews, Alan Dixon and Stephen Hackett 12 months after another Dub, Glen Crowe, and Dominic Foley from Charleville in north county Cork had signed as apprentices.

"It was not like London where there are half a dozen clubs," says Crowe. "Wolves was the only club in the area so it was a great family and community club and run in the right way. Having me and Dom Foley there probably helped those four lads when they arrived."

Keane stayed at Josie Edwards's digs at Willenhall, close to Wolverhampton and although he naturally suffered pangs of homesickness, he soon settled into life at the club as a YTS apprentice. He even elected to remain with the Edwards family after securing a place in the Wolves first team a year later, remarking: "I'll not be tempted to live away, not yet anyway. I know there's nothing better than a friendly family for me.

"Josie's a brilliant cook and friend and I love the way she does chicken!"

The Wolves that Keane signed for was a club that had survived a brush with extinction in 1982 and 1986 due to financial problems but was now firmly re-established in Division One (later re-named the Championship) under owner, multi-millionaire Jack Hayward, and manager Mark McGhee.

Local man made good Hayward, who had made his fortune in property and other businesses, was determined to steer his beloved Wolves back into the top flight of the game where Stan Cullis's uncompromising side of the 1950s had claimed the league championship in 1953-54, 1957-58 and 1958-59.

Hayward would plough more than £70m of his own money into Wolves during his 17 years as proprietor, transforming Molineux into a modern stadium and personally bankrolling transfer fees and salaries. The impact that Hayward had on the club should not be underestimated and today he remains an honorary life president of Wolves and their training ground in Compton is named in his honour.

Having purchased the club in 1990, Hayward had big plans for one of the founders of the Football League and Keane would quickly find himself a key figure in that quest in the late 1990s.

Crowe, who had also adapted well to life at the club, was instantly impressed by Keane, whom he played alongside in the youth and reserve sides.

"Robbie would have come over during the 1995-96 season on trial — maybe already signed up for Wolves — and would have trained with the youths and reserves," outlines Crowe. "He played a couple of games for us and although he was only a skinny little whippet, he would glide down the wing with the ball with two or three players around him but still jink past them.

"He looked special from the first time I saw him. There are some players that way. He has always been good on the ball and that helped compared to me — I wasn't beating players with the ball when I went over to Wolves first.

"I was in the box looking to score while Robbie was outside the penalty area looking for the ball. Robbie was always comfortable on the ball and he was only there a few days when he was demanding the ball from his teammates in training. That's the type of personality he has always had.

"You knew from the first day and the first training session that Robbie was a good player. He stood out and I have never seen any shyness in him. I don't think there is any.

"In that first season he was at Wolves, we had a very good season in the youths and finished second in the league behind Aston Villa. As a small, skinny little lad you probably would not have expected him to develop as quickly as he did. But you felt he would do very well."

McGhee's side boasted Keith Curle and the late Dean Richards at centre-half, strikers Steve Bull, Iwan Roberts, Don Goodman and Darren Ferguson, and Steve Froggatt in midfield but would lose to Crystal Palace in the 1996-97 promotion play-off semi-finals after finishing third in the table, four points behind runners-up Barnsley.

By the time the 1997-98 campaign began, there was a new face in the Wolves attack. McGhee's men headed to East Anglia to take on Norwich City on the opening day, with Keane pushing forward from a wide right position to assist Bull and Goodman. McGhee had kept an eye on Keane's progress with the youths and reserves during the 16-year-old's first season at the club but was startled by what he saw in pre-season in July, 1997.

"As a manager, you wander over and have a look at the youth team," explained McGhee. "Robbie looked a different class to the players he was with so I said I would take him in the first team training session.

"Again he looked a different class — he was the best player. So we then decided we were going to take him to Scotland and we gave him bits of games. He again looked our best player.

"The thing that stood out was his ability to keep possession. Seasoned defenders were unable to get near him because he moved the ball too quickly, he could see things early and he could finish. By the time we got to the Norwich City game it seemed like the obvious thing to do even though he was only 17. We had to play him."

Keane recalled the pivotal week in his career that would fast-forward his development at club level.

"I got taken and put in the first team, they seemed to like me," said Keane. "I went to Scotland on pre-season and played against Dundee United and Stirling.

"It was such a huge bonus when Mark McGhee told me that I was in the first team for pre-season. After that, I was on my way and things just kept happening. Mark took a chance on me and I'd like to think that I didn't let him down."

Choosing the Dubliner against Norwich proved to be a wise move by the manager, as Keane scored in the 34th and 64th minutes in a 2-0 success. It also heralded the arrival of Keane's trademark celebration routine on British and Irish television screens.

"I was on the bench the day that Robbie made his debut at Norwich when he scored two goals," recalls Crowe. "That was the first time that he did his little cartwheel celebration for Wolves and, from what I remember, he nutmegged two players before scoring the second goal!

"Scoring two goals away from home on your debut was some start. That was basically the making of him."

Crucially, Keane was now handed a role in the Wolves team just off the two strikers that allowed him to develop at a natural pace and to lay the basis for his future as both a creative force and a finisher. McGhee's assistant, Colin Lee, believes the decision to play Keane in this position was to the youngster's benefit.

"We established a role for Robbie in Scotland when we felt he wasn't quite strong enough yet to play up front and yet he was not athletic enough, in terms of his development, to play in midfield," said Lee. "So we found him a role just behind the striker and that is where we played him initially. He was not a wide player and he wasn't quite ready to play up front.

"At one stage we thought of playing him in an advanced midfield role but in the end we decided to play him in between. I think it was the right decision. If we had stuck him up front initially, I think it would have been too much for him at that stage of his development."

And Wolves' youth team coach Chris Evans — who, along with fellow coach Rob Kelly, had been hugely influential in developing Keane during his first 12 months at the club — was even able to ensure that Robert and Anne Keane were present at Carrow Road to see their son make his senior debut.

"Wolves flew the family across and I was lucky enough to score two goals in my first professional game," said Keane. "We went back to my mam's hotel afterwards but that was it. Just went to bed early."

The Wolves fans had followed Keane's progress with the youths and reserves through the match day programme and the few paragraphs that the Wolverhampton Express and Star would carry on their games. So apart from the couple of hundred die-hards who would turn up for such games, this was the first glimpse that Wolves supporters had got of their new teenage sensation, whose two strikes against the Canaries was the club's first debut double since Ted Farmer netted two in the 3-1 league win against Manchester United at Old Trafford in September, 1960.

Farmer's promising career would be over by the age of 24 after he failed to recover from a badly-broken leg. Keane, in contrast, would be blessed with a near-perfect absence of major injuries as he progressed.

That McGhee was willing to throw the still waif-like Keane into the hard-hitting and frequently brutish surroundings of Division One said much about the youngster, who had only celebrated his 17th birthday a month prior to his competitive debut at Carrow Road.

When Keane spoke to Stephen Finn of the Irish Daily Star in early October, 1997 ahead of an Ireland youths qualifying match, Keane was surprised by his rapid progress at Wolves but not intimidated by his new surroundings.

"Everything is going so well for me recently and I hope it continues with this game," said Keane. "Everything has happened so fast since making my debut in the first team in a preseason tour in Scotland against Dundee United.

"I didn't know it was coming. I was training with the youth team but their manager told me to go over with the first team. I couldn't believe it when I was called up for the Norwich game but it was great because my mam and dad were there to see it. It's hard to take all this in as I had said to my friends that I'd like to make the first team at the end of the season.

"The coin has turned round completely and I'm getting a lot of attention, although I'm coping with it alright, trying to take each day as it comes. I'd like to use this game to show Mick McCarthy and Ian Evans what I can do. It's always exciting to get called up for Ireland, it's my homeland."

A month later and Ireland senior team captain Andy Townsend had become a fully paid-up member of the Robbie Keane fan club.

"Robbie is a superb player and he could be playing for us in the World Cup finals provided we make it there," declared Townsend after Keane's lob for Wolves had beaten Townsend's Middlesbrough 1-0 at the Riverside Stadium.

"He is an exceptional player for his age and if he can keep producing that kind of form he will go all the way."

Ireland manager McCarthy and his assistant Evans were

preparing for the upcoming World Cup play-off that would see them edged out of a place at France 98 after a 3-2 aggregate defeat by Belgium. But McCarthy believed that introducing young players at such a decisive stage of the qualifiers would be unfair on them and his team.

"Damien Duff, Robbie Keane, Mark Kinsella and Graham Kavanagh are young, exciting players who have big careers ahead of them," said McCarthy. "But I don't think this is the time or the place to blood them. Some people will suggest a lot of things between now and the Belgium match but that's one option I won't be pursuing."

Keane would make his senior international debut in the spring of 1998 and would go on to play in 38 (34 starts) of Wolves' 46 league games that season, finishing as the club's leading league scorer with 11 goals — one ahead of Dougie Freedman, three more than Goodman and four better than Bull.

Keane's status at the club was confirmed by the greater number of starting teams he made during the nine months compared to Freedman (25), Goodman (29), Bull (24) and Mixu Paatelainen (10).

"That shows the quality that Robbie had," says Crowe. "Wolves was the sort of club that had money, so if they were struggling they would spend a few bob to bring in a player on loan or sign a new player if a key player was going to miss a long spell through injury."

If Jack Hayward was the off-pitch local hero, then Bull was the playing equivalent having served the club he supported as a boy from its days in the old Fourth and Third Divisions.

Though Bull had once played for hated rivals West Bromwich Albion, the lad from Tipton had established himself as a bona fide Wolves legend. A club record haul of 306 goals in all competitions and a Wolves all-time best of 250 league goals was sufficient to persuade the club to rename one of its stands in his honour in 2003.

"Robbie was different class. He was a young, up-and-coming

player who was a bit cheeky," recalled Bull. "He had to have the odd squeeze now and then to bring him back down.

"My first impression of Robbie was that he left me feeling frustrated. He was one of these tricky players who does 10 skills but only one comes off. So I'd be in the box for the other nine and the ball would never reach me.

"Then the one time the ball did get there, I would not be there to score so it was a frustrating time. I used to have a go at him to begin with but he couldn't understand me," added Bull as his strong west midlands accent failed to register with Keane.

"But as the games went on, we got to know each other and I knew where he was and where he'd put the ball. That was it, we just clicked."

Crowe believes Bull had a positive influence on Keane. "You could not say a bad word about Steve Bull," recalls Crowe. "He was quiet but if you were training with the first team then he would give you little pointers and tips. He didn't say much but you would listen when he did.

"Steve would have helped Robbie just as he would have with all the lads. He was the club legend then. Robbie was also great friends with Dougie Freedman and Carl Robinson."

Surrounded by familiar accents and looked after by the club's attentive network of landladies, Keane settled quickly into life in the Black Country.

"In my first year at the club, I was on my own in digs," explains Crowe. "But for the second season Stephen Hackett and Robbie moved into digs just around the corner from me that was run by my landlady's mother. They would have dropped dinners around to each other's houses and we were well looked after."

And the down-to-earth nature that remains a key part of Keane's fabric was already firmly-rooted in his attitude off the pitch in those days, according to Crowe.

"As a person, Robbie has not changed since I first met him in 1996. When I was called into the Ireland squad in 2001 and had not seen Robbie for a few years, he was still the same lad I trained with, enjoyed a few drinks with in Wolverhampton and had called around to his digs for dinner."

But if Keane and his Ireland teammates later developed a reputation for enjoying themselves when there was appropriate down time, Crowe is equally emphatic about his then colleague's ability to know when to start and, more significantly, when to stop.

"Robbie was always a good trainer and would push himself to the limits. That meant closing people down in games and doing the right things. And that also meant living his life the right way off the pitch as well. At Wolves, of course we went out for a few drinks but Robbie was never one to over-do it or to go out at the wrong times. Professional football always came first for him."

Wolves found it hard to reproduce the form of the previous season and although Keane scored the winner against Middlesbrough in November and the equaliser against Ipswich Town in the same month, they were still only flirting with sixth place that would secure them another bash at the play-offs.

And a terrible three-month finale to Keane's debut season — four wins in 17 games — saw Wolves slump to ninth after the final day 2-1 defeat away to Tranmere Rovers. Keane's form had also dipped, with only thee goals in his last 11 games of the campaign. But Wolves would march into the semi-finals of the FA Cup with victories over Darlington, Charlton Athletic, Wimbledon and Leeds United in the quarter-finals, when Goodman's late winner at Elland Road would secure a place in the last four.

Keane was now in and out of the Wolves side and was introduced as a substitute for Bull against a Leeds outfit that included Harry Kewell and Jimmy Floyd Hasselbaink and was being groomed by manager George Graham for greater success under David O'Leary.

"Towards the end of his first season Robbie had started to run out of energy simply because we had asked too much of him," admitted McGhee. "Perhaps we had asked too much of him because he was practically carrying the team. Physically, he got tired but mentally, there were never any problems for him."

When McGhee sat down on April 8 to select his team for the Villa Park semi-final showdown with Arsenal, Keane was again left on the bench but he would replace Kevin Muscat as the underdogs chased an equaliser to Christopher Wreh's 12th-minute strike. It was an equaliser that would never come.

If the season ended on a disappointing note, there was no disguising the fact that Keane had arrived as a star of the future at Wolves and his performances saw him elected by his fellow professionals on to the PFA First Division team of the season — the only Irishman to achieve that feat in the top two divisions that year.

Keane was also on the move with Ireland, for whom he made his debut in March, 1998 in the 2-1 friendly defeat to the Czech Republic in Olomouc. Mick McCarthy would introduce the young striker as a half-time replacement that afternoon in the remote northern Czech city.

A month later the Dubliner was scaring the daylights out of Daniel Passarella's World Cup-bound Argentina at Lansdowne Road as Keane started the friendly.

If promotion had again evaded Wolves, Crowe is adamant that the foundations for Keane's career had been solidly driven into the west midlands earth.

"In the dressing room, Robbie was always the one having the laugh and cracking the joke. He was never overawed by his surroundings. He was simply that cheeky, lovable fella that if there were gags going on, he was involved. I'm sure that's helped him wherever he has gone."

Keane was not shy to approach Kylie Minogue in the hospitality room prior to appearing on the Kenny Show on RTE television, showing that his confidence was building off the pitch too.

"Some players, like myself, take time to settle when they go to a new club. I can't imagine that being the case with Robbie, as was proved when he was quickly scoring goals for Aston Villa after his loan move from LA Galaxy," says Crowe.

Keane's quick rise through the ranks at Wolves prompted the club to ensure that they kept their most valuable asset satisfied in monetary terms, and he signed two new contracts within two years of moving to Molineux having agreed an original four-year professional deal.

"I got a good four-year contract when I went to Wolves," said Keane. "Next year, that was ripped up and they gave me another. I was quite clued-in as a young-fella. I needed a bit of advice but I knew what I was doing."

In the summer of 1998, Keane and the rest of the football world marvelled at the French flair of Zinedine Zidane as Les Bleus captured their first ever World Cup crown by beating Brazil 3-0 in the final in Paris. Keane, however, had his own international exploits to reflect on before returning to Wolves for pre-season training ahead of the 1998-99 campaign.

As part of Brian Kerr's Ireland Under-18 squad, Keane had played a key part in the team's UEFA European Youth Championship win in Cyprus in July as Ireland defeated Germany in a penalty shoot-out in the final.

It helped to complete a truly remarkable national double following the UEFA European Under-16 Championship win by Kerr's side in Scotland two months earlier.

That success would not bring the curtain down on Keane's underage success with his country but from now on, it was the hard graft of league points and competitive qualifiers in Mick McCarthy's team that would form the mainstay of his blossoming career.

Premiership managers and chairmen were also now taking a real interest in Wolves' attacking star, with McGhee fending off questions about his availability in the transfer market. When Wolves played Barnet in the League Cup in late August, Arsenal boss Arsene Wenger was present to check on Keane, who had an off-night in a 2-1 first-leg defeat.

Keane was on the mark on the opening day of the 1998-99 season, with the first goal in the 2-0 home win against Tranmere. With four victories and one draw in August, Wolves appeared to mean business in their bid to achieve promotion to the promised land of the Premiership. However, McGhee would be replaced as manager by Colin Lee following a poor run of results in October and early November.

Keane's absence with a knee injury — that required minor surgery — hardly helped McGhee or Wolves as he missed seven league games between mid-October and mid-November.

Despite the manager's departure, Wolves struggled to produce a consistent run of form and they would finish the campaign one place and three points behind Bolton Wanderers for the last of the four play-off spots. If Keane had failed to repeat the feats of his debut season with Wolves, he was still their top striker and ended the campaign with 11 league goals from 33 appearances.

His two goals away to Bolton saw Wolves advance to the fourth round of the FA Cup on a 2-1 scoreline, where they would face holders Arsenal, who had ended their hopes at the semi-final stage the previous season. The pre-match build-up included plenty of speculation about Keane's future, with some talk again linking the Dubliner with Arsenal and Middlesbrough, although earlier speculation about a Spurs bid had waned.

Wolves officially confirmed that Middlesbrough boss Bryan Robson had tabled a £5m offer prior to the cup tie, with Managing Director John Richards stating that the bid had been rejected point-blank.

Keane had a quiet match against the Gunners, as Dennis Bergkamp struck a deserved winner in the 69th minute to give the visitors a 2-1 margin of victory.

A knee injury — originally sustained the previous autumn — was now causing Keane some irritation and he required injections prior to games. His league form was patchy as the season turned into spring and he failed to find the net following his goal in the 1-1 home draw against Oxford United on February 6. Not helping Keane at club level was his absence for a three-week spell to mid-April when he was on duty with Kerr's team at the FIFA Under-20 World Cup in Nigeria.

If Wolves and other European clubs bristled with anger at FIFA's failure to play the tournament outside their main club season, Keane and his teammates were anxious to emulate their predecessors of 1997, who had claimed the bronze medals in Malaysia.

Ireland youth team boss Brian Kerr and the FAI were adamant that Keane should travel to Nigeria, and FIFA's laws and statutes made it clear that clubs had to release players who were selected by their countries.

Keane recognised the dilemma all three parties faced. "I'm hoping someone else makes the decision for me," said the Dubliner in March. "If I go to the tournament I will be missing matches which could decide whether Wolves reach the play-offs or win promotion.

"If I don't go, I could be seen to be letting Ireland and its people down. I don't want to let anyone down."

Wolves boss Colin Lee made his own anger clear and Wolves appealed to the FAI in a written submission to allow Keane to remain on club duty.

"Robbie is a full international and we feel this should be taken into account," stated Lee. "But we are aware that if our appeal is turned down there is nothing we can do as they are within their rights to call him up."

There was no way that the FAI and Kerr were going to allow one of their stars to stay at home and Keane would miss five crucial league matches. On his return to Molineux, he appeared short of energy and Lee was again annoyed when his striker was called up for the 2-0 friendly win over Sweden at Lansdowne Road on April 28.

"I hope that Ireland treat him as we have," said Lee. "Robbie's whacked and it would be crazy for him to play in a friendly when we are leaving him out of crucial games."

Mick McCarthy, sympathetic to Wolves' plight, only put Keane in for the final 12 minutes for Niall Quinn. With Wolves missing out on the play-offs by three points, many at the club felt that the loss of Keane at such a vital stage of the season had been a major setback to their promotion hopes.

And before the precious 1-0 home win over Macedonia in the Euro 2000 qualifier in June, 1999, Keane admitted that his lengthy season — that began in Cyprus the previous July — had taken its toll.

"I felt a little flat in last month's friendly against Northern Ireland and that was reflected in my play," he said. "But I've been on the go all season and travelling to Nigeria with the Under-20s in April took a lot out of me."

However, Keane was able to depart for his summer holidays content in the knowledge that his international career was moving forward, while speculation mounted over his club future. Throughout July, Keane was seriously linked with Leeds United, Middlesbrough, Newcastle United and Aston Villa, with Wolves making it known that a large offer would bring them to the negotiating table.

"Sooner or later, most players move on," said Managing Director Richards. "In Robbie's case it could well be sooner. There have been no firm bids yet but if someone offers us the kind of figure we are seeking, then we probably won't be in a position to refuse."

And Colin Lee's statement on his own transfer budget only reaffirmed the belief that Keane would soon be on his way.

"It would be better if Robbie went quickly," outlined Lee. "Otherwise, I don't have a single penny to spend in the transfer market, which makes it difficult to bring in the players I want."

However, when the 1999-2000 season kicked-off in August, Keane was still very much a Wolves player and the constant media talk had certainly not ruffled the now 19-year-old's focus. Having secured promotion from Division Two just three months earlier by virtue of an extraordinary play-off final win over Gillingham at Wembley, Maine Road was almost full to capacity for the club's first match of the season, the visit of Wolves.

Keane's goal on the half-hour mark silenced the home support and gave the visitors all three points. Six days later, Keane notched the second-half equaliser in the 1-1 home draw against Portsmouth. Manager Lee, Keane's teammates and the player himself could surely look forward to a season where his goals could finally inspire the club to promotion, either automatically or through the play-offs. But it wasn't to be.

Joe Royle's Manchester City would achieve promotion the following May while Wolves would again fall short, with another seventh-placed league finish. Keane, however, would fast-track his own move into the Premiership before August was out as Coventry City finally matched their talk with a firm offer for the hottest teenage property outside the top flight.

As Villa's £5.5m offer in late July fell short of their neighbours' valuation of Keane, Coventry manager Gordon Strachan insisted that his board go the extra mile and tender a bid of £6m. Reluctantly, Wolves agreed to sell Keane just two years after he had made his debut for the club.

"I was not surprised at all when a Premier League club came in for Robbie as he had built up a great reputation with Wolves," says Crowe. "The only thing that surprised me was that Wolves had not cracked it because they had put a lot of money into the team. That was the hardest part, I always felt, because once they went up, they had the money to spend to stay there."

Keane was now really in the big time, even if the club he had joined had claimed only one major trophy — the FA Cup in 1987.

Strachan was more than satisfied that he had made a shrewd investment. Two of football's most crucial assets — goals and money — would prove the Scot right.

Chapter 5
Boy in Green

EVEN prior to Robbie Keane's accelerated progress at Wolves, the waif-like centre-forward was making waves in the green shirt.

Few footballers enjoy successful careers without being the recipient of the occasional stroke of good fortune. Keane was no different although, like all great players, it was talent and application to his trade that formed the foundation for glory.

As Keane continued to hammer home goals for Crumlin United in the Dublin and District Schoolboys League, it appeared that an Irish call-up was only a matter of time away. However, Under-15 national team manager Joe McGrath was not completely convinced about Keane, and when he moved on to play in the Under-16 schoolboy grade, he was again overlooked when the team successfully embarked upon the European qualifiers in the autumn of 1995 for the finals to be staged by Austria in the spring of 1996.

But when the Irish Daily Star's Derek Foley reported on the Under-16 side's preparations for the opening group match of the finals against hosts Austria on April 29, 1996 in St Polten — located less than an hour's drive west of Vienna — he noted that there was a change to manager Liam O'Brien's expected starting eleven. It would prove to be a pivotal moment in the young attacker's formative teenage years.

"There has been a late call-up for Robbie Keane who will start following the withdrawal of Paddy Fitzpatrick," reported Foley. "Stephen McPhail, Niall Byrne and newcomer Gerard Crossley, in particular, have been making big progress at their clubs."

And manager O'Brien was confident that Keane — still playing his football with Crumlin United although destined for Wolves in little more than two months — would adapt to his new surroundings.

"Robbie has grown up so much in the last year," stated O'Brien. "The preparation has been excellent and from going to tournaments and playing twice in two days at Lilleshall recently, we know who is able to dig deep." And just as Keane would later make a habit of creating an impact on his debuts, this first competitive outing for his country would be no different.

"Sixty nail-biting seconds into injury time, Robbie Keane raced 30 yards to the edge of the Austrian box," said Foley in his match report. "And with time practically frozen, he tucked the ball under the out-coming keeper. It was a dream debut, dream goal and a dream start for Ireland."

The home side protested as the final whistle sounded just seconds later, but the Israeli referee was dismissive of claims that Keane had been offside.

"I was coming back from a run but tracking sideways when Niall won the ball," said Keane. "I knew there was a lad chasing back behind me but I was sort of waiting to see what the goalkeeper would do before I made up my mind.

"In the end I just hit it and because he spread himself so big it went under his body, through his legs — I think!"

Two days later, Ireland crashed 2-0 to Portugal at Atzenbrugg with the slick Portuguese worthy winners, although Keane had a great chance to give Ireland the lead just before the break when the match was scoreless. But with Austria and Poland ending level at 0-0, a win or a draw in the final group match against Poland would see the Irish into the knockout stages.

O'Brien's side strode confidently into the quarter-finals thanks to a 64th-minute winner from Stephen McPhail, who was selected by UEFA's Scottish coaching guru Andy Roxburgh as the most skilful player among the 16 nations.

Now France — who had beaten Croatia, Spain and Switzerland in the group phase — awaited Ireland in the last eight back in Amstetten. A tense, well-contested encounter failed to produce a goal during normal time or extra time, although Clive Clarke's electric 60-yard run almost produced a breakthrough and substitute Richie Partridge fired just over.

France's first spot-kick was saved and when McPhail, Clarke and Sean Mannion all converted their penalties, Ireland were on the verge of going through. But Richard Dunne — majestic alongside Tim McGrath in the heart of the Irish back four in all of the games — saw his effort saved, with France then levelling the score at 3-3. Ger Crossley netted, as did the French, and it was the unfortunate David Freeman who missed to see Les Bleus advance as their first effort in sudden-death was converted.

It was a numbing moment for the Ireland players but many of this squad would go on to enjoy glory with the youths while Keane had announced his arrival in a green shirt. He, too, would progress to savour the winners' podium for his country. Keane would have to wait 17 months for his next Ireland call-up when Brian Kerr selected a squad for a youth friendly against Northern Ireland at Tolka Park in October, 1997.

Kerr had taken over as Ireland youth and Under-16 manager earlier in 1997 following his appointment by the FAI as its national director of coaching. It was a hugely popular decision within the game, for Kerr had won League of Ireland titles with his beloved St Patrick's Athletic in 1990 and 1996 when operating on limited financial budgets. He also played a key role in saving the club from oblivion in the early nineties when debts mounted. Kerr was one of those whose hard work ensured that the Saints returned to Richmond Park in the autumn of 1993 after five years as tenants at Harold's Cross Stadium, where the greyhounds' underfoot conditions on the dog track were infinitely superior to the bumpy, rutted surface on the football pitch.

The feisty and jocular Dubliner from the southside area of Drimnagh had served part of his apprenticeship at underage level and had been Liam Tuohy's assistant when Ireland competed in the 1985 FIFA Under-20 World Cup in the USSR, where Ireland lost all three group games in the Georgian capital of Tbilisi.

Tuohy and Kerr had quit their posts in the spring of 1986 just weeks after the appointment of Jack Charlton as Ireland senior team manager after a run-in with the Englishman at half-time in a youth friendly international at Elland Road.

Kerr would start the transformation of coaching throughout the country and tackled his jobs as Under-16 and 18 national team coach with gusto. And he enjoyed immediate success by guiding the Ireland Under-20 side to third place at the FIFA World Cup finals in Malaysia in June, 1997. That squad included Damien Duff, Glen Crowe, Dessie Baker and Trevor Molloy, although Kerr seriously considered adding Keane — just short of his 17th birthday and still eligible to play in the next finals in 1999 — to his 18-strong panel after the Wolves youth team star impressed in a number of warm-up matches staged in Limerick.

"We called in a few of the younger lads to train with us when we prepared the Under-20 side for Malaysia in Limerick last May," said Kerr. "Robbie showed then that he was clearly a talented player.

"He was a skinny fella. I knew about him in Crumlin because Crumlin was my original team. But I had not seen him until that day and I genuinely thought about taking him to Malaysia but it was too late," added Kerr, who had adjusted his thinking only a week or two earlier to accommodate Molloy, who had impressed in training to build on his outstanding stint on loan with Athlone Town from Shamrock Rovers in the season just ended.

"We were taking Damien Duff, who was a year older, and we had the squad picked."

Another highly-regarded coach, Maurice Price, had been the team's manager during the European Youth Champion-ship finals, jointly hosted by France and Luxembourg in 1996, when the French triumphed with a side that numbered Thierry Henry, Nicolas Anelka, William Gallas, Mikael Silvestre and David Trezeguet.

In those finals, Ireland drew 1-1 with Italy and played out

a scoreless draw against Spain before David Thompson's lone strike gave England — boasting Michael Owen, Rio Ferdinand and Frank Lampard — victory in the final group match. The Irish failed to reach the semi-finals but did claim the last of the six berths on offer for the World Cup in Malaysia thanks to their goal difference of minus one!

In the World Cup finals during June and July, 1997, Ireland's youngsters grabbed the attention of the nation to claim the bronze medals having qualified for the quarter-finals after a group phase that saw them beat USA (2-1) and draw with China (1-1) in the wake of an opening day 2-1 setback to Ghana. Morocco were despatched 2-1 in extra time in the quarter-finals, with Molloy's first-half penalty sending Ireland into the uncharted territory of the semi-finals where Argentina — boasting Juan Riquelme, Esteban Cambiasso and Pablo Aimar — would finally end the Irish dream thanks to Bernardo Romeo's 55th-minute goal.

There was still the matter of the third/fourth place play-off to be decided, and on July 5 goals by Baker and Duff earned Ireland revenge over Ghana in a 2-1 victory. Third place in the tournament had been secured — the nation's highest ever place in a major global finals in any field sport.

A few hours later in the same Shah Alam Stadium in Kuala Lumpur, Argentina defeated Uruguay in the final by the same score.

Ireland had been gripped by the team's success and Kerr vowed that this was just the start of long-term success at under-age level. A few weeks later in Iceland, Kerr's team finished fourth in the UEFA European Under-18 finals.

So in October, 1997, Kerr assembled his squad for the warm-up match against Northern Ireland ahead of the forthcoming Under-18 qualifiers with the ultimate intention of clinching the World Under-20 crown in Nigeria in April, 1999. Ireland strolled to a 4-0 win over Northern Ireland with Ryan Casey and Barry Quinn each scoring but it was Keane's two-goal barrage in the 34th and 75th minutes that stole the show.

And Keane — now playing week-in, week-out for Wolves, stunned the crowd of less than 1,500 present with a truly exceptional first-half strike. Receiving the ball on the edge of the box with two defenders in front of him, he feigned to shoot but instead flicked it past the two opponents. He then ran around the pair, and as the keeper advanced to narrow the angle, Keane dinked the ball over him.

It was the perfect tonic for Kerr's troops prior to the three-nation qualifying group to be staged in Moldova later that month involving the hosts and Azerbaijan. But Wolves manager Mark McGhee was not happy that his rising star was making the trek to the former Soviet Republic.

"It's a scandal that Robbie can be taken away to an obscure tournament like this," moaned McGhee. "It's wrong for the player and it's wrong for us."

But the FAI were not for turning and, backed by UEFA and FIFA laws, Kerr selected Keane for the competitive games.

On October 22 in the Moldovan capital of Chisinau, Ireland secured a merited 4-2 victory over Azerbaijan. Liam George scored the first and third goals while Damien Lynch notched the second before Duff and George combined to set up Keane for the last goal. Two days later, Keane's 83rd-minute strike was enough to claim the three points and send Ireland into a two-legged play-off against Greece.

Kerr kept faith with the same side apart from Casey for Duff, although he introduced Richie Partridge for O'Brien in the 75th minute and then put on defender David Billington for midfielder Casey just after Keane's winner. It was a thoroughly professional success for the Irish, who had been provided with less than desirable hotel accommodation. The lift would stop 14 inches above the floor when destined for the lobby level — requiring guests to 'jump' the final part of their descent. Requests by the FAI to switch hotels met with a negative response as the hosts claimed that hotel rooms were extremely scarce due to a summit of CIS (the successor of the old Soviet Union) heads of state in Chisinau.

By the time the first leg against the Greeks was played on March 25, 1998, another manager wanted Keane in his squad — not McGhee, but Ireland senior manager Mick McCarthy, whose team was playing a friendly against the Czech Republic in the small city of Olomouc on the same day.

So while Kerr took his squad to the northern Greek town of Veria close to the Macedonia border, Keane was joining up with a new-look senior panel for the first time. Kerr had asked McCarthy if he would release Keane for the youth side but McCarthy — who had seen his and the nation's 1998 World Cup qualifying dreams end in bitter disappointment the previous November in Brussels with a 2-1 second leg play-off defeat by Belgium — was adamant that he needed to use this friendly to blood new players.

Keane would make his debut against the Czechs, replacing one of the other five senior debutants, Alan Maybury, in a 2-1 defeat that saw Mark Kinsella and Damien Duff also start their first senior games for their country, with Graham Kavanagh and Rory Delap joining them as second-half substitutes.

It was easy to have sympathy for both managers, whose initial cordial relationship following Kerr's appointment 14 months earlier would slowly disintegrate to a point where they seldom spoke. Kerr believed this youths side could make an impression at the finals if they qualified, while McCarthy wanted to build a new senior team for the Euro 2000 qualifying campaign that had landed Ireland with the Balkan giants of Croatia and Yugoslavia.

Ronnie O'Brien's 26th-minute winner would be enough to earn the Irish a valuable win over the Greeks, with the Middlesbrough striker joined up front by Liverpool's Richie Partridge and Luton Town's Liam George in a flexible unit that could drop to form a five-man midfield. The second leg would take place at Dublin's Tolka Park on May 14 and, once again, Keane would play no part. This time, however, an ankle injury picked up in a league match against Middlesbrough would rule him out.

"He's not fit and his ankle is too sore," explained Kerr on the eve of the game. "But when I get Curtis Fleming I'm clattering him because it was his tackle that put him out of this match," joked Kerr about his former St Patrick's Athletic star, who he sold to Boro for £70,000 in 1991.

Kerr would also lose Duff for the game, with Blackburn Rovers stating that the winger was suffering from a groin injury. For Kerr and his assistant, the late Noel O'Reilly, the game came just a week after they had steered the Ireland Under-16 team to glory in the UEFA Championship finals in Scotland with a squad that included John O'Shea, Jonathan Douglas, Liam Miller and Andy Reid.

The Greeks had learned lessons from their first-leg defeat and they caused the home side its share of problems. It was only when Sheffield Wednesday's Alan Quinn replaced the injured Stephen McPhail in the 57th minute that Ireland began to assert control. Quinn scored the crucial opener in the 79th minute and Ryan Casey's cross was pushed into his own goal by Nastos for an injury-time insurance second. Ireland were on their way to Cyprus in July for the finals.

Keane — who had marked his home senior bow in April with an outstanding display against Argentina in the 2-0 friendly defeat — would win his third senior cap against Mexico at Lansdowne Road nine days after the Greece encounter, before departing for a well-earned holiday after an event-filled first season in the senior game.

When Kerr's squad departed to Cyprus in mid-July, they did so from a country that had been seduced by the heroics of the players in the previous year that had finished third in the FIFA Under-20 World Cup in Malaysia. The European Under-16 success in Scotland added to the sense of anticipation. If there was disappointment with the senior international team's failure to qualify for back-to-back tournaments, teenage kicks were filling the void to some extent. The presence of established club and senior international stars Duff and Keane in the panel only increased the level of expectation. And Kerr's Midas touch further fuelled this optimism, although the loss of Duff through injury for the finals was a definite setback.

Once again, Kerr's preparations were carried out to the nth degree and the players were brilliantly briefed as to what awaited them under the baking, cloud-free skies of the eastern Mediterranean.

"The first priority is to qualify for the Under-20 World Cup in Nigeria but obviously we are going out to Cyprus to try and win the tournament as well," said Kerr, whose long-term aim was equally as important to him as short-term success.

A warm-up game against a team comprised of local United Nations troops ended in a 22-0 victory, with Keane notching six and the manager appeared pleased that his star striker had settled back in quickly prior to the opening group clash with Croatia.

"Robbie has only played the two competitive matches against Moldova and the Northern Ireland friendly so we have not had him for the last six matches," said Kerr.

If the cool conditions of Scotland were a home from home for the Under-16 players, then Cyprus was more akin to Malaysia. And UEFA's extraordinary decision to insist on a group stage programme of games on Sunday, Tuesday and Thursday with a final between the two group winners the following Sunday flew in the face of all logic. It also went against medical opinion in such testing conditions.

"This is the hottest environment I have ever played football. But I aim to make it hot for all the other teams in Cyprus," said Keane. "Brian gave us a training programme to follow and I went back to Wolves three weeks early, where Mark McGhee made sure I carried it out.

"Playing for the youths is as important to me as playing for the Ireland senior team — you're representing your country."

In the opening group game against Croatia in the noisy and brash tourist haunt of Ayia Napa, Keane and the Irish delivered as the striker scored, set up a brace and Kerr's lads won 5-2. Within nine minutes of the kick-off Keane found the net having earlier presented the chance that allowed Liam George to net inside 45 seconds. The Croats battled back to level, however, before Keane's cross gave Stephen McPhail the opportunity to restore Ireland's lead on the stroke of half-time. Partridge extended Ireland's lead midway through the second period and George sealed the win with the fifth.

With England beating the hosts 2-1, the Ireland-England meeting on Tuesday, July 21 was rightly regarded as potentially decisive in determining who would reach the final as group winners. A closely-contested clash saw Howard Wilkinson's team triumph 1-0, with a former club protégé of the manager at Leeds United, Alan Smith, netting the only goal five minutes from full-time.

But the Irish had enjoyed their moments, with O'Brien volleying over and Barry Quinn going close, although Keane and George found the England central defence of Matthew Upson and Jonathan Woodgate hard to make progress against.

"We completely dominated the second half and battered their goal — we were all over them," said Kerr. "The goal came from a little lack of concentration but we had enough chances to make that goal irrelevant and not taking them was our costliest mistake.

"There is a glimmer of hope — Croatia will be determined," added Kerr about the final group games, although he must have held out only a slim hope that Croatia would defeat England to allow Ireland progress if they saw off Cyprus.

Kerr's forecast proved uncannily accurate, and as Ireland cruised past Cyprus 3-0, Croatia were beating Wilkinson's side by the same scoreline in Derynia. Keane grabbed two goals in the 45th and 78th minutes to add to Barry Quinn's early opener in a thoroughly professional Irish display. Keane's superb contribution led to Marios Elia being sent off for kicking the striker, but Kerr revealed that Wilkinson — regarded as one of Europe's leading coaches — had committed a basic psychological blunder in the days prior to the final group matches.

"Howard Wilkinson was moaning to me about how UEFA

wanted him to bring his players to a reception for three hours just two days before the final," smiled Kerr. "We thought that if we got to the final, we wouldn't care if we were taken away for 10 hours!"

Keane was elated after the win and was in no doubt that England's demise was the correct outcome after five days of frantic action in the sun.

He said: "I'm on such a high. It was so nerve-wracking waiting for the final whistle to come through from the England game. We were the best team in the group and we've proved that because we are in the final.

"It took a combination of results on the night but first and foremost we had to do the business and beat the host nation. We are all delighted with the result and, personally, I am well pleased because I have now scored three goals at this level. I kept thinking to myself that England might get two penos or something like that because they usually do."

Ireland were already assured of a place in Nigeria by virtue of their top-three finish in the group, and going into the final against Germany there was a real sense in the Ireland camp that they could win the match, even if they were underdogs.

The Germans had trounced Lithuania 7-1 in their opening group encounter and then cruised past Spain 4-1. But a 2-0 defeat to Portugal in the final game meant Germany required goal difference to reach the final after a three-way tie involving the three major nations. Sebastian Deisler — who would enjoy a short, dazzling career at senior international level before succumbing to major injury — was pulling the strings in midfield while Andreas Gensler was also hugely thought-of by the Germans.

"We will respect the German team but there will be no fear," declared Kerr. "It's a beautiful place but the lads had no problems with going to bed when they were supposed to, staying out of the sun, drinking the isotonic solutions we prepare for them and eating the right food.

"Some of our football has been brilliant and all of the eight goals came from play, usually from a bit of classy movement."

On the eve of the final, in a feature article by Stephen Finn in the Irish Daily Star, Keane spoke about his status as the star of the side even though he was the third youngest member of the panel.

"My confidence is sky high at the moment. If you play first team every week and have three senior caps you should be confident at this level," insisted Keane. "The attention won't bother me. This is a big game for me but after sharing a pitch with the likes of Ortega and Batistuta, I'm experienced enough to deal with the situation.

"Wolves didn't really want me here because they had a tour to Austria and Germany but the situation was out of my hands and thankfully it got sorted out. I felt this was an honour that was not going to come along very often and I wanted to make a big impression."

Kerr's assistant, the late Noel O'Reilly, was a soft-spoken member of the management set-up who would make his point quietly to a player. He was also a gifted guitarist and singer whose ability to create a family atmosphere with his evening sing-song was a central plank in creating an unbreakable spirit in the Irish camp. This was the case during the week prior to the games and then throughout the hectic week of action.

Keane, too, had the singing bug and readily took up the challenge from teammates to bash out a few numbers on the guitar.

"My dad played guitar in a band and my housemate, Stephen Hackett, has one too so I thought I'd learn how to play. It's just good craic, I'm a terrible singer so I won't be following in Nicky Byrne's footsteps by joining a boy band!" added Keane about the former Leeds United FA Youth Cup medal winner, who had traded life on the pitch for a career with Westlife.

Keane also revealed that his trickery on the ball and his somersault celebration were inspired by Brazil at that summer's World Cup finals in France. "I watched the Brazilians and decided I wanted to do their tricks so I went into the back garden and gave it a lash.

"I've been doing somersaults since I was at Under-10 level with Fettercairn United and I kept doing them at Crumlin United. I played Gaelic football too for Noamh Eanna but I didn't do any flips, I was scoring so many points that I would have been exhausted!

"We were upset about losing to England. We tried to put a brave face on it but it will be hard for fellas going back to their clubs having lost to England. We didn't play as well as we could have against England and we will always regret that if we don't win the tournament."

It was a brave admission to make on Keane's part ahead of such a huge game but it once again proved that he was not overawed by such occasions. By now, Keane's dad Robert and mam Anne had travelled to Cyprus and immediately fitted into the family atmosphere created by Kerr, O'Reilly and the FAI party.

Robbie would be the only Ireland player to miss from the penalty spot in the shoot-out to decide the destination of the trophy after 120 minutes of football in Larnaca's Zenon Stadium. Germany dominated the first half, with Deisler magnificent. But it was Ireland who took the lead after 71 minutes when Keane — with neat footwork — set up substitute Alan Quinn, whose introduction at the interval changed the course of the game.

The Irish would hold out until deep into injury time, when Gensler sent the game into extra-time. No further goals meant penalties, and West Ham keeper Alex O'Reilly emerged as the Irish hero as he saved Germany's first effort from Andreas Voss. When Ryan Casey netted with Ireland's first spot-kick and Tobias Schaper struck the post with Germany's second, Paul Donnelly then put Kerr's side two goals clear. Christian Timm reduced the arrears to 2-1 with Germany's third shot before Keane's poorly-struck penalty allowed Timo Hildebrand to save. Manuel Majunke found the net to level the scores at 2-2 but Barry Quinn restored Ireland's lead. Thorsten Schramm again restored parity at 3-3 with his side's final spot-kick before Liam George stroked home the decisive penalty to give Ireland a 4-3 victory and create European football history by becoming the first country to win the Under-16 and 18 crowns in the one season.

"We were all saying afterwards how Liam George looked like David O'Leary," joked Keane afterwards, with reference to the former Arsenal and Ireland star whose spot-kick had beaten Romania in the 1990 World Cup.

"I don't care that I missed my peno because we still won. But after the Germany equaliser I nearly fainted."

Kerr said: "Our attack of Robbie Keane and Liam George was the best of all the participating teams."

There were few who would challenge that assertion.

As the squad and FAI party returned to Dublin for an official reception by the Lord Mayor of the city, Senator Joe Doyle, another Keane was giving his verdict on the Tallaght man's impact in Cyprus.

"Robbie is excellent — he'll be world class by the time he gets to 24," said Roy Keane in Norway ahead of his return to action for the first time since his cruciate knee ligament operation the previous September.

The elder Keane's judgment would not be found wanting. His only miscalculation would be the length of time it would take Robbie to make his mark on the highest stage of the world game.

Chapter 6
Tropical storm

ROBBIE Keane signed off a glittering youth and underage career with Ireland in a tournament that English football wanted to ignore.

The FIFA Under-20 World Cup staged in Nigeria in April, 1999, would see the Irish make the third of the nation's four appearances at a championship that has become a key staging post for many players on their way to stardom.

FIFA's decision to award the tournament to sub-Saharan Africa for the first time — the inaugural FIFA tournament at this age level had been hosted by Tunisia in 1977 — sparked a chorus of protests from many European clubs. Apart from their annoyance over the timing of the finals during the run-in to domestic league championships, there was a fear of random violence. Regions of Nigeria were extremely volatile at the time, although the nakedly sectarian killings that would become commonplace in the following decade were less prevalent.

Aside from politically-motivated attacks, there were fears over the general high level of crime in the country. With England, Spain, Portugal and Croatia also making the journey from Europe, the voices of discontent from big clubs became louder as the days counted down to the opening game on April 3, between the hosts and Costa Rica.

Ireland manager Brian Kerr, his staff, the FAI official party and the players all adopted a pragmatic and softly-softly approach to the security issues. Fearful of both upsetting and insulting their hosts, they did not speak publicly about any privately-held negative views. Anyway, the FAI had been keen to face down British clubs wishing to withdraw their players from Kerr's squad and correctly believed that any reservations on their part about the finals or Nigeria would only assist those clubs' wishes to hold on to their players.

FIFA's laws clearly stated that national federations had the right to call-up anybody they wished. Leeds United boss David O'Leary had been particularly vocal in his criticism of the venue and the timing of the tournament, with Stephen McPhail's Elland Road teammates Jonathan Woodgate, Alan Smith and Lee Matthews all omitted from boss Howard Wilkinson's squad for the finals. The three players had featured in the European finals the previous summer.

However, Leeds were not the only Premiership outfit to get their way with the FA and Wilkinson. Another rising teenage star of English football, West Ham's Joe Cole, was also excused duty. Matthew Upson, another member of the team in Cyprus, was also missing. The strength in depth of English football, however, meant that Ashley Cole, Stephen Wright, Peter Crouch and Paul Rachubka all came into Wilkinson's plans.

In mid-January, Wilkinson had all but admitted that he had written his country's top young established stars out of his squad, stating that of the 66 players he considered, 28 featured in first-team squads in the Premiership and First Division (now Championship) and were unlikely to travel to Nigeria.

"Clearly we have to live in the real world and the demands made on young players in the Premiership and Football League," said Wilkinson. "Young players who are involved in first-team squads on a week-to-week basis are unlikely to go. It would be futile trying to start a war concerning the release of first-team players."

Even FIFA began to have concerns as the opening game approached, with the hiring of two British Airways 737 planes to be used to ferry teams from venue to venue across this vast country. And the planned sale of tickets through a large local bank network also failed to materialise until the eve of the tournament.

There were no such hang-ups about the finals among senior FAI officials and Kerr, who saw the tournament as a crucial stage in the development of young players and the spread of the football gospel throughout Ireland. The squad flew to Nigeria on March 29 and set up base camp in the city of Ibadan — a sprawling metropolis of more than 1.3million people located 125kilometres inland from the former capital of Lagos — where the team would play its three group games against Mexico, Saudi Arabia and Australia. The Irish travelled in confident mood, with Damien Duff upbeat about the finals having been forced to sit out the Under-18 European victory nine months earlier with a groin injury.

"Hopefully we do the business again in Nigeria," said Duff, who was joining an elite group of players to feature in two Under-20 World Cup finals. "I don't want to stick my neck out and say we are going to win it but we are going out to do well."

If there was still a degree of apprehension about the security situation, the Irish were intent on making the best of their circumstances. Within 48 hours of arriving in Ibadan, they had established a close relationship with the Irish Embassy in Lagos, ex-pat workers in the country and, crucially, the large number of Catholic missionaries operating there. And it was the locally-based SMA Fathers — through Fr Tim Cullinane and Fr Damian Bresnahan — who provided a makeshift, small-sized but well manicured pitch for a much-needed impromptu friendly with South Korea the day after arriving.

The match lasted 74 minutes and left many players flat-out with exhaustion, but Kerr was now armed with a clear-cut view of the problems he and his squad would face. Keith Doyle suffered severe dehydration and had to receive prompt medical attention on the sideline, and Richard Sadlier — who had missed the Cyprus victory with a persistent groin injury — found the heat extremely oppressive.

"I had never experienced heat like that before or played in those conditions before," recalls Sadlier. "I remember when we played Nigeria in the second round, even the Nigerian lads had to warm-up in the stand to get into the shade, it was incredible."

With FIFA and the local organising committee petrified of

an incident happening involving players or visiting federation officials, the team hotel, The Premier, became a fortress due to the massive security that ensured nobody could penetrate.

However, it meant that the Irish group became virtual prisoners inside. Kerr was even forced to abandon plans to attend a local television station to discuss the finals after the local security guards were unable to find a plain-clothes policeman to accompany him on his journey.

"It was a joy to be there, it was a brilliant experience but there were real frustrating elements to it as well because of the climate and the security risks," adds Sadlier. "There was also the difficulty in contacting home, the length of the trip and the boredom, as you couldn't leave the hotel. But it was a really great trip and the majority of the lads bonded well."

A three-minute phone call home cost about £10 and getting a connection was not easy. Irish and British mobile phones did not work on the local Nigerian system, although that was the case in many other European countries and in the USA at that time.

"There are a couple of standout memories. We were over there during Easter so for Easter Sunday we tried to arrange to have mass said together. We could not get a meeting room anywhere as the people we were dealing with were not great at organising things. That frustrated the life out of Brian," says Sadlier.

"We had got to know an Irish priest from Belfast. So somebody got a table and put it in the middle of the corridor, dressed it up as an altar and we had mass in the corridor. Noel O'Reilly had the guitar out at one point and sang a couple of songs. I remember Brian being in tears. At the time I said to myself that I was going to remember this for a long time because even then you knew that this was so unique and that these experiences don't really happen.

"Not being able to leave the hotel, the difficulty in contacting home and the fact that the mobile phones did not work in Nigeria — it all added to the unique feeling. It took ages to get through to home on a landline and a big wad of local notes to pay for it! There was nothing to watch on the television so there were no distractions. You had each other and that brought us together very, very quickly.

"On most trips I was on, there would be lads trying to sneak out of the hotel or get up to some bit of devilment, particularly at the underage level. But there was none of that as it was not safe to do so. We had an armed guard at the end of our corridor. We shared a hotel with Mexico, Saudi Arabia and Australia and each had a corridor to themselves as well as an armed guard posted by the fire exit. So we weren't going to mess around with that."

Keane was already connecting with the local children after staging an exhibition of ball control during a training session at the Liberty Stadium, where Ireland would meet Mexico in their opening game and, indeed, play all three group matches.

"There was an open training session and about 2,000 locals came to watch us," says Sadlier. "Robbie was doing keepie-uppies, juggling the ball and heading it up, just putting on a show. They loved it and cheered him. And he was so comfortable and enjoyed football so much. He appeared to thrive on the attention and the pressure, or that's the way it looked."

Ireland lost their first game to the Mexicans, with Rafael Marquez — who would go on to become one of that country's greatest ever internationals and a star with Barcelona — scoring the seventh-minute winner with a well-struck free-kick from 20 yards. Before the kick-off, the Irish players unfurled a banner that read 'Ireland loves Ibadan people' but the gods were hardly smiling in return.

Keane saw his lob drop inches wide while the Mexican keeper saved his close-range shot. Duff was ruled out of the game with a hamstring strain, while Liam George and Gary Doherty also failed to take chances that came their way. In the final 10 minutes Keane had two more efforts on goal but failed to score.

But it was events off the pitch that grabbed most of the post-match focus. Jason Gavin had been dropped from a stretcher while being carted from the pitch in the 73rd minute — seven minutes after the game had resumed following a 21-minute stoppage due to a floodlight failure when both generators broke down. Amusingly, FIFA president Sepp Blatter had spent the interval telling the media that the finals were going according to plan, only to find himself and the rest of the 7,000 attendance plunged into darkness midway through the second period.

Although the opening 90 minutes had not gone Ireland's way, Saudi Arabia's 3-1 defeat by Australia in their opening game left centre-half Gavin more than optimistic about his side's chances against the Saudis three days later.

"They looked very weak at the back and with Robbie Keane up front we should be able to score against them," remarked Gavin about his teammate and long-time friend from Tallaght.

"I think we are adjusting to the conditions. Anyway, we have better players than them and if we can get on the ball, we can punish them. We have to win the next two games, if we don't then we might be struggling."

The punishing climate had seen Gavin lose three pounds during his 74 minutes on the pitch, with Keane shedding a full half-stone from a frame that was not exactly carrying much excess baggage to start with.

For the second group game, Kerr made sweeping changes to his side. He started the fully-fit Damien Duff on the left wing with Colin Healy dropping out, opted to retain Sadlier in attack beside Keane at the expense of George, dropped Donnelly at right-back in a move that saw Thomas Heary switch to that position and Keith Doyle operating at left-full. And the manager was also forced to replace keeper Alex O'Reilly with Everton's Dean Delaney after his first choice was stricken by a nasty stomach bug.

The changes paid off for Kerr and although the Saudis — cleverly using the oppressive weather to their advantage by playing a game based on possession that forced the Irish to chase them — held out until the 42nd minute, McPhail eventually beat keeper Mabrouk Zaid with a 30-yard scorcher. The goal broke Saudi hearts and, more importantly, their resistance. Duff completed the scoring in the 65th minute after a pass by McPhail, who looked more comfortable in his familiar central midfield role.

It was a key victory but a far from convincing one as the Saudis appeared to have been denied an early goal when a shot looked as if it had bounced down off the bar and across Delaney's goalline. Then, five minutes from full-time, Gary Doherty conceded a penalty but Bandr Al Mutairi blazed over from 12 yards.

"Liam George and Robbie started up front in the first game and I went there expecting very much to be a substitute for the whole tournament," adds Sadlier. "He and Liam had started in attack when they won the Euros and it's difficult to expect to break that up.

"But Liam had an off-night in the first game against Mexico and I came on for the last half-hour and subsequently started each of the remaining four games with Robbie. Nothing that I instinctively wanted to do clashed with what Robbie instinctively wanted to do.

"He was easy to play beside and it's a good starting point in any partnership if you want to instinctively do different things. You are not going to clash and the idea is that hopefully you will complement each other.

"McPhail was brilliant, Barry Quinn was very good and he was the captain — a very good one. All the lads had a lot of time for him. Duff, Robbie, McPhail, Barry Quinn, Healy, myself and Gary Doherty went on to play in the senior squad, with three or four of them winning a load of caps. And we all know what Robbie has done since then."

Mexico's 3-1 win over the Aussies that afternoon in the same stadium left the Australians complaining bitterly about being forced to play two games in the even more difficult conditions of that time of the day when the mercury tipped 100.

Ireland and the Aussies would now meet during the afternoon in this heat on the Saturday to decide who would advance to the knockout stage, where 16 teams would do battle. With goal difference used to separate sides on the same number of points, Ireland only required a draw to proceed, although their opponents boasted a squad blessed with players who would go on to forge impressive club and senior international careers. Brett Emerton, Vince Grella and Marco Bresciano all started but the Irish enjoyed a match to savour as they romped to a 4-0 win, with Sadlier's 20th-minute opener followed by strikes from Duff (73), Healy (74) and Gerard Crossley (90). It was Ireland's most convincing performance to date and it left Keane purring with satisfaction.

"The whole team was magnificent and nobody put a foot wrong," declared Keane. "It's the best I have experienced with Brian and that includes the European Championship in Cyprus last year.

"The heat at the start of the game was a bit of a killer but we are starting to get used to it now. To be honest, I would prefer to play in the afternoon, as we will against Nigeria, than at night when you have to deal with swarms of flies and other insects.

"A variety of people scored against Australia and I am delighted for them. My time will come and I'm not really bothered about not scoring yet."

Keane was playing well but it was Duff — shrugging off his hamstring problem — who was Kerr's jewel. The Irish squad was thrilled that Duff was delivering for his country because he was experiencing a difficult period at Blackburn Rovers. Without a club goal prior to departing to Nigeria and with new manager Brian Kidd not using him every week, Duff was unsure about his long-term future at Ewood Park. By the time that he returned to Rovers, they were in the vortex of an eight-match winless Premiership streak, stretching to the final day of the season that would see them relegated, fully six points adrift of safety.

"Anybody who scores two magical goals, and they were magical, must be rated as the tournament's best performer to date," gushed Kerr. "I have not seen anything better."

Duff set up Sadlier's opener and then beat three defenders to grab the second for himself while his natural relationship on the pitch with Keane — a potent force for Ireland at senior level for many years to come — was flourishing. Keane might not have found the net in three games but Sadlier recalls that his strike partner was in scintillating form and a joy to play beside.

"Robbie had already played for the senior team and there was a question mark as to why he was involved at all with our age group because I don't think Mick McCarthy approved of him coming with the Under 20 squad. It was seen that he had elevated to the senior level and that this type of stuff was beneath him at this stage.

"But you never got that impression from him. There was no sense at all that 'this is only the Under-20s or 19s'. He was certainly the best I played with at the time in comparison with the lads I played with at Millwall, who were nowhere near Robbie's level. I remember him being so bloody enthusiastic to get out playing.

"Robbie was brilliant, very lively and, even then, seemed very intelligent with the runs he would make and the decisions he would take. The thing that really struck me was that nothing seemed to faze him. Any pitch he was on, he was the focal point due to his reputation and achievements to date with Wolves.

"Mentally, he seemed to be so strong and so tough which, at the time, was staggering for someone who had so much attention on him and was so young. Robbie was so comfortable, even with the attention on him as he was the big name. He had senior caps and it was known that Premiership clubs wanted him."

As Ireland travelled to the northern city of Kano to play Nigeria on one of the British Airways planes, England were departing for home having lost all three group games to USA (1-0), Cameroon (1-0) and Japan (2-0). They had the unwanted record of being the only side of the 24 competing nations to complete their section with neither a goal nor a point. Wilkinson and the FA's stance now looked extremely ill-judged.

"I think England took their third or fourth-choice players to Nigeria, but for such a big country and such a strong league, you would have thought that they would do a lot better," suggested Duff.

"Malaysia played a significant part in shaping my career and Roy Hodgson included me in the side when I returned to Blackburn. I believe Nigeria '99 will take me along another couple of steps as a player. You never stop learning while playing against teams like Nigeria, and working with Noel and Brian will help us to become better players."

Ireland's form left the party in buoyant mood as they switched cities and the hosts' own problems further boosted their hopes of reaching the last eight. Nigeria joined them on the flight but without coach Tunde Disu, who had been replaced by senior team technical adviser, Dutchman Thijs Libregts, in the wake of the 2-1 defeat to Paraguay that only saw the hosts scrape through on goal difference.

"The Flying Eagles are disorganised, indisciplined and chaotic — a mirror of Nigerian society," proclaimed Libregts as he assumed control with hardly a vote of confidence in his squad and their officials.

On a more worrying note, however, police, many on horseback and using whips or bamboo-type canes, waded into Nigeria supporters who hurled bottles and cans at the bus carrying the Nigeria team away from the National Stadium in Lagos following the defeat. Violent clashes were reported in several areas of the city. These disruptions followed an incident in Port Harcourt where hundreds of fans blocked streets with burning tyres to protest against the difficulty in buying tickets. The protests had prevented several teams from leaving their hotels to train.

Kano — with a population of more than two million and situated in the mainly Muslim north close to the border with Niger — offered a welcome relief to the Irish group. They could now watch Sky TV, enjoy a dip in the hotel pool and even take a stroll around the nearby streets. Keane's Sony Play-Station was no longer the sole method of relaxation.

"Yes, we are confident that we can beat them — there is no fear in this squad at all," stated McPhail on the eve of the game. "I think there is a lot more to come from the team as we have adjusted well to the heat."

After 120 minutes of toil under the searing heat of the afternoon sun that produced one goal apiece, it would take penalties to decide who went through.

Crossley and Paul Donnelly both scored but when Nigeria keeper Sam Okoye saved Heary's spot-kick, Barry Quinn's successfully-struck fourth effort was of no consolation as Nigeria's third, fourth and fifth attempts were all successful to put them through 5-4. The Irish collapsed to the ground in a mixture of inconsolable disappointment and sheer exhaustion. Sadlier had put the Irish ahead after 35 minutes as he finished off a sweeping move involving Duff and Quinn — a lead that Ireland held until Plus Ikedia levelled in the 70th minute.

"We were very disappointed to lose in the second round because we had thoughts of advancing like the lads in Malaysia two years earlier," says Sadlier. "So there was all this hype and loads of interest in the underage teams, particularly with Brian in charge.

"To lose the way we did, particularly on penalties, was a sickener and Robbie's miss late on added to the feeling. He had a header from a few yards out at the back post and it went a couple of inches wide. We had to deal with the conditions and it was very much 'us against them'. The entire stadium was Nigerian, with this tiny little pocket of white faces. You could see them up in the corner — some locals, some missionaries, some Irish people who had been there for years and the small section of the Irish media who travelled just stuck out a mile!

"I scored the goal to give us the lead and I didn't celebrate because the place went completely silent, which is not what normally happens when a team scores because somebody cheers. You're thinking 'has this been allowed or has the ball gone in?' A few of the lads came up and said 'he's given it'. We all looked around and trotted back to the halfway line as slow as we could to get a rest."

Keane had strong appeals for a penalty turned down when he was fouled in the penalty area while Kerr's assistant O'Reilly, as mild-mannered as he was knowledgeable about the game, was sent off for having a small disagreement with the fourth official. Keane had been lined up as the fifth penalty taker, but would not be required. However, such statistics were forgotten about as the joyous home fans invaded the pitch, provoking a scary police response, as Sadlier recalls.

"We lost the penalty shoot-out and there was a pitch invasion. The armed police started shooting into the air to disperse the crowd! I remember Noel O'Reilly calling out 'close in, come in close' so we huddled in a group. But all these ecstatic Nigerians were jumping about celebrating and then the police start shooting their guns into the air! The whole thing was bizarre. You don't normally expect to be on a pitch with police shooting in the air, but that's where we found ourselves.

"The biggest memory I have of that match is the disappointment of losing because we went there as European champions. If we had beaten Nigeria that would have put us into the quarter-finals against Mali."

If Sadlier was relatively relaxed about the surrounding mayhem, Kevin Fahy — the head of delegation as FAI Youth Committee chairman at the time — was more concerned.

Fahy — who would later hold the role of acting FAI general secretary in early 2003 following Brendan Menton's decision to pursue his career with FIFA and the Asian Federation — explained his fears.

"The stadium was absolutely jammed and when they scored

the winning penalty there was an invasion of the pitch," said Fahy. "Naturally, we were really concerned for the players. They were charging at some of our players and I ran on to the pitch. There were numerous soldiers and police present and, in fairness, some of them went out to protect the players.

"So we got the players into the dressing room as quickly as possible but it was still a bit hairy. The crowd was leaving the stadium and that took them behind the dressing rooms. They were banging and hammering on the windows. I spoke to Brian Kerr as we were so concerned about the situation.

"We got the FIFA representative who was there and they eventually made two lines of soldiers, police, officials and stadium stewards to escort us out to the bus. At this stage most of the crowd had gone out of the stadium but it was hairy. When we drove out of the stadium on to the road, there was a ferocious bang as rocks and bricks were thrown at the bus.

"There was a fantastic atmosphere in the stadium and we had a really good chance of winning the game near the end but missed it."

Following earlier disappointing results against Costa Rica and Paraguay, Nigerian fans had applauded the opposition from the pitch. Fahy is not convinced an Irish victory would have been greeted with the same response.

"Looking back, I often wonder and think that maybe it was as well that we didn't win given what happened when Nigeria won the game."

Keane returned to Wolves and reflected on the outcome of a tournament in which he had failed to score but had seen him enhance his status on the world stage.

"Yes it was disappointing to go out on penalties after we had played so well in the tournament and against Nigeria," said Keane. "But nobody can say that we did not do well because the lads were a credit to themselves and the country. I thought we were going to win the game when Richard got the early goal and that we would hold on.

"Then after they equalised, we could have clinched it in extra time. But that's football, it's over and done with now. We won the European Championship last year in a shoot-out. In all the excitement I didn't feel sorry for the Germans, but now I feel how they must have felt. It's not something that I want to go through again.

"It has been hardest on Thomas Heary, but he deserves credit for going up and taking the kick and for doing ever so well in the tournament. He has so much to be proud of. It's cruel how a little thing like that can cause so much upset. He's a hell of a player and man enough to take it on the chin."

Spain — with Xavi, Pablo, Gabri and Iker Casillas in their side — would go on to hammer Japan 4-0 in the final to cap a tournament that had weathered predictions of trouble and strife to give the planet a glimpse of Ronaldinho, Mali's Seydou Keita, Paraguay's Roque Santa Cruz, Diego Forlan of Uruguay and Ireland's own Robbie Keane and Damien Duff.

Two days after returning to London, Sadlier would experience more disappointment, albeit on a lesser scale, as he played for Millwall in the 1-0 Auto Windscreens final defeat to Wigan Athletic at Wembley.

Like his colleagues, Sadlier hoped one day to graduate to Mick McCarthy's senior squad. He would go on to win one cap at that level before a series of injuries put paid to his playing career prior to moving into the administrative side of football and a role in the media.

Keane, too, desired to continue his progress in the green shirt. Three years later he would again grace a World Cup finals — this time in the greatest show of all.

Chapter 7
Blue-eyed boy

"IF I could buy Robbie Keane for £500,000, I wouldn't hesitate to sign him," mused Alex Ferguson with a broad grin. "Then I would give him a run in the reserves and if he measured up, he would get a chance in the first team."

The well-fed guests at the sportsman's dinner in the Lancashire coastal town of Fleetwood in early August, 1999, lapped it up as the Manchester United manager answered questions from the floor.

Given the informal surroundings of the event, the famous guest's comments were delivered tongue-in-cheek and expected to be received in the same manner. Yet there was also a slightly dismissive tone to Fergie's words as he assessed the fee of £6m that Wolves were seeking for Keane. Nine years later, when Liverpool splashed out £20m to Tottenham for the Dubliner, Ferguson would again query the size of the transfer fee.

It wasn't always that way and two years earlier Ferguson had expressed a strong interest in the 17-year-old on the day that he announced his arrival in the English game with a brace of goals in Wolves' 2-0 victory at Norwich City. News of that opening-day-of-the-season double was relaid by Sky Sports News to the watching Ferguson, who was enjoying a cup of tea in his club's hotel base near Epping for the following afternoon's Premiership meeting with Spurs at White Hart Lane.

After the second goal went in, Ferguson turned to a number of friends and a group of United supporters and asked 'who is this lad Keane?'. On Keane's return to Wolves' Compton training base in the first week of July, 1999, speculation over his future at the club quickly resurfaced. Leeds United, Middlesbrough, Newcastle United and Aston Villa had all made enquiries to Wolves, who had now taken a board room decision to allow Keane to leave once their £6m valuation was met.

Club chief executive John Richards and manager Colin Lee

both knew that a sale was inevitable, but Richards remained adamant that the asking price would not drop. By the middle of July, Middlesbrough's bid to land Keane appeared doomed. While Boro's wealthy owner and chairman Steve Gibson had sanctioned manager Bryan Robson to meet Wolves' price, Keane was less than enthusiastic about moving to the Riverside Stadium despite the Premiership club's form in the previous few seasons that saw them beaten in both the FA and League Cup finals in 1997 and the League Cup final in 1998.

Robson had steered his side to a very respectable ninth in the table in 1998-99 with a side that contained Mark Schwarzer, Andy Townsend, Paul Gascoigne, Gary Pallister and Brian Deane. By the end of September, 1999, Brazil star Juninho would return to the club where he had starred a few years earlier. But Keane was waiting for an offer from a London, Lancashire or Yorkshire club and maybe he was influenced by the words of his Ireland youths teammate Ronnie O'Brien, who had just been released by Boro after two years but had been snapped up by Juventus in one of the most curious moves ever involving an Irish player.

Robson had stated that he was unsure if O'Brien was capable of making it at Premiership level. That was a judgment that would be ultimately proven to be accurate, although O'Brien naturally did not see it that way at the time.

"By letting me go, Robson let it be known that he did not rate me," said O'Brien after exiting Boro. "I was surprised he said what he did. If in a year or two I play in Serie A, it will be a kick in the teeth for him."

With the help of teammate Paul Merson — who had also been released by Boro — O'Brien secured the Juventus move, with Merson calling upon his agent Steve Kutner's expertise.

"I found out that Juve scouts had noted me during the World Under-20 Cup in 1997 and the next thing I was talking over a deal with Roberto Bettega. He was shocked when he found out that I had been released by Boro."

By July 13, the Irish Daily Star was reporting that Villa were now willing to cough up £5m for Keane, who would command £10,000 per week in wages. With Steve Bull reluctantly calling time on his glittering career 24 hours later, the impetus increased at Wolves to finalise a move for Keane and use the money to rebuild their team.

A week later, Villa boss John Gregory's optimism on concluding a deal on Keane led to Villa sources suggesting that a triple signing of Coventry City midfielder George Boateng, Israeli-born striker Nagram Garayeb and Keane was imminent. But no deal had been completed by Tuesday, July 20 when Keane played for Wolves against Liverpool in a pre-season friendly at Molineux. And two days later, Gregory was forced to depart with his squad to the USA for a pre-season tour without Keane as Wolves again rejected Villa's £5.5m offer. Keane was playing it by the book, refusing to be publicly drawn on his hopes of securing a move to a Premiership club while privately praying that his ambitions of starting the new campaign in the top flight would be realised.

At training, Keane remained one of Colin Lee's most committed players and the manager could not accuse his star turn of anything other than being fully focused. However, the humdrum schedule of pre-season games was shattered during the early hours of Tuesday, August 2 when Keane found himself spending several hours in a police station after teammate Kevin Muscat was arrested on suspicion of drink-driving. On Monday night the pair had attended a friendly between Wolves reserves and Telford United, which had to be abandoned due to torrential rain.

Keane and Australian international Muscat decided to continue the wet theme and adjourned for a few drinks. Keane was not charged with any offence but Wolves were furious with both players' behaviour and chief executive Richards stated that the pair "had let the club down very badly".

"It's hardly the way you would expect professional players to behave in the week leading up to the season," added a clearly unhappy Richards.

Club sources suggested that Keane would be hit with a fine of two weeks' wages that would sting the striker for approximately £12,000, and the manager was equally scathing in his comments.

"Professionalism is something that I demand at this club and the players have let me and Wolves down," declared Lee.

While Robbie Keane waited for his club future to be decided, his namesake from Cork was digging in over the terms of his new contract at Old Trafford. Manchester United skipper Roy Keane was seeking £40,000 per week in salary, with the club offering £28,000 over the duration of the proposed five-year deal. Naturally, the impasse alerted Chelsea, Inter Milan and Juventus, who had each discovered to their own cost in recent seasons that Keane's presence in Ferguson's side was the rock upon which the treble-winning team was built.

With his contract due to expire on July 1, 2000, United were playing a risky game of poker even if Keane was very settled at the club. Back in the Black Country, Robbie Keane's transfer saga rumbled on with no end in sight.

"We still believe that Wolves are asking too much and we have made an offer which we believe to be realistic," argued Villa manager Gregory. After Keane's well-taken first-half goal earned Wolves a 1-0 opening day win at Maine Road on August 8, Manchester City boss Joe Royle grumbled about the outcome but paid tribute to the match-winner.

"It was a smash-and-grab and there's no way we deserved to lose," said Royle. "The difference is that Wolves had a striker worth £6m and we did not. Keane only had four kicks of the ball but one of them ended up in our net. And that's all that matters." By the following Saturday, Manchester United had agreed to meet Roy Keane's demands that now included an Old Trafford testimonial as the term of the contract would bring the player's stay at the club through the decade-long mark in July 2003.

However, the trail appeared to have run cold at Molineux for the other Keane, although there was no pressure on any of his suitors to finalise a deal by the end of August as the FIFA-imposed transfer window system was still a few years off.

What Keane required was a change of heart by Wolves over his price tag or a Premiership manager to increase their offer. Fortunately for the Dubliner, the spark required to ignite Keane's departure from Wolves was lit by Leeds United manager David O'Leary's £4m acquisition of Darren Huckerby from Coventry City on August 12. This meant that City needed a replacement for Huckerby — who had a decent goals ratio of scoring almost one in every three games for the club — and were now armed with the money to buy one.

Finally, on Thursday, August 19, Sky Blues chairman Bryan Richardson confirmed that Coventry City were willing to match Wolves' financial demands.

"We have agreed a fee with Wolves for Keane and transfer terms have also been agreed," stated Richardson following parallel talks with Keane's agent Tony Stephens and Wolves chairman Richards.

"We have received an offer from Coventry that is acceptable to the board but we are not prepared to reveal the fee involved," said Richards, as Keane signed his five-year contract.

The spotlight fell on Aston Villa, who had been outbid by their smaller midlands neighbours by just £500,000 and Gregory indulged in a bout of self-protection, even if he was privately fuming with his own board's refusal to stump up the extra half-a-million pounds to land Keane.

"We could have pursued it 48 hours ago but we decided that we didn't want to," said Gregory. "I made my bed and I will have to lie in it. I just didn't feel right about the whole thing — I didn't have good feelings about it.

"I have seen Wolves four times this season and I have to assess a player and feel he would be totally capable of coming straight into our side. I had bid as high as £5.5m and now it appears that he has been sold for £5m, with £1m after so many games," added Gregory, who did at least say he was pleased for Keane that his future had been sorted out. "I am delighted for him that it has been resolved."

The smile etched on Keane's face accurately reflected the player's inner feelings when he was introduced to the media.

"I had a long talk with Gordon Strachan before I signed and he told me about Coventry's hopes and ambitions," said Keane. "He told me about the new stadium and it is all very exciting. I want to be part of it.

"I also knew of Mr Strachan's reputation for improving younger players and he has also played football at the highest level so that came into it. I'm pleased that my future is settled because it has been going on for a long time.

"I did want to play in the Premiership for Wolves but it was not to be. They are a big club and I am sure they will get there. Maybe the money they have got for me will enable them to do it."

Keane was joining a club that had been enjoying one of its more fruitful periods in the top flight given that it had frequently spent many seasons battling relegation since its promotion to the old First Division in 1967. Following Gordon Strachan's appointment as manager in November, 1996, the team had finished a healthy 11th in his first full season in charge, although they had dropped to 15th when the final table was calculated for the 1998-99 campaign.

However, Strachan's strong personality, his passion for the game and personal ambition to match his playing career with success in the dugout, meant that there was a buzz about Highfield Road, a commodity not always associated with the club or, indeed, the city. Yet, Coventry knew that they would always have to consider substantial offers for their big-name players and in November, 1998, they had been unable to turn down Aston Villa's £5.75m offer for their then leading scorer Dion Dublin. It was a deal that saw the club receive its largest ever transfer fee to that point. It was a standard that would not last for long.

Strachan had built a workmanlike side that included defender Richard Shaw, winger Steve Froggatt and midfielder

Carlton Palmer but also boasted the creative midfield force of Moroccan internationals Youssef Chippo and Mustapha Hadji. Crucially, the fiery Scot had inherited his old Leeds United teammate Gary McAllister, who was pulling the midfield strings and adding a touch of class.

McAllister would start every single one of Coventry's league games in the 1999-2000 season and be substituted in just three. Now the boss was adding British football's most expensive teenager to his squad and was excited at the prospect of having Keane at his disposal.

"Mark McGhee is my best mate in football and I used to go and watch his team so I know all about Robbie," said Strachan with regard to the respective managers whose relationship dated back to their six years together from 1978 as Aberdeen teammates under Alex Ferguson.

"I used to watch Robbie's progress with envy because I could not have him in my team," added Strachan. "When the chairman phoned me to say he was on the motorway on his way to make a big signing, I must admit that I did not realise there was so much money in the coffers.

"Speculation about Robbie's future has been going on for over a year and I was impressed with the way he handled it. There was a lot of pressure on the young man but he still improved as a player. That showed me he is mentally strong." And Strachan pinpointed Keane's twin assets of being able to find the net and create chances for teammates as two of many reasons why he smashed through his club's transfer record to land him.

"I see him either as a goal scorer or a goal creator, he can do either job. A few people may scratch their heads and wonder why he has come to us. Well, we are having a bash at it and people should say 'good for them'. Some people talk ambition but we set out to try to do it, action not words.

"Any transfer is a gamble and this is a courageous move by us. We watch players for a long time but we have done more homework on Robbie than anyone else."

Among the faces of his new colleagues that Keane knew well were fellow Ireland youths and Under-20 stars Barry Quinn and Barry Ferguson, while senior international Gary Breen had been with the club since his £2.4m move from Birmingham City in January, 1997.

"Robbie won't be left hanging around in the reserves for months until there's a vacancy in the attack," predicted Breen a few days after Keane's capture. "He'll get his chance early on which is important and I reckon he's capable of making the step up. For me, however, it's the opportunity to learn more about his trade which makes this move the right one. Gordon is the master when it comes to helping young strikers develop their game."

Breen's assessment of his manager's plans for Keane and his international colleague's ability to deliver would prove correct. But all three must have been somewhat taken aback by the impact Keane would make on his Coventry debut at home to Derby County on Saturday, August 21, 1999. Keane was on a mental high ahead of the match as he was able to forget the tribulations of his club future and concentrate on playing. After all, pulling on a football shirt was his only real interest in life.

"My confidence could not be higher going into the game and I am really looking forward to it," said Keane at the time. "These are the sort of matches I have come to the Premiership to play in."

As Aston Villa and Gregory were losing by the only goal at Chelsea, Keane was repeating his debut day feat at Norwich two years previously with both goals for his new club in the 2-0 Highfield Road victory over The Rams. In a tight encounter, Keane broke the deadlock just before the break when mesmerising defender Jacob Laursen with his skill before squeezing the ball under keeper Mart Poom from a tight angle. Midway through the second half, Keane raced on to Froggatt's pass, rounded the advancing Poom and slotted the ball home for his second. "I always dreamed of scoring in the Premiership and I can't believe it has happened," beamed Keane after the match in which he had received a standing ovation from the home fans a few minutes from the final whistle when replaced by Strachan's son, Gavin.

"Coventry are a great team and Gordon Strachan is a great manager. I am not thinking about the transfer fee, I am just thinking about playing football and concentrating on my game above anything else," added Keane when asked if the £6m fee might affect him from settling at his new club.

Strachan added his congratulations to his new signing. "It's unfortunate that he was not here at the start of the season," quipped the Scot. "I knew his character was strong as I have been watching him for two years and know what he's like. I also think he lifted the players around him, they respected his work rate and his attitude was spot on."

Noel Whelan started up front with Keane that afternoon and he was both impressed by his new teammate and slightly surprised by the teenager's strong presence on the pitch.

"Robbie was a dream to play alongside because he talked so much, I was amazed," admitted Whelan. "I'd got it in my mind that he's only 19 and was preparing myself to help him through his debut and take the senior role, especially as he seems to be quiet off the pitch. But once he got out there, he was shouting at me the whole time, telling me where he wanted me to go and how he wanted the ball!"

First day on the new job, first goal. And who were Coventry's next opponents in the league? Champions Manchester United, who were top of the pile with three wins and a draw in their first four outings, including a 2-1 success at Arsenal the day after Keane's Coventry debut in a game that saw the other Keane claim both goals for Ferguson's men.

Highfield Road rarely enjoyed football's limelight and had lived an existence where it usually found itself living in the shadows of midlands rivals Villa, Birmingham City, Wolves, Nottingham Forest and West Bromwich Albion. Now, Strachan's presence as manager, the team's improved fortunes and the arrival of Keane had given the club and its fans a tangible lift.

And the visit of United brought the usual pre-match banter about the fact that Ferguson and Strachan enjoyed a somewhat strained relationship given the manner of Strachan's exit from United as a player in 1988 and their subsequent verbal exchanges, with Strachan one of the few managers who challenged his former boss. Now, Keane's signing and Ferguson's well-aired recent comments about the Dubliner added another layer of intrigue to the encounter.

It was little surprise that a crowd of 22,022 — still 1,500 short of capacity — turned up for the midweek fixture that was played in early evening sunshine. United's impressive start to the season encouraged Strachan to be cautious and he opted to use Keane as a lone attacker to ensure that the visitors did not cut through the home side's midfield. It was a tactic that worked until the 62nd minute when substitute Paul Scholes put United ahead with Dwight Yorke adding a second 13 minutes later. Substitute John Aloisi's reply in the 80th minute ensured a tense finale to the match and Keane tested Raimond van der Gouw in the dying seconds but the shot lacked power. United held out for the three points to leave Coventry in the lower half of the table after an opening five games that had produced two defeats by Southampton and Leicester City and a 1-1 draw with Wimbledon prior to Keane's arrival.

Yet, Keane had reason to be cheerful having reflected on his first two games for his new club that had yielded two goals and the assist for Aloisi against United. Even Ferguson was willing to add his voice to the chorus of praise.

"Robbie worked very hard tonight and I thought he had a good game in a difficult role," said Fergie, who also claimed that his after-dinner comments about Keane three weeks earlier had been taken out of context. Strachan also gave the club's most expensive ever signing a rattling good review.

"Robbie was absolutely phenomenal — he played against two world-class defenders in Jaap Stam and Henning Berg and gave them a torrid time."

Keane was clearly revelling in his new surroundings and, like a giddy child in a playground, marvelled at the company he was now keeping.

"Playing against world-class players like Stam, David Beckham, Denis Irwin and Roy Keane is the sort of challenge I wanted," said Keane. "Their style of one-touch, two-touch football is unbelievable. That's what I have got to aim for. It's really a bit of a relief to have moved because it was going on for so long. Now I can concentrate on playing football."

Keane's form in August saw him chosen as Carling Young Player of the Month and Cisco Young Player of the Month, with the latter award's judging panel — chaired by Bobby Robson — comprising the senior international team bosses of England, Wales, Ireland and Northern Ireland. Barring a major dip in form or the intervention of injury, it was clear that Keane was going to have a real impact on the Premiership. And his international manager was also set to benefit as Ireland prepared for a hectic finale to their Euro 2000 qualifying campaign that would see the team play Yugoslavia, Croatia and Malta in the space of seven days in the first week of September.

"Robbie's only played a few games but from what I saw on TV last Saturday and in the flesh against United, he's done very well," said Ireland manager Mick McCarthy. "When people publicly doubted his ability I'm sure Robbie thought to himself that he'd played against Argentina and he was the best player on the park as he ran their defence ragged.

"That's bound to help because he will know that Premiership defenders will be no better than the Argentinians he faced on that occasion."

Three days before the visit of Yugoslavia to Lansdowne Road, Keane was once more on the mark for City when notching the opening goal in the 1-1 away league draw against Sunderland. Keane's 33rd-minute effort looked set to give Coventry their second win of the season but another serial goal-scorer, Kevin

Phillips, would salvage a point for the home side. However, Keane missed a gilt-edged opportunity to earn his side maximum spoils when sending a 92nd-minute effort over the bar.

Spurning the relatively easy chances would become part of the overall Keane package, but so too would be his response to such setbacks. When other players dropped their heads in the middle of a poor patch of form, Keane simply stayed in automatic gear and seemed to have a psychological DNA where the last bad miss never registered with him. It would become a trait that every teammate who played alongside him and every manager who picked him would comment upon in the years that followed.

The perfect illustration of this unfolded between the dying moments of the game at the Stadium of Light and the final whistle of the crucial 2-1 win over Yugoslavia the following Wednesday night. Yugoslavia had inflicted a 1-0 defeat on the Irish in Belgrade the previous November when one defensive error allowed Predrag Mijatovic to pounce at the far post. Amid the turmoil caused to the group games by the horrific events in the Balkans, this rearranged fixture in Dublin was one that McCarthy's men needed to win to stay in contention to qualify for Belgium and Holland in June, 2000.

Niall Quinn and Keane were now McCarthy's first-choice attack and from the opening minutes they gave the visitors a torrid time as they set about their task with vigour on an unusually sweltering early autumn evening. And it was Keane — completely unburdened by his late, late howler three days earlier — who put Ireland ahead in the 54th minute with a stunning finish. Irwin's measured, angled diagonal pass from right-full was flicked on by Quinn with the deftest of touches and Keane, without altering his stride, met the ball with his right foot just as it touched the ground to send an unstoppable right-foot shot past Aleksandar Kocic. However, Dejan Stankovic levelled on the hour mark and it required Mark Kennedy's stunning 30-yard drive to ensure the Irish of the win they required to keep their ambitions on track.

To a man, Ireland had been magnificent and Keane was the equal of any of his colleagues, most of whom — apart from Kevin Kilbane, Mark Kinsella, Gary Breen and Kennedy — were between nine and 18 years his senior. Keane was omitted from the Ireland side that lost 1-0 away to Croatia three days later but he was restored to the attack when Ireland secured a vital but unconvincing 3-2 success in Malta on September 8. Keane was among the Ireland scorers along with Coventry teammate Breen and Steve Staunton. The Dubliner was in a rich vein of form for club and country and he would go on to play 23 consecutive Premier League matches for Coventry, taking him up to the 1-0 home defeat by Spurs on February 26.

His status at Highfield Road within a few weeks of his arrival could be gauged by the fact that his absence due to being cuptied from both legs of Coventry's Worthington Cup second-round exit to Tranmere Rovers was keenly felt. The Merseysiders hammered Strachan's side 5-1 at Prenton Park to ensure the Premier League team's 3-1 success in the return leg counted for nothing. John Aldridge's side — which contained Ireland international David Kelly and budding Dublin youngster Alan Mahon — would go on to contest the Wembley final the following February when Martin O'Neill's Leicester City claimed the trophy after a 2-1 victory.

Inconsistency was the word that summed up the Sky Blues' form throughout the 1999-2000 season as they fluctuated between 11th and 16th in the table before playing out the final few months in the comfortable but scarcely inspiring 14th position. From a Coventry point of view it was a qualified success and from Keane's it was a definite period of progress.

In November, Keane scored the goal in Ireland's 1-1 Euro 2000 qualifying play-off first leg against Turkey at Lansdowne Road. However, he was ruled out of the scoreless second leg in Bursa for picking up a second booking of the campaign that earned him a one-match ban. Keane's absence was felt on a tense night of few chances at either end. With Coventry, Keane was maturing with each passing month, especially as he did not have the luxury of playing in a regular 4-4-2 system or with a co-striker when Strachan did opt for two men in attack.

Whelan suffered from injury and occasional loss of form while Belgian forward Cedric Roussel and Froggatt were also unable to pin down permanent places up front. So Keane's frequent appearances on the scoring charts owed much to his own application and craft on the pitch. By the turn of the year he had netted against Derby County (two), Sunderland, Spurs, Newcastle United, Watford, Aston Villa and Arsenal, when he got the crucial third goal in a 3-2 St Stephen's Day defeat of the Gunners, live on Sky Sports.

Keane had skinned Ireland teammate Shay Given when scoring in the 4-1 demolition of Newcastle at home in early October and when his display in the 4-0 Highfield Road hammering of Watford included a goal and two assists, Strachan was more than obliged to give the press a few gold-star quotes.

"Robbie Keane is definitely one of the greatest talents in British football," declared his manager. "He is better than I realised when I bought him and he can go right to the top. He's been phenomenal and if you put him in any side in Europe he'd be able to play for that team. He's a great talent and sometimes you have got to watch what you are doing in training with him because I don't think there is much you can teach him."

Keane was chuffed to receive the plaudits for his display against the Hornets but was anxious to deflect the praise to the entire team. "I think I did alright but it was the team who played absolutely brilliantly," said the modest youngster.

"It is quite flattering for the manager to say what he said but things are going well and long may that continue. People were wondering whether I could make the step up from the First Division to the Premiership but I had played nine games for Ireland so I have always believed in myself. I've always had confidence in my own ability. Obviously I want to become a bigger and better player and that is why I have come to the club, so Gordon Strachan will help make me a better player. I am still only young and learning."

Keane had now moved from Telford to the small, upmarket town of Balsall Common where he would be able to unwind and not be hassled on a constant basis given his status as one of British football's rising young stars. And his status as a local celebrity meant that he and Whelan were asked to switch on the Coventry city centre Christmas lights in November.

A few days later he was scoring the winner against Villa at Villa Park. The goal against the Gunners was followed by another in Coventry's next league match, the 2-2 home draw with Chelsea, before Keane rattled in another in the 2-0 Highfield Road win against Wimbledon.

In the first weekend of February, Coventry travelled to Old Trafford to play Manchester United in the league, with Ferguson naturally asked if he had revised his earlier verdict on the visitors' young star.

"He's got nothing to prove to me — there was all that stuff in the papers saying I didn't rate the boy, which is absolutely untrue and everyone knows that," said Fergie. "What I said was that if I spent £6m on a player I would need to put him in my first team. And at 19 years of age with Yorke, Andy Cole and Teddy Sheringham, that would be very difficult."

United won 3-2 but Keane and Roussel — who claimed both Coventry goals — produced a strong display in attack. Keane was now driving a Jaguar XK8 and admitted that he was fulfilling another childhood dream. "Ever since I was a kid I would dream of having a car like this and as soon as I could afford one, I started looking around. This was my first choice."

Yet Keane was anxious to deny that his wealth and status had changed him in any way. "I like to see my name all over the place and it's good to be talked about," said Keane. "Anybody would want to better themselves and I want to be the best I can be. But I have not changed. I am just the person I was three years ago. A lot of people watch me now and talk about me but it's something I don't worry about. Don't get me wrong, I don't mind the attention.

"It's just that I was brought up in the backstreets of Dublin and I think I have to remain the person I have always been. If I am not and I get too big for my boots, then I'm sure my parents and all the people I know back home would let me know. I wouldn't like to think that fame would get to me anyway.

"It's the type of person I am. I think I am just a down-to-earth guy who loves to play football."

But Keane's form would dip as winter gave way to spring, though a knee injury did him no favours. Having missed the away defeat at Leeds on March 5 before being substituted at half-time a week later, Keane then sat out the next three games before returning to the bench for the home match against his beloved Liverpool on April 1.

The joke was firmly on the home side, who lost 3-0 and introduced Keane for the injured Whelan just after the half-hour mark. At least Keane was back in action and a fortnight later he claimed the winner in the 2-1 Highfield Road victory over Middlesbrough. McAllister paid his own tribute to his young teammate after the match.

"Robbie is a very special player and I cannot think of anybody who has been better at his age," declared McAllister. "I don't want to build him up too high but he has a special talent. He's up there with Ryan Giggs and Michael Owen but he is not playing at a club which has the same profile as Manchester United or Liverpool."

Keane would finish one goal ahead of McAllister as the club's leading league scorer that season, with the Scot benefitting from four penalties in his tally of 11. Hadji was next on six. And Keane's fellow professionals voted him runner-up to Harry Kewll in the PFA Young Player of the Year category.

Robbie had more than proved himself in the Premiership in his first campaign and Strachan was looking forward to working with his star attraction in pre-season. However, moves were already afoot to lure Keane elsewhere. Inter Milan and their gregarious president Massimo Moratti had been following Keane's progress at Coventry, having been alerted to his talents by a £20 video compiled by his agent.

Moratti wanted Keane at the San Siro and Strachan never stood a chance of keeping him, due to the mounting debts at Highfield Road. So less than 12 months after Strachan took the plunge to sign Keane for £6m from Wolves, he was reluctantly agreeing that the Sky Blues had no alternative but to sell the now 20-year-old forward to the Serie A club for £13m.

"The chairman reckons every player has his price and in an era of increasing uncertainty about the future of transfer fees in European football, I can understand that point of view," mused Strachan as the deal was confirmed by Bryan Richardson. "But I shall be desperately sorry to see Robbie go because you are not given the opportunity to work with that sort of talent very often. If it was down to me, I would sell the training ground and everything else to keep him.

"I have been at Highfield Road for the past five years and selling Robbie Keane will definitely be the worst thing that has happened during that period. Robbie is something very special and I believe he deserves the description 'great'. I'm just hoping that Robbie doesn't like the San Siro, doesn't like the wages, and wants to come back here!

"Robbie Keane is a genius and the other players are disappointed to lose him from the squad. I tried everything I could do to keep him but sometimes decisions have to be made above you."

Keane's departure for Inter would prove to be the beginning of the end of the Strachan era at Coventry City. By the following May, after a wretched 2000-01 campaign, Coventry's stay in the top division — dating back to 1967 — would end as they finished second from bottom of the table some eight points from safety.

By the time the 2001-02 campaign began in the First Division, Strachan had been replaced by one of his coaches, the Swede Roland Nilsson. Like his timing in the penalty area, Keane's decision to depart Coventry was perfectly judged.

Chapter 8
Czeching in with Ireland

AS Keane started to firmly establish himself in the Wolves side in the autumn of 1997, Mick McCarthy's primary concern was to qualify for the 1998 World Cup finals in France following a campaign that had scaled a few heights but dipped alarmingly on more than one occasion.

On his appointment in February, 1996, few people envied McCarthy's task in succeeding Jack Charlton,. The Englishman had steered Ireland to its first ever major tournament when qualifying for Euro 88 in West Germany and then secured a place at the 1990 and 1994 World Cup finals. Only a late Gary Lineker equaliser for England away to Poland in Poznan prevented Ireland from reaching Euro 92 and a collapse of form in the second part of the group stage led to a 2-0 Euro 96 play-off defeat to Holland at Anfield in December, 1995.

To have qualified for three out of four major tournaments between 1988 and 1994 was still a superb achievement by Charlton and his players. However, many believe that had Ireland pipped England to win their Euro 92 qualifying group — only the winners progressed to the eight-team finals in Sweden — they might well have triumphed in a tournament that was won by Denmark, who only received a late call to compete after a United Nations sporting embargo forced UEFA to expel Yugoslavia.

In 1992, Big Jack boasted an overwhelmingly experienced squad that numbered Packie Bonner, Paul McGrath, McCarthy, Denis Irwin, Steve Staunton, Terry Phelan, David O'Leary, Chris Morris, Roy Keane, Andy Townsend, Ray Houghton, John Sheridan, Ronnie Whelan, Alan McLoughlin, Kevin Sheedy, Niall Quinn, John Aldridge, Tommy Coyne and Tony Cascarino.

It was a squad that was also playing with a formidable intent that saw them embark upon an unbeaten competitive run between June 1990 (1-0 to Italy in the World Cup quarter-final in Rome) and October 1993 (3-1 group qualifying defeat to Spain in Dublin).

There are those who suggest that large-scale interest among the Irish public only began when Charlton tasted success in the late eighties, but even a casual glance at previous campaigns proved this to be untrue. In the campaign to reach the European Championships in 1976, Johnny Giles' Ireland hammered the USSR with a famous Don Givens hat-trick in front of 45,000 people at Dalymount Park in their opening match.

Their bid to reach the last eight was undone by a 1-0 away loss to Switzerland on the second part of a trip that had seen the Irish lose 2-1 to the Soviets in Kiev. Without live television for most Ireland matches in that era, fans tuned in to listen to the magnificent RTE Radio commentary provided by the late Philip Greene. The loss in the capital of the Ukraine was heroic and not unexpected against a side almost completely comprised of the great Dynamo Kiev side that included the legendary Oleg Blokhin. The defeat by the average Swiss was the real killer.

Giles' side would defeat France at Lansdowne Road in the 1978 World Cup campaign although the bid to reach Euro 80 proved to be less enthralling and it petered out limply with home draws against England and Northern Ireland and away defeats by both.

Eoin Hand succeeded Giles in 1980 and went within a whisker of guiding the country to the 1982 World Cup finals in Spain. The 1978 tournament runners-up Holland, and France, were both beaten in Dublin while the Dutch were held to a 2-2 away draw. Although France inflicted a 2-0 defeat in Paris, Ireland would have qualified as one of the two top teams but for two truly shocking refereeing decisions during the 1-0 away defeat to Belgium in Brussels in March, 1981.

On that infamous night, Portuguese referee Raul Nazare disallowed a perfectly headed and onside goal by Frank Stapleton for reasons that remain unclear and then allowed Jan Ceulemans' last-gasp winner to stand despite a clear foul on Ireland keeper Seamus McDonagh.

RTE Television broadcast that game and the entire nation was gripped by the drama, the quality of the Irish performance and incensed by the game's key decisions. Significantly, there was massive away support for the Boys In Green in Brussels, Paris and Rotterdam during that campaign, with as many as 8,000 fans making the journey to the match in the Heysel Stadium. In an era of domestic austerity and expensive air fares, it was a remarkable and accurate reflection of the interest that had existed for decades in the international senior team.

So while Charlton had taken up the coaching cudgel in early 1986 at a low point in the side's history, there was both a large pool of quality players and a fervent fanbase to tap into. Once Charlton engineered the breakthrough, both emerged to play their part in the decade that ended in Liverpool just prior to Christmas, 1995.

In spring, 1996 McCarthy inherited a squad that still had Townsend, Houghton, McGrath, Quinn, Cascarino, Irwin, Staunton, Phelan, McLoughlin and Aldridge, while Roy Keane was now one of the European game's midfield power-houses with Manchester United. Gary Kelly, Jason McAteer, Phil Babb, Alan Kelly, Jeff Kenna and Mark Kennedy were all capped at senior level by Charlton while Ian Harte, Curtis Fleming, Shay Given, Kenny Cunningham, Kevin Kilbane, Gareth Farrelly, Gary Breen and David Connolly would be blooded by McCarthy in the glut of friendlies between March and June of 1996.

The bid to reach France in 1998 began brilliantly, with the 5-0 away hammering of Liechtenstein — where the wheels seriously began to buckle for the previous manager only 14 months earlier in a scoreless draw — and the easy 3-0 home win over Macedonia.

However, the 0-0 Lansdowne Road stalemate against a dour Iceland team in November sparked a few boos from the terraces to echo the ones heard before kick-off for Roy Keane, who was making his return to the side fully six months after he had failed to show for the end-of-season US Cup matches.

McCarthy chose to deploy Keane as one of the three centre-halves — alongside Breen and Babb — in a 3-5-2 formation that struggled badly to break down the Icelandic blanket defence. McCarthy's decision to ignore Aldridge on the bench when making his final substitution that saw midfielder Alan Moore replace David Kelly 11 minutes from time, prompted 'Aldo' to retire from international football the following day.

McCarthy's two other changes from the bench that day — defenders Cunningham and Harte — had puzzled and perplexed the fans but worse was to follow in April, 1997, when Ireland were beaten 3-2 away to Macedonia in Skopje. McAteer was sent off for a kung-fu kick on an opponent while the 3-5-2 system — even with Keane back in central midfield — was torn apart by the home side's passing game.

Four weeks later in Bucharest, McCarthy abandoned the formation and opted for 4-5-1 with Connolly as the lone forward. Roy Keane missed a penalty and the impressive home team's 1-0 win meant that Ireland were now chasing the runners-up spot that would guarantee them a play-off spot in November. But at least there was a shape to the side and the players had turned in a reasonable display.

The team was less than impressive in securing the two-legged showdown with Belgium as it drew 0-0 at home to Lithuania and claimed away wins against Iceland (4-2) and Lithuania (2-1) before rounding off the qualifiers with a 1-1 home draw with Romania, who were dropping their only points in the 10 group games.

The play-off proved a massive disappointment, with an average if experienced Belgian side managed by Georges Leekens securing a 1-1 draw at Lansdowne in the first leg and then triumphing 2-1 in Brussels in the second game. The return leg saw Houghton mark his farewell international appearance with Ireland's equaliser and Connolly was sent off within a few minutes of being introduced as a substitute to leave the visitors with only 10 men for the last eight minutes of the tie.

Robbie Keane watched the events of Brussels unfold on his television screen back home near Wolverhampton having scored Wolves' goal in that afternoon's 1-1 league draw with Ipswich Town at Molineux. While McCarthy was well aware of Keane's form for his club — he had netted four times in his first 11 league matches prior to McCarthy naming his squad for the first leg on October 29 in Dublin — he felt that it was not the time to throw a rookie into the pressurised surroundings of such an occasion.

"I went up to see him at Wolves and also to meet him — it was simply to meet him and speak to him," recalls McCarthy, who was also facing some calls from the media and public for Damien Duff to be included, who was playing well at Blackburn Rovers.

"It was probably typical of when some good young players come through. Everybody wants them in. I'm saying it against the media without any bitterness but journalists always want the new fellas because they get sick of the other ones. Nobody is ever happy with a squad and it's always the ones who are out that create more talk than the ones who are in.

"Damien and Robbie had done alright with their clubs. If they had ripped it up and looked like the best things since sliced bread internationally I would have put them in the squad. But I was obviously not convinced of them internationally and we were involved in a World Cup play-off against a very experienced Belgium team."

In the wake of the World Cup exit, Townsend also hung up his Ireland boots to join Houghton, Aldridge and McGrath — who had retired in mid-campaign — as ex-internationals. It meant another stint of rebuilding prior to the Euro 2000 qualifiers, that would start against Croatia the following September. McCarthy took on the task with renewed energy.

In an era when the FIFA international calendar had friendly dates set aside throughout spring, the Czech Republic was confirmed for Olomouc in March, Argentina were secured for

Lansdowne Road in April with Mexico also including Dublin on their itinerary en-route to the World Cup finals in France.

However, with a significant departure of senior players, McCarthy wisely opted to arrange a rare B friendly for February 11, 1998 at Dublin's Tolka Park, with Northern Ireland providing the opposition.

So on January 27, McCarthy named a 20-man panel for a 90 minutes that offered young players the opportunity to stake a place in the manager's plans for the next two years. The standout stars were Keane and Duff while fellow uncapped (at senior level) players Richard Dunne, Graham Kavanagh, Nicky Colgan, Stephen Carr, Neale Fenn, Rory Delap, Gareth Farrelly, Steve Finnan, Sean Devine and Mark Kinsella were also included.

Apart from the mesmerising 4-1 victory by Ireland B against England B at Turner's Cross in March, 1990 and a 2-0 defeat by the same opposition at Anfield in December, 1994, this level of international football had been largely ignored by the FAI and other national federations over the decades in preference to playing often meaningless Under 21 games.

Injury ruled out Carr and Jim Crawford of Newcastle United while Cork City's Gareth Cronin, St Patrick's Athletic's Colin Hawkins and Alan Maybury of Leeds United were added to the original panel. A packed house of 10,000 fans — with hundreds outside unable to secure a ticket — turned up to get their first glimpse of Keane and Duff but a sluggish match saw Roy Millar's side win through George O'Boyle's only goal.

"Before we played the B friendly against Northern Ireland at Tolka Park, Robbie was brilliant in training," adds McCarthy. "Robbie just lit the place up with his ability, his infectiousness and his desire to play football. From the start his talent shone like a beacon."

A month later, McCarthy flew into Dublin to announce his squad for the March 25 trip to Olomouc to face the Czech Republic, with eight uncapped of the 22 players named. Of that new bunch, Keane and Duff were joined by Carr, Maybury, Phil Hardy, Kavanagh, Kinsella and Delap while Crewe Alexandra's Gareth Whalley would be added a week before the game.

This squad provided six senior debutants including Keane, Duff and Kinsella. However, there was another aspect to the game and McCarthy's preparations for it.

Keane was part of Brian Kerr's plans for the first leg of the UEFA Youths Championship play-off in Greece but McCarthy was — and still is — adamant that he was right to select the 17-year-old for senior duty.

"There was no controversy from my point of view. The senior team is the one that is important. Whatever you do qualifying or winning at youth level, if the first team is not doing well then nobody is bothered about it. It's great at the time and fantastic but I needed (him) in the senior team.

"I cannot remember what happened but I'm certain I would have said 'no, it's a first-team game'. It's only two years into my tenure and I'm trying to build a new team. If I was in the same position now and I wanted to play Robbie Keane and Duffer in a friendly based on me trying to build my squad, I would put them in because that is what youth teams do.

"They get players through to the reserves and to the first team and if it's to the detriment of the youth team, then it's unlucky. It's just unlucky."

Such are the problems that can face underage international managers, although Kerr was given full power to name Keane in his squad for the return leg against the Greeks in Dublin and then for the panel confirmed for that summer's finals in Cyprus. McCarthy's contention that youth, Under-20, Under-21 and B teams exist for the ultimate benefit of the senior side is borne out by a statistic from the Under-21 squad that lost 3-0 to their Czech counterparts in Drnovice on the night before the senior encounter.

Of the 17 players named by Ian Evans in his squad, only one, Alan Mahon, would go on to win senior caps, with friendly appearances against Greece and South Africa in 2000. Mc-

Carthy handed senior starts to Maybury, Kinsella and Duff on that grey afternoon in Olomouc in front of 9,405 people with Delap, Keane and Kavanagh brought on during the game.

Keane replaced right-full Maybury at the interval in a switch that saw Gary Kelly move to right-back to accommodate the new kid on the block, who became the second youngest Ireland senior debuatant after Jimmy Holmes.

"Against the Czechs, we went 1-0 up through Gary Breen. The team was probably the youngest and most inexperienced team I have ever been involved with," added McCarthy.

Kelly — only aged 23 but a near veteran as he clocked up his 26th senior cap — was instantly impressed by Keane, who he had only played fleetingly against a few weeks earlier when Wolves shocked Leeds United 1-0 in the clubs' FA Cup quarter-final at Elland Road, when the pair had been used as second-half substitutes.

"The first game that Robbie played in was the away match against the Czech Republic," says Kelly. "He had a brilliant goalscoring record at Wolves so Mick brought him in. You just knew from day one that he was going to be special, he was just one of those special players. When he got a chance he shot and he was always trying to do something amazing on the ball.

"With Robbie on the pitch you always knew that you would get a chance. And when you look at where he has been and the moves he has got, he's enjoyed a fabulous career. He's a really lively character and one of those players who came into the squad and gave us all a new lease of life. There was plenty of banter out of him.

"During games he would be making tongue-in-cheek remarks to the centre-halves, driving them mental."

Shay Given earned his 15th senior cap on that evening when Karel Poborsky's outstanding midfield display inspired the home side to overturn the visitors' ninth-minute lead and secure the win with second-half goals by Vladimir Smicer and Edvard Lasota. The Irish public's appetite was whetted for the visit of Daniel Passarella's Argentina side to Lansdowne Road on Wednesday, April 22. A crowd of 38,500 turned up to take a look at a team tipped to go a long way at that summer's World Cup finals against the rising stars in green.

Argentina boasted a truly stunning array of players with Roberto Ayala of Napoli, Roberto Sensini of Parma and Matias Almeyda of Lazio comprising three of the back four with Claudio Lopez (Valencia), Diego Simeone (Inter Milan), Juan Veron (Sampdoria) and Ariel Ortega (Valencia) in midfield. River Plate's Sergio Berti partnered Gabriel Batistuta — the man that many present had come to see — in attack. And 'Batigol' did not let them down with a scintillating 90 minutes that included the opening goal after 27 minutes in a 2-0 victory.

Ortega added the second five minutes before the interval to cap a stunning display that would become the norm for the attacking midfielder in the years to come for both club and country. Argentina had Batistuta, Veron and Ortega but Ireland could boast Keane, who — in the absence of the injured Duff — was the football public's new golden boy. And the 'Tallaght Tiger' did not disappoint in a game that saw Kinsella retain his place in central midfield.

Partnered with Niall Quinn in attack, Keane needed no time to adapt to his new surroundings and was soon dropping deep to pick up the ball, sniffing around the box for half-chances and rattling the top of keeper German Burgos's crossbar. Keane resembled a jack-in-the-box with his frantic darting around the pitch that thrilled the home supporters and proved irritating to his opponents. But there was a lot more to Keane's game that night, for he showed a deft touch on the ball, could spot a pass and made intelligent runs off the ball.

Naturally, the second-half tempo died down as neither set of players — especially the visitors — were keen to pick up any injuries at a vital stage of the season. But the home fans went home happy having given Keane a standing ovation on the final whistle. Many observers — including most of the home media — gave Robbie the man of the match award.

"Robbie was the bright spot that evening at Lansdowne, he stood out," adds McCarthy. "And before that game he again had some impact on the squad."

Keane partnered David Connolly in attack against Mexico — also on their way to the World Cup — a month later in a forgettable scoreless draw at Lansdowne Road as McCarthy opted to allow several of his players a rest ahead of the start of the Euro 2000 qualifiers with the visit of Croatia.

When the Croats arrived in Dublin for the September 5 clash, they did so as the third best side on the planet having won the third and fourth place World Cup play-off in Paris six weeks earlier with a 2-1 triumph over Holland. That capped a wonderful tournament by Croatia, who had been unfortunate to lose out 2-1 to the hosts in the St Denis semi-final having swept Germany aside 3-0 in the quarter-final in Lyon and defeated Romania 1-0 in the second round.

A team based on a solid work-ethic, Croatia were blessed with players of true quality such as Davor Suker, Robert Prosinecki and Zvonimir Boban. Lady luck had hardly been kind to Ireland at the previous January's qualifying draw in the Belgian city of Ghent, with McCarthy's side asked to claim a top-two place in a section that included Croatia and Yugoslavia and also contained the Macedonians and a strong enough fifth seed in the shape of Malta. With the worst of the nineties' brutal Balkan conflict now over, the biggest hurdle to mount would be seeking to push either Croatia or Yugoslavia out of the top two.

Yet, for once, the gods smiled down on the Irish before the visit of the Croats to Lansdowne Road with neither Suker nor Prosinecki able to feature and McCarthy able to welcome back Roy Keane to competitive action having recovered from the cruciate knee ligament injury that had laid him low for most of the 1997-98 season. McCarthy opted to start Robbie Keane in attack beside Keith O'Neill, who had been plagued by a succession of injuries since making a stunning entry into club and international football in the latter part of the 1995-96 season.

On the back of six friendly caps won during the glut of friendlies in May and June, 1996, O'Neill had started in attack beside Niall Quinn for McCarthy's first competitive game in charge, the 5-0 away hammering of Liechtenstein in September of that year.

O'Neill scored, kept his place beside Tony Cascarino for the subsequent home win over Macedonia and then played as a substitute for Cascarino in the 3-2 defeat away to Macedonia, though an injury forced him to be replaced by David Kelly 31 minutes after he came into the match. O'Neill would not be able to feature in the rest of the World Cup campaign, nor any of the spring and summer friendlies in 1998, but McCarthy believed he and Keane could form a winning partnership.

"I thought Keith O'Neill and David Connolly might have been our partnership for a long time after they played up front in 1996 when they looked a real handful," says McCarthy. "But both of them had injuries. And when Robbie came into the team in 1998 he was the best by far.

"But Keith was a real handful and it was very disappointing when he missed all those games, he was always injured."

On an Indian summer's afternoon, Denis Irwin's penalty after four minutes and Roy Keane's 15th-minute strike gave Ireland a dream start to the qualifying campaign. But by the time that Keane scored, O'Neill was already off the pitch having being injured after only nine minutes. It was the end of what might have proved to be a wonderful relationship with Robbie Keane.

In mid-October, Ireland demolished Malta 5-0 in Dublin. Robbie Keane opened his Ireland account with the first two goals in the 16th and 18th minutes, while Roy Keane, Quinn and Breen completed the rout. Robbie also broke a record set by Johnny Giles in 1959 to become the youngest ever Ireland international to score for the senior side — and he was thrilled with his evening's work.

"To get one goal, let alone two, was a bonus and becoming

the youngest player to score for Ireland was even better, smiled Keane. "I'm absolutely delighted. Niall Quinn is always helping me in attack and I'm very lucky to be playing alongside him. If I keep scoring goals like I did tonight then I will keep doing my cartwheels!"

And McCarthy was also pleased that Quinn and Keane looked capable of developing an understanding that would stand the test of a major qualifying campaign. "Niall and Robbie had a really good partnership, they instinctively knew where the other was. Quinny could read him as he was an experienced player," explained McCarthy.

"Robbie got himself into positions, would go for the first ball, then leave it for Quinny, who would then set up it and spin the ball around the corner. Robbie would feed off him. And Quinny was a great supplier of passes for other forwards for ages. It was evident from the start that Robbie would break Quinny's record by a mile. That was jumping out that he would pass it."

Quinn and Keane were now the first-choice attack and although O'Neill would be used as a substitute in the 1-0 defeat away to Yugoslavia in Belgrade the following month, he would win just two more caps — a friendly against Northern Ireland in Dublin and on the night in Skopje when Ireland conceded a 93rd-minute equaliser to Macedonia in October, 1999 that prevented them from taking the automatic tickets to Belgium and Holland.

Injuries would ruin O'Neill's career and force him into premature retirement by 2004 at the age of just 27. As the lad from the northside suburb of Finglas contemplated life outside of football, Keane was now making serious inroads for both Wolves and Ireland, although he missed the key away match with the Yugoslavs due to a knee injury sustained in the win over Malta.

Sadly, Group Eight now became the victim of the horrendous events unfolding in Kosovo. Even the match in Belgrade had been played a month later than planned due to the fact that NATO was planning air raids on the regime of Slobodan Milosevic, whose forces were now attacking sections of the Kosovan population. In the spring of 1999, NATO finally did unleash a ferocious aerial bombardment on Yugoslavia as growing evidence mounted of atrocities by Serbian troops and their allied militias on civilians in Kosovo.

Football would rightly take a back seat, with the scheduled March 27 away trip to Macedonia — a former part of the greater Yugoslav state that borders Kosovo — postponed. In early June, the offficial Yugoslav party was refused entry visas to Ireland for their game in Dublin as part of the EU's response to the actions of the Milosevic regime.

The Macedonians, however, were given a warm welcome a few days later for their match that was settled by Quinn's lone goal. The postponements of the two matches left Ireland facing a hectic week at the start of September, with Yugoslavia visiting Lansdowne Road on September 1 and Ireland taking on Croatia and Malta away in the next seven days.

On a humid, incredibly warm evening in Dublin, Ireland produced one of their best ever performances in a competitive game with a thoroughly convincing 2-1 defeat of the Yugoslavs, with Robbie Keane scoring a peach of a goal with his right foot as he met Denis Irwin's cross with a sweetly-struck half volley.

Mark Kennedy's thunderbolt clinched the points and left Ireland as favourites to claim top spot in the group and so advance automatically to the finals. However, three days later in Zagreb, McCarthy sacrificed Keane in attack to leave Tony Cascarino as the only forward in a 4-5-1 formation. McCarthy argued — with a strong degree of evidence — that the conditions in Dublin had sapped many of his players of energy and that he needed to play a containing game.

Irwin, Kennedy, Kevin Kilbane and Quinn were also rested while Roy Keane was forced out through injury. The manager's plan worked effectively in a tense, dour battle in front of Croatian president Franjo Tudman — who would die three months later — until the 91st minute, when Croatian pressure finally produced a winning goal for Suker. The goal rocked the Irish and they were fortunate to beat Malta in Valletta four days later when a 74th-minute free-kick by Steve Staunton confirmed the three points. Goals by Robbie Keane and Breen in the first 21 minutes had given Ireland a comfortable cushion but the side — with Keane and Quinn restored as the two-pronged attack — became ragged in the sunshine and allowed the Maltese to level by the 69th minute.

However, Ireland now knew that a final night win away to Macedonia on October 9 — a date originally set aside for an away friendly with Denmark — in their rearranged match would secure them at least second place in the group with Croatia facing Yugoslavia in Zagreb at the same time.

Quinn put Ireland ahead after only 19 minutes and with the Zagreb game level at 2-2 as both matches entered stoppage time, McCarthy's men were set to top this most competitive of groups and so qualify without the hassle of a two-legged play-off facing the runners-up.

However, the football gods would now conspire to wreck Irish dreams as a combination of the manager's decisions and poor defending by a number of Ireland players allowed Goran Stavrevski to equalise with a stunning header to a 93rd-minute corner. No blame could be attached to keeper Alan Kelly but both Cascarino and Keith O'Neill — who had replaced Quinn and Keane during the final quarter — were each found wanting for failing to either mark or designate a marker for the towering Macedonian right-full as he ambled unmarked into the Irish penalty area.

McCarthy, too, had made a strange decision to replace Mark Kennedy with Matt Holland in the 85th minute. Holland was making his Ireland debut and although he appeared to get into the tempo of the match fairly quickly, it was the loss of Kennedy that had a greater impact. Kennedy was a player whose performances exasperated both McCarthy and the left-winger's club managers on more than one occasion, but on that night his strong physical presence on the ball and his clever running

By the end of the Euro 2012 qualification campaign, Robbie Keane had scored an astonishing 53 goals for his country. Closest to Robbie in the Ireland scoring charts is Niall Quinn with 21, so it's no surprise that the Tallaght man has well and truly made the number-ten jersey his own

Robbie makes his senior international debut for Ireland (*above*) away to the Czech Republic in March 1998 and (*below*) he scores his first goal for the Boys In Green against Malta at Lansdowne Road seven months later

A brace of goals against the Faroe Islands saw Robbie Keane become Ireland's record goal scorer and (*below*) he netted his 50th and 51st against Macedonia

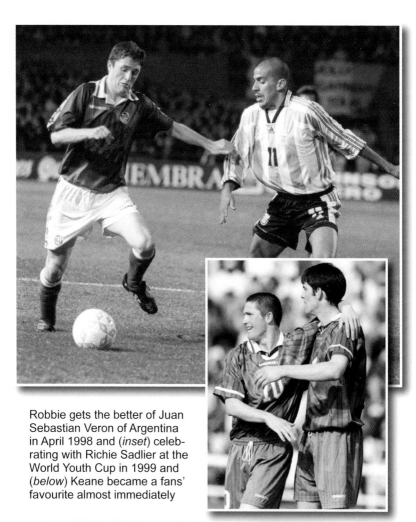

Robbie gets the better of Juan
Sebastian Veron of Argentina
in April 1998 and (*inset*) celebrating with Richie Sadlier at the
World Youth Cup in 1999 and
(*below*) Keane became a fans'
favourite almost immediately

Robbie scores against France in Paris to draw Ireland level in the 2010
World Cup play-offs and (*below*) celebrating with Aiden McGeady after finding the net against Estonia as his side cruised to a 4-0 victory in Tallinn

Robbie celebrates after scoring against Liverpool during Tony Cascarino and Steve Staunton's joint testimonial at Lansdowne Road in 2000 and (*below*) arm in arm with his old pal Damien Duff after qualifying for Euro 2012

Keane fires past Germany keeper
Oliver Kahn to secure a famous last-
gasp draw at the World Cup in 2002
and (*below*) the Tallaghtman enjoys
a lighter moment as he celebrates
in Japan with some local police and
(*right*) showing his delight after finding
the target during the qualifiers against
the Dutch at the Amsterdam ArenA

No other Ireland international has ever been so clinical in front of goal — and no Ireland international has ever performed such a memorable goal celebration. Robbie Keane's cartwheel has been put into semi-retirement, but he's more than willing to bring it back on a special occasion. Watch this space...

in possession was the visitors' best 'out' when they needed to relieve pressure in the concluding stages of the game.

With Kennedy now off the pitch, Ireland had 37-year-old Cascarino and an out-of-sorts O'Neill up front with a far from mobile central midfield of Kinsella and McLoughlin. It was little surprise that Ireland conceded a lot of territory in the final minutes of the game, with the sucker punch then added by Stavrevski.

McCarthy, the players and the management team flew for home that night completely shattered, with the consolation prize of a play-off of little appeal. They feared the worst and the draw did them no favours when the side was paired with a rapidly-improving Turkey in the two-legged affair on November 13 and 17, with the crucial second leg away from home.

On the day that Paul Scholes' brace at Hampden Park effectively settled the Scotland-England play-off, Robbie Keane shot Ireland into a 79th-minute lead at Lansdowne against the Turks. But Lee Carsley was harshly penalised for accidentally handling the ball inside his own area four minutes later and Tayfur levelled from the penalty spot.

Robbie Keane would miss the second 90 minutes having picked up a silly yellow card — his second of the campaign that earned him an automatic one-match ban.

"With Robbie playing on a regular basis, we would have missed him. And he had scored in the first leg in Dublin," says McCarthy.

The following day the players, management, FAI officials, backroom staff, media corps and a hardy band of Ireland supporters set off on a marathon trip to the city of Bursa for the return clash. A near five-hour flight proved to be the most comfortable part of the journey as a 45-minute coach trip was followed by a 90-minute ferry expedition across the Sea of Marmara where other buses completed the final 75-minute leg to Bursa.

The Turkish federation had already used Bursa to play Germany in a key group match — winning 1-0 — so the FAI had no real grounds to object to the venue, that may have adhered to UEFA rules on the staging of games within a certain radius of international airports, but broke every gentleman's agreement in terms of sportsmanship.

However, the visitors' complaints about the journey were tempered to a large degree when they passed thousands of people living in makeshift tented villages by the side of the road in the wake of the August earthquake in the region of Izmit that reportedly killed up to 45,000 inhabitants.

If the people of Bursa had offered a curious and friendly welcome on the streets of the city, then it was a different story inside the home of Bursaspor, where the hostile fans in the attendance of 25,000 created an intimidating atmosphere for the visitors and the couple of hundred travelling supporters.

An early injury to Stephen Carr did not help Ireland's cause and while they contained the home side without too much difficulty, they seldom looked like scoring the goal they needed to win the tie. Ten minutes from full-time, McCarthy threw in Cascarino for Jeff Kenna — who had replaced Carr — to form a three-pronged attack with Quinn and Duff, who had come in for Connolly midway through the second period.

But the Irish could still not create the opening they needed and the Turks advanced on the away goals rule to the finals, where they would lose to Portugal in the quarter-finals. Amid disgraceful scenes on the final whistle in Bursa, a lack of security saw Irish players attacked by fans, with Cascarino fighting a one-man battle with several of his hosts.

UEFA laughingly handed Cascarino a four-match ban that still stands as he announced his retirement from international football a few weeks later. But just as the FAI searched in vain for real justice when Irish fans were viciously attacked in Istanbul in 1991, the subsequent UEFA investigation into the incidents on and off the pitch in Bursa left a lot to be desired.

So for the second time in two years and for the third consecutive qualifying campaign, Ireland had come up short in a play-off. Surely the worm had to turn for the team and McCarthy?

Chapter 9
'Baby Irish'

ON July 8, 1980, a future Ireland football legend arrived into this world just as one of the nation's most established sporting heroes was realising an ambition to play in Italy.

Robert David Keane was born into a country that was increasingly gripped by a recession that would lead to hundreds of thousands emigrating by the middle of the decade. For Liam Brady, however, that summer month must have seemed like the first days of a great new adventure having signed for Juventus from Arsenal.

Twenty years later Keane was now following the same path as Brady, albeit at the age of 20 compared to Brady, who had been 24, and with a price tag of £13m — 26 times the £500,000 Juventus had paid Arsenal. Once the dust settled on Keane's move to Inter Milan for a five-year contract, Ireland fans and the British game alike eagerly anticipated his start to life in the challenging new surroundings.

Thanks to Channel Four's live Sunday game, the broadcaster's Saturday morning highlights package and the advent of the Champions League during the 1990s, Italian football now enjoyed a large following in Britain and Ireland. And Keane's transfer from Highfield Road to the San Siro — with reported wages of £30,000 per week — inevitably invited questions as to how the youngster would fare in what has always been regarded, from a tactical and technical viewpoint, as the toughest domestic league to play in.

Brady made a success of his seven years in Serie A as he won two league titles in his two years at Juventus, and he remained one of the game's most revered midfielders during his subsequent seasons at Sampdoria (1982-84), Inter (1984-86) and Ascoli (1986-87) before he returned to the English top flight with West Ham in 1987. The gifted midfielder had cherished ambitions for several years of playing abroad and turned down a lucrative new contract from the Highbury club and an equally attractive offer from Manchester United, who Frank Stapleton would join from Arsenal 12 months later in a £900,000 deal.

Juventus coach Giovanni Trapattoni had singled out Brady as a transfer target for some time. His pursuit accelerated after watching Brady contribute a key role in the Gunners' 2-1 aggregate semi-final victory over Juve in the Cup Winners' Cup earlier in the year. Brady's late free-kick in the first leg at Highbury had glanced off Roberto Bettega's head on its way to the net in the 1-1 draw. Hundreds of cheering Juventus fans greeted Brady on his arrival at Turin airport and Trapattoni's new signing was hoisted shoulder high and carried through the arrivals' hall.

It was not the welcome that the modest Brady had sought but it would prove to be uncannily prescient in predicting how the Irishman's career would pan out at 'The Old Lady' of Italian football. Quickly learning the language — ironically with the help of new room-mate Bettega — and with his skill on the ball and passing ability shining through, Brady soon established himself in Trapattoni's midfield. Juventus lifted the league championship in 1981 for the third of six times during Trapattoni's stewardship. Brady finished his first season as the team's leading scorer and 12 months later, Juventus and Brady were retaining the title with Brady stroking home the penalty against Catanzaro for a 1-0 win that would secure the crown for the holders.

However, the Dubliner had already been informed by Trapattoni that his contract would not be renewed at the end of the season. Instead, France's Michel Platini and Zbigniew Boniek of Poland would fill the two 'foreign' slots then allowed at each Italian club for the 1982-83 campaign. Brady moved to Genoa-based club Sampdoria.

So, although two full decades had passed since Brady had trekked across the Alps to Lombardy, it was inevitable that comparisons would be made between the pair. It was also undeniable that Keane had a very hard act to follow.

Internazionale of Milan regard themselves as a cut above their great city rivals AC Milan, referring to their neighbours as upstarts who relied on the generosity of wealthy business-man Silvio Berlusconi, who would later become Prime Minis-ter of his country. Berlusconi's business empire would fund AC Milan's ascent to the summit of Italian and European football during the late 1980s and the early part of the following de-cade. During the initial eight seasons of Berlusconi's first 18-year term as club president, coaches Arrigo Sacchi and Fabio Capello would win four Serie A crowns (1988, 1992, 1993 and 1994), three Champions Leagues (1989, 1990 and 1994) and two Intercontinental Cups (1989 and 1990). And although Inter landed the 1989 Italian league title, it was AC Milan who were very much on top even if Inter felt that they themselves were the more prestigious club.

It's not by chance that Inter's commercial, legal and administra-tive operations are based in plush downtown offices at Via Durini. With its marble staircase and valuable antique furni-ture and paintings, Inter's offices resemble a high-end auction-eers rather than those of a football club.

It was into this world on Friday, July 28, 2000 that Keane — billeted in the opening few days at a nearby five-star hotel — stepped along with his agent Tony Stephens. Wolverhampton might have its honest toil of heavy industry and Coventry its car plants, but Milan's economic strength was certainly more aesthetically appealing. The club's training ground of La Pineti-na also had the feel of old money, set in the Plain of Lombardy at Appiano Gentile, situated about an hour's drive out of Milan on the road to Lake Como.

Established for the 1961-62 season by the late Helenio Her-rera, the coach who in the 1960s led Inter in their greatest era prior to their recent domination of Italian football, the train-ing ground was way ahead of its time. When Keane arrived in Milan he scarcely had time to unpack his bags before jumping on a plane for a pre-season friendly the following evening.

Crucially, the pictures from that game, in which Keane did not feature but was introduced to the crowd at half-time, focused on two people: the Dubliner and club president and owner Massimo Moratti, rather than coach Marcello Lippi.

Club presidents have long held powerful roles in the way European football clubs are run, with these figures often deciding what players should be brought to their club. Depending on the relationship that exists between the president and first-team coach, the latter will be consulted prior to a transfer deal but may not always have the power of veto.

Moratti was happy to reveal that he had spotted Keane's goalscoring exploits for Wolves, Coventry City and Ireland on a video supplied to Inter by Keane's management team at the SFX Agency some six months earlier. His debut brace for Coventry against Derby County in August 1999 particularly caught his eye. "We chose Robbie for his quality of being in the right place at the right time," said Moratti. "We'll give him time to improve but we rate him very highly."

So there could be little doubt that Moratti had instigated the move, with Inter's managing director Gabriele Oriali then completing the deal with Sky Blues chairman Bryan Richardson. The previous Saturday, Keane had asked to be brought to the San Siro on his way from the hotel to the training ground, as Inter press officer Giuseppe Sapienza explained. "He had taken only three steps on the grass when he stopped and said 'wow, this is incredible — I want to play here," said Sapienza.

On Monday, Keane was back at Appiano Gentile where he gave his first media interview following his whirlwind move. Barely 20 years of age, there was a definite strain of bewilderment in Keane's voice as he reflected on the events of the previous few days. Yet there was also a steely resolve to do well and his self-confidence shone through in an interview he gave to the Irish Daily Star.

"I would have been a fool to say no to the opportunity of talking to Inter, never mind joining them," declared Keane. "Gordon Strachan helped me progress to be the player I am today but, surrounded by world-class players and coaches, I can only get better. Some people may wonder if I can succeed at this level of the game but there's no doubt in my mind that I will.

"There will definitely be pressure on me but I have thrived on pressure up to now. I've taken the challenges in my stride so this should be no different. It has made me a better player and I know that I will become a better player by playing for Inter Milan. The last few years have not fazed me so I won't be fazed by this move.

"They have spent a lot of money on me and I'm confident in my own ability. I would not have signed for Inter Milan unless I thought I would be playing regularly. Yesterday was the final day to register players for the Champions League and they wanted me to be signed in time. That's encouraging.

"I saw the talk about a move in the papers but it wasn't until Thursday that I was told that there was something definitely going on. When I went into training on Friday morning, Gordon Strachan told me that Coventry had accepted an offer from Inter Milan for me and asked did I want to speak to them?

"It only took me a few seconds to say 'of course I will'. I have watched plenty of Champions league and Serie A matches at the San Siro on television and always dreamed of playing there. When I left training for the airport on Friday, Gordon said he would not shake my hand because the deal had not gone through yet. But then he said that he knew and I knew that I would not be coming back. Gordon became a friend to me and I would not be at Inter but for him.

"Twelve months ago I was preparing in the First Division at Wolves and now I'm playing for a club that has Ronaldo, Christian Vieri and Hakan Sukur."

If Keane arrived at a swift decision on Inter's offer, he still consulted those he had grown to trust in the few short years he had spent in England, including Alan Shearer, with whom he shared an agent in Tony Stephens.

"I spoke to Mick McCarthy, Alan Shearer and David Platt last week when Coventry confirmed Inter's offer. Alan has been great to me over the past few years so I took his advice very seriously. His record in the game and his knowledge of it makes his views very important. He told me that I had the ability to make the step up to Serie A.

"David was a success over here with Sampdoria so he knows what it takes to make the grade in Serie A. He told me that it will be a lot different to England, in particular the lifestyle. But as a young lad he felt I can adapt, especially as I moved from Dublin to England when I was only 15. He said that I would be well able to tackle the changes and that he would always be at the end of a phone if needed.

"According to David, I will emerge a better player than when I arrived here in Milan no matter what happens. Mick has been brilliant to me in the past two and a half years and was also supportive of the move."

The cheeky-chappy persona that had quickly surfaced in the Molineux dressing-room was already evident.

"I asked if there was any chance of wearing the number nine shirt," he quipped. "But they told me that Ronaldo wears that shirt so I agreed to accept another. It was worth a try and now there's talk that I may be handed the number seven shirt.

"I met Laurent Blanc, who gave me a warm welcome to the club. After spending the last four days in hotels, planes, coaches and taxis I'm looking forward to getting back to training. Last Wednesday I was playing a pre-season game against Wolves. Now I'm an Inter Milan player," added Keane with a broad smile.

"People are entitled to their opinions but I'm sure I'm going to prove myself. I'm just so happy to be a player with this famous club. Life is incredible at the minute. Let's just say many great players are now my teammates."

Lippi was also satisfied that Keane would become a key player for him and the club.

"You can always see the difference in quality in a player when he moves from England to Serie A," Lippi outlined. "Quality is the most important aspect of a player to us and I believe Robbie has plenty of that. We are very happy to have signed him and I have told him that he will be a very important player for us.

"Robbie may be only 20 but his efforts on the pitch and the way he conducts himself off it make you think he is 25 or 26. That's an element of a player that is important to Inter Milan and Robbie has impressed us with his maturity.

"Keane's a quality player and he's also from a country within the EU, which is significant. He seems a nice guy and a great player even if the language barrier is set to be an initial problem. Hopefully, it won't be for too long with Robbie already taking lessons."

And his international manager, Mick McCarthy who was on holidays in Fitzpatrick's Hotel in New York when the deal went through, also gave the striker his full backing in the wake of his decision. He said: "This is a great move for Robbie Keane. It can only benefit him as a player and us as a country to have one of our brightest young talents learning his trade in the toughest league of them all.

"I know that Robbie will thrive in Italy. Even if Robbie only lasts a year in Italy he will learn from the experience and his financial security will be sealed. There are no downsides to the move as far as I am concerned and he cannot come back from Italy as a failure. He will be a better player for Ireland because of his time on the continent."

Keane's arrival in the bustling home of Italy's thriving fashion trade caused a stir even though Inter already employed Brazil's Ronaldo, Turkey striker Hakan Sukur, Italy defender Javier Zanetti, Dutch midfield genius Clarence Seedorf, Croatia defender Dario Simic, Italy striker Christian Vieri, France World Cup giant Laurent Blanc, Vladimir Jugovic of Yugoslavia, 31 times-capped Italy midfielder Luigi Di Biagio, Uruguay's attacking midfielder Alvaro Recoba, Chilean forward Ivan Zamorano and a budding midfielder by the name of Andrea Pirlo.

It was now 11 years since Trapattoni had guided Inter to the last of their 13 Serie A titles, with a team largely comprised of Italians such as Giuseppe Bergomi, Aldo Serena and Nicola Berti, but laced with the German steel of full-back Andreas Brehme and midfield genius Lothar Matthaus.

The 1990s had been dominated by city rivals AC Milan, who won five league crowns, with Juventus weighing in with three while Napoli and Sampdoria had bagged the opening two titles of the decade. However, with the financial muscle of the Moratti family still driving them on, Inter began the first full season of the new millennium anxious to recreate the glory of the 1960s when 'La Grande Inter' annexed three Serie A wins, became the first Italian club to win two European Cups (1964 and 1965) and claimed the Intercontinental Cup in 1964 and 1965.

The impressive list of players was augmented by the presence of coach Lippi, who had emerged as the Italian game's latest managerial Don by winning three league championships, an Italian Cup, the Champions League, the UEFA Super Cup and World Club Championship in the five seasons to 1998-99 when in charge of Juventus.

Lippi had arrived at Inter 12 months before Keane and the pressure was now firmly on him to deliver the silverware that the fans and owners craved. But before a ball was kicked in the defining league campaign, there were ominous signs that Lippi and Inter would struggle. A lengthening injury list meant that Ronaldo — who had played little part in the previous season because of a serious knee ligament injury that was now receiving treatment in his native Brazil — and Vieri were unavailable in the opening months of the season. It was still felt that there were enough quality players available to ensure that the hassle of reaching the group stage of the Champions League via the preliminary round tie with Helsingborgs of Sweden would not present a major problem.

However, a shock 1-0 aggregate exit to the Swedish club added further pressure on Lippi before a ball had even been kicked in the league and sparked rumours that the coach would do well to keep his job until Christmas. At the end of the 1999-2000 season, Lippi had tendered his resignation to Moratti after a fourth-place finish in the league, with a place in the Champions League only secured via a play-off win over Parma.

However, the owner refused Lippi's offer and told the 52-year-old coach to prepare for the next campaign, sanctioning another raft of big-name signings that included Sukur from Galatasaray, Keane, Vampeta (Corinthians) and Francisco Farinos (Valencia). National hero Roberto Baggio, however, was allowed to leave the club. Indeed, the fees for Keane and Farinos of £13m each represented Inter's joint-fifth highest ever expenditure until then on a player, behind Christian Vieri (£31m to Lazio in July 1999), Ronaldo (£18m to Barcelona in July 1996), Vampeta (£14.6m to Corinthians in August 2000) and Clarence Seedorf (£13.5m to Real Madrid in the summer of 1999).

The summer recruitment programme had now brought Inter's total spend on new players over five years, since Moratti's election as president, to a staggering £150m. That left Lippi — according to most pundits — boasting the most powerful squad in the Italian game.

However, it was hard to escape the feeling that the manager was operating on borrowed time. While Lippi was no boy scout venturing forth, statistics on his predecessors made for interesting reading and must have caused him a degree of discomfort.

In the eight years from July, 1991 — when Trapattoni exited having just guided Inter to the club's first ever UEFA Cup success — to July, 1999, when Lippi took charge, Inter had employed no fewer than nine coaches. Corrado Orrico, Osvaldo Bagnoli, Giampiero Marini, Ottavio Bianchi, Luis Suarez, Roy Hodgson (twice), Luciano Castellini (twice), Luigi Simoni and Mircea Lucescu had all taken either permanent or temporary charge of the club's first team during that period.

It was little wonder that Trapattoni had compared the final part of his successful five years as akin to working 'in a spin dryer'. Keane was adapting well to life in Italy with the presence of his long-time friend from home, John Ledwith, helping him as he made a plush apartment close to the San Siro a home from home. In the same building, Ronaldo had put down roots although he was now undergoing rehab in Brazil.

'Baby Irish' — as the Inter fans had christened their new signing — only missed one thing: brown sauce that he liked to mix into his mashed potatoes.

Keane figured in the embarrassing European exit and partnered Sukur up front in the 1-0 first leg away defeat to Helsingborgs — the club's first competitive match following his arrival just over a week previously. Despite the defeat and with the second leg back in Milan to rectify matters, Keane was able to give a positive assessment of his competitive debut in Sweden where he had been one of the few Inter players to play well, despite missing one of his team's few scoring opportunities.

"It's incredible, everything happened so quickly that it all seems like a dream," admitted Keane. "I was so happy to play for Inter in the Champions League — a competition I have only seen on television before. Even though I played well I am disappointed that we lost."

Lippi — whose side was fortunate not to lose by more than one goal — also gave an upbeat post-match statement about Keane. "Keane and Sukur did very well and all of our new signings were impressive, which goes to show we have spent well."

With Ronaldo and Vieri both injured, Keane was very much in Lippi's plans to claim a starting place in the attack when the league started on October 1, and scoring the winner in the August 14 friendly win over Real Mallorca did his hopes no harm. Before then, however, there was the return leg against Helsingborgs and other domestic games to play.

Keane was dropped from the Inter attack for the second leg at the San Siro on August 23, as Lippi decided to partner Sukur with Zamorano. At the interval with the game scoreless,

Lippi sent in Keane for Pirlo, while Recoba replaced Zamorano. Inter dominated possession and Keane's back-heel struck the post. Yet the home side lacked a cutting edge in the final third of the pitch and when they finally looked like making a breakthrough, Recoba missed a 90th-minute penalty to send the tie into extra-time.

"It is the worst evening of my life," stated a rueful Lippi who defended his selection of Zamorano ahead of Keane. "Zamorano has great character and attributes, I thought he could bring what we missed in the first leg.

"Keane is a superb player but he still needs time to settle in," added Lippi, whose grip on power at the club was slipping by the day. He ran the gauntlet of verbal abuse from many of the 49,949 fans present at the final whistle.

Keane had signed for a team thrust into early season turmoil. He was restored to the Inter frontline on September 8 for the Italian Super Cup clash against Lazio in Rome's Olympic Stadium, and within two minutes Keane was celebrating his first competitive goal for the club with a neat lob.

Operating alongside Recoba behind target man Sukur, Keane appeared to enjoy his role, although Lazio would recover and claim the cup with a 4-3 victory in front of 65,000 spectators. Keane was again on the mark on September 14 in the 3-0 away win over Ruch Chorzow in the UEFA Cup first round first leg when he started alongside Sukur.

Undoubtedly, his confidence had been boosted by his key role in Ireland's 2-2 away draw with Holland in Amsterdam in early September. On that day, Keane headed one of the side's goals in a game that marked the start of the international team's eventual qualification for the 2002 World Cup finals.

For the return leg two weeks later in Chorzow, Keane was in the dugout but played the second half of a 4-1 victory, setting up the third and fourth goals for Seedorf and Corrado Colombo. Between the two UEFA Cup games, Keane started against Lecce in the 1-1 third round, first leg of the Italian Cup when he was replaced at the interval. Keane found the net in the 3-1 second leg away win when he chipped the keeper for the crucial second goal.

Despite the club's hit-and-miss beginning to the season, Keane's own start to life in Italy had been relatively impressive with three goals to his name. While Sukur had yet to score for his new club, Keane was living up to expectations. Along with teammate Recoba, the pair were regarded as potential saviours for Lippi, whose popularity remained tarnished with many fans due to the Champions League horror shows. Taking daily Italian lessons, Keane was quickly engaging with colleagues in the dressing-room and training ground banter.

The fact that Seedorf and Vieri both spoke good English helped. "Christian and Clarence have both helped me settle in and have been brilliant around the dressing-room," revealed Keane. "Before the Ireland-Dutch game, Seedorf was winding me up and we were both looking forward to playing each other.

"David Platt told me how important it is to learn the language quickly, so I have an hour of lessons every day. I always carry a dictionary about with me but some of the phrases Clarence used during the Holland game cannot be found in the phrasebook!"

Back at Inter, the embattled Lippi — who would lead Italy to their fourth World Cup success just six years later against France in Berlin — remained defiant. "I won't resign even if they decide to put bombs under my house," he declared a week before the first Serie A engagement of the campaign.

That opening game of the season away to Reggio Calabria saw Keane named in the Inter attack only to be replaced by Colombo after 72 minutes. By full-time, Lippi's fate was sealed by a 2-1 defeat as Moratti's patience finally drained away.

"I'm ashamed — if I was the president, I'd get rid of the players and the coach," said Lippi. Moratti stated: "Lippi admitted to me that he did not have a solution to the problems."

Keane was stunned by events at the club that saw Lippi axed within 24 hours of the defeat.

"It's quite a shock, the Italians certainly don't mess about," said Keane. "But I don't think it will affect the players and, more importantly, me. I would have preferred a settled environment having only just got here."

Ex-Argentina coach and the then manager of Uruguay, Daniel Passarella was initially approached about the post but it was Marco Tardelli who was recruited from his role as Italy Under-21 boss in the wake of his success in guiding them to the European title the previous year.

"I love impossible missions even if I have to say that I don't think it will be too difficult to turn things around," said Tardelli on his appointment. "It will either be heaven or hell."

The new boss had words of encouragement for his Irish striker. "Robbie Keane is a player who really impresses me. I have seen him a lot because I was youth coach with the Italian national side and Keane was involved with Ireland. One of the things he has going for him is youth. With luck, he has many years ahead of him in the game."

Tardelli retained Keane for his first match in charge as Napoli were defeated 3-1 at the San Siro, although Recoba replaced him midway through the second period. A week later the Tardelli honeymoon ended abruptly with the 3-0 reversal at Udinese, with Keane only lasting until the interval before Recoba came in for him.

On November 1, it was Keane who was brought on from the bench for Recoba after 79 minutes in the 2-0 home success against Bari. Not involved in the 2-2 draw with Verona, Keane returned to the attack for the 1-0 home loss to 10-man Lecce on November 12, with Pirlo replacing him on 68 minutes.

Robbie had yet to score for Inter in the league after five appearances but that was hardly a crime given the upheaval at the club, the change in coach and the inconsistency of displays and results.

Rumours of a return to English football surfaced and Serie A side Reggina tried to sign him on loan. He would play just one further Serie A match — a foot injury ruling him out of three league games.

Significantly, he was already beginning to doubt if his long-term future lay in Italy, as evidenced by an interesting exchange at the San Siro when Inter were not even playing.

When Leeds United arrived in the city on November 7 for the following night's Champions League group stage match against AC Milan, there was one very interested spectator in the stands.

"Robbie came to see us training in the San Siro the night before we played AC Milan in the Champions League," recalls Gary Kelly, who was then almost ten years with the Yorkshire club and had developed a close bond with Keane while on Ireland duty.

"He obviously knew the Irish lads who were with Leeds — me, Ian Harte, Alan Maybury and Stephen McPhail. Tongue-in-cheek, he went to David O'Leary and said 'any chance of getting me to that club or what?' And within a matter of weeks, David, out of the blue, said 'get on to Robbie and make sure he comes here'.

"We were all on to him — me, Stephen, Alan and Ian. We knew that he wanted to come to Leeds, especially with all the Irish lads there. There was some craic at the club then. At that time, David would say that he wanted somebody and Peter Ridsdale would just get him."

And get 'him' is what Ridsdale did on December 20, despite strong interest from West Ham, Aston Villa, Chelsea and Liverpool, who all made enquiries for Keane in late November and early December. A few weeks earlier Keane had wisely publicly declared his intention to stay with Inter.

"No-one said it would be easy here but you have to challenge yourself and I am determined to get into the first team," said Keane on December 4. "I would be foolish to return before I have given Serie A a good shot. I am happy to fight for my place at Inter.

"It's quite flattering to think that people like Chelsea and Leeds United are interested in me but I'm very happy at the moment. I just want to get myself fit and hopefully work my way back into the team. It's different from England and Milan is a wonderful city. But I didn't come here to go shopping, I came here to play football."

Keane initially signed for Leeds United on loan, with the clubs and the player agreeing to a clause that allowed Leeds to permanently purchase him for £12m the following July. If Inter, Tardelli and Moratti were satisfied that Keane's exit from Inter was the best move for all concerned, the forward had still made a hugely favourable impression at the club.

More than a decade after Keane moved to Leeds, Tardelli stresses that he would have been happy had the Irishman stayed. "It was not my decision to ask him to leave, it was a decision taken by the club and by the player himself," says Tardelli. "Robbie played well at Inter. He was very young and we had many players so we needed to decide some things. It was not that he played badly, he played well but we had other players.

"I would have liked to keep him but he was young and maybe had he stayed it would have been possible for him to play."

Of some consolation to the Dubliner was the fact that his direct replacement, Uruguayan Antonio Pacheco, would make no impact while Tardelli would also exit at the season's end following more poor results and a UEFA Cup exit to Spain's Alaves.

When Inter did finally decide to allow Keane to leave on loan, it was again Moratti who confirmed the news. "Inter are evaluating offers from several English clubs interested in Robbie Keane," said Moratti. "During the Christmas break, negotiations could come to a successful conclusion, naturally, with the consent of the player and a sum equal to that which we signed him six months ago from Coventry."

Eleven years on, Moratti's wife Emilia would speak fondly of Keane during Inter's participation in the Dublin Super Cup at the Aviva Stadium. Keane may not have lasted long at Internazionale, but he had made friends in Milan and the rest of his career would benefit from the short stint at the famous club.

Chapter 10
Leeds reunited

HAVING endured several months of turmoil at Inter Milan, Keane rejoiced when Leeds United agreed a deal with the Italian club to initially sign him on loan in December, 2000 — with a £1m arrangement fee changing hands — and the option to complete a permanent transfer in the summer of 2001

Keane arrived at Leeds at a time when there were tangible signs that manager David O'Leary and chairman Peter Ridsdale could steer the club into another successful era to rival the glory decade between the mid-sixties and mid-seventies, as well as the early 1990s. Don Revie's side had won two league titles in 1969 and 1974, one FA Cup in 1972, the 1968 League Cup and two Fairs Cup (the predecessor to the UEFA Cup) crowns in 1968 and 1971.

They were beaten finalists in the 1975 European Cup final when a series of dubious refereeing decisions helped Bayern Munich to the second of their hat-trick of successes with a 2-0 win in Parc des Princes in Paris. That defeat marked the end of that side, by then managed by Jimmy Armfield. But Howard Wilkinson's no-nonsense team of the late 1980s and early nineties — tempered by a classy midfield of Gordon Strachan, Gary McAllister, David Batty and the late Gary Speed — saw the club claim its third league crown in 1991-92 when it lifted the last ever Football League First Division, prior to the creation of the Sky Sports-backed FA Premier League.

After Wilkinson's departure in the autumn of 1996, George Graham took charge of the first team and began to gradually blood the hugely talented crop of young players emerging from the club's academy, where legendary former winger and manager Eddie Gray was in command. Graham's sudden exit to Spurs in October, 1998, saw Leicester City boss Martin O'Neill resist overtures by Ridsdale to become the new manager before Graham's assistant, ex-Ireland international O'Leary, was appointed.

O'Leary immediately gave youth its head with Harry Kewell, Stephen McPhail, Jonathan Woodgate, Alan Smith, Ian Harte, Michael Bridges, Lee Bowyer and Eirik Bakke becoming established first-team stars. A fourth-place league finish in 1999 secured a UEFA Cup place the following season. That campaign's demise at the semi-final stage in April, 2000, with a 4-2 aggregate defeat to Galatasaray, would be tragically overshadowed by the horrific murders in Istanbul the night before the first leg of Leeds fans Christopher Loftus and Kevin Speight.

During the 1999-2000 campaign Leeds would top the Premier League for all but a few weeks of October, November, December and January before eventually ending the season in third place, which earned them the last of the three Champions League places for the following autumn. By the start of the 2000-01 season O'Leary had added midfielder Olivier Dacourt, striker Mark Viduka and defender Dominic Matteo to his strong squad, with Rio Ferdinand signing from West Ham for £18m in November.

Leeds' league form was baffling, however, and they were 12th in the table when Keane arrived on December 20. However, impressive European displays against AC Milan (1-0 win at home), Besiktas (6-0 at home), Barcelona (1-1 at home) and AC Milan (1-1 away) would see them qualify for the second group phase of the Champions League. In the weeks just prior to Keane's signing, Leeds defeated Lazio 1-0 in Rome to offset their 2-0 home setback by Real Madrid in the opening game of that second phase.

Keane was certainly joining a club that could mix it with the best in Europe even if it was struggling domestically. He was honest enough to state that he was leaving Italian football somewhat reluctantly and not in the circumstances that he had imagined. However, with Christian Vieri now back from injury at Inter, Ronaldo making his first tentative steps towards a return and coach Marco Tardelli believing that Keane was not sufficiently experienced to start games in what was becoming a relegation battle to avoid the drop into Serie B, Keane knew that his best option was a return to the Premier League.

Chelsea had matched Inter's £12m asking price in early December and, initially, Inter favoured a deal that would see them regain almost their entire outlay on the forward. But Keane wanted to join Leeds who, in a pre-Roman Abramovich era at Stamford Bridge, he thought represented a better punt for honours. Robbie was also aware that a prolonged spell without first-team football could damage his international ambitions. With no reserve team football in Italy, his prospects appeared bleak if he stayed with Inter.

Ireland manager Mick McCarthy valued Keane immensely, and Keane and Niall Quinn were the first-choice pairing up front in the green jersey when McCarthy played a 4-4-2 system — which he did most of the time.

But the Ireland boss also liked the fact that Damien Duff was more than comfortable operating as a striker and David Connolly was also pushing for a place in the side. Quinn and Keane started the 2002 World Cup qualifying campaign in sparkling form in the autumn of 2000 as Ireland drew away with Holland (2-2) and Portugal (1-1) and then defeated Estonia 2-0 at Lansdowne Road, with Keane netting in Amsterdam.

However, that would be Keane's only goal in the 10 group games until he ended his famine with a priceless strike in the 2-0 first-leg victory in the World Cup play-off with Iran in Dublin in November, 2001 — fully 14 months after his goal against the Dutch.

Indeed, Keane was dropped by McCarthy for the one and only time for the 2-0 win in Estonia in June, 2001. Six months prior to this, Keane was anxious to prevent such a rarity becoming the norm and that played a part in his decision to move to west Yorkshire. It would be a wise move in international terms, for McCarthy did indeed start Duff up front at the World Cup finals — but it was beside Keane rather than Quinn.

"I have mixed emotions. When I joined Inter I thought I would be spending some years in Italy," admitted Keane when introduced to the media at Elland Road. "I have settled in well over there and was learning the language and had made a number of friends. But the most important thing is that I had only been picked for half of the Serie A games and, as any footballer will tell you, playing is everything.

"I wanted it to work there and things were going well under Mr Lippi but we all know that things change in football and when the new manager came in, he had his own ideas. I've nothing against Mr Tardelli. He is a great man and a great manager but unfortunately I just did not figure in his plans.

"Last week, Inter officials told me that there had been a lot of interest in me from Premiership clubs and indicated that they would be considering offers. They asked me which team I would join if I had the choice and I told them it would be Leeds United.

"I have a lot of friends at Elland Road and I have heard from them what a fantastic spirit David O'Leary has created. Even though I only spent a few months in Italy, I have improved and matured and now I am looking forward to help bringing silverware to the club. I don't think I have a point to prove. I went over to Italy and unfortunately it didn't work out. I'm just grateful that they gave me the chance.

"It was an experience for me and something that I will never forget and will never regret. A lot of clubs came in for me but Leeds were always the ones I wanted to join. They are a club in the Champions League and I have come here to win things."

For a squad built solidly on the flair of youth, Keane revealed that he had been unable to convince Leeds to sign him six years earlier.

"It seems like a long time ago that I came to Leeds on trial but I remember it well. I was 14 at the time and I came over with two other Irish lads. It was a big thing, especially as my dad is such a massive Leeds supporter. I scored that day but never got the magical phone call.

"I think my dad was a bit disappointed but he never let on because he wanted the best for me and going to Wolves was a good thing. And Leeds have got a much better player."

O'Leary was thrilled to land Keane, whom he felt would act as the perfect foil for Mark Viduka, who had been signed from Celtic in July, 2000 for £6m and was now developing into a feared marksman.

"Robbie is not eligible for us in the Champions league but that will leave him fresh for our league games," stated O'Leary. "He is a player who is mentally very strong. He has a hunger to do well and wanted to stay in Italy to prove himself. Robbie is not yet the finished article. We have bought potential but I have no doubts about how good he can be. The lad is out of the Alan Shearer mould in terms of his mental attitude."

And the chairman confirmed that the greening of that part of Yorkshire had been no harm when it came to attracting Keane to Elland Road.

"I think Robbie has chosen us because David is Irish and there are a number of Irish lads here who he knows well," said Ridsdale.

Keane would be forced to sit out the remaining exciting games of the Champions League due to his appearances for Inter against Helsingborgs the previous August, but set about his league duties with gusto. However, his debut as a substitute for Lucas Radebe two days before Christmas did not work out as planned with Aston Villa inflicting a 2-1 Elland Road reversal. He fared no better on St Stephen's Day when he replaced Kewell in the 2-1 loss away to Newcastle United.

New Year's Day at home to Middlesbrough heralded Keane's first start for Leeds, and his first goal, as his 55th-minute penalty salvaged a 1-1 draw. In the next league match he scored twice as a substitute in the 4-0 Maine Road hammering of Manchester City. Keane started the next eight league matches and scored three times as Leeds moved into sixth place in the table and set their sights on finishing third once more, which would secure another Champions League experience.

On January 31, he netted the winner against his old club Coventry City. Now first-choice up front, Keane was reproducing the quality of football that had lit up Coventry City 12 months earlier, although he could still misfire, as was the case when he squandered two opportunities in the 2-0 FA Cup fourth-round defeat away to Liverpool.

In the league, Keane was a revelation and a run of six goals in as many games helped him secure the Carling Player of the Month award for January.

"For £1m, Robbie has been a great buy for the rest of the season," enthused O'Leary. "He could be the key to a European place. He's had a massive impact in terms of scoring vital goals in games where we desperately needed points and I am in no doubt that he has helped us turn our season around."

With Keane unable to play in Europe, O'Leary paired Viduka with Alan Smith and they formed an outstanding spring partnership that saw the team record home and away wins over Anderlecht, a 3-2 defeat to Real Madrid in the Bernabeu and a thrilling 3-3 Elland Road draw with Italian champions Lazio. Leeds comfortably reached the Champions League quarter-finals, where a 3-0 hammering of Deportivo La Coruna at home was enough of a cushion to weather a 2-0 reversal in Spain.

Smith's Champions League form was giving O'Leary a problem as to who he should select beside Viduka. Keane found himself on the bench for several league matches, including the 2-1 win at Anfield on April 13. Leeds moved into the top three on two occasions in the final two months of the campaign, but the 2-0 home win over Chelsea on April 28 — with Keane again on target — was nullified by the 2-1 defeat at title-chasing Arsenal three games from the end.

On the final day of the season, with Keane sitting out his second consecutive game through injury, Leeds needed to beat Leicester City at home and hope that Liverpool failed to take all three points away to Charlton Athletic to nail third place in the table. But the Reds — celebrating a treble of FA Cup, League Cup and UEFA Cup — held their nerve at the Valley to win 4-0 and so render Leeds' 3-1 success over the Foxes as meaningless in terms of Champions League ambitions.

As the dust settled at Elland Road, few people were aware of the financial implications of the failure to make it back into club football's most glittering competition, and the loss of tens of millions of pounds that accompanied it.

Keane, however, had every right to feel content with his efforts that had yielded nine goals in 18 league appearances. So he was happy to make his move permanent in July for the extra £11m as he looked forward to next season in which he hoped to drive on Leeds' ambitions and to help Ireland qualify for the 2002 World Cup finals.

After three moves in the space of two years, Keane was also relieved to be putting down roots in Yorkshire, where he had been met with the warmest of Irish welcomes from Gary Kelly, Ian Harte, Stephen McPhail, Alan Maybury and manager David O'Leary.

"There was a great bond that existed between the players at Leeds, it was a real family bond," explains Gary Kelly, who was now a senior and hugely popular figure in the dressing room.

"And it was a home from home because every weekend Robbie's mam and dad were over, or mine or Stephen's, Alan Maybury's or Ian's. It was just brilliant. We always enjoyed the banter and that never changed. When we went to Miami for his stag, we still enjoyed that same craic as we had when we played for Ireland and Leeds."

The social aspect of life as a first-team player at Leeds certainly appealed to Keane, who still happily hops up on stage to sing in public at the first invitation.

"We had a great local called the Bingley Arms in Bardsey that was close to the training ground at Wetherby. It kept us all out of town, it was in the sticks and we all lived in the area," adds Kelly. "Shay Given loves a song and Richie Dunne loves a song but Robbie fancies himself to have a go in Pop Idol.

"If he wasn't a footballer then he was always going to end up in Take That or Westlife. But I still think I'm better than him!"

It was during these impromptu sing-songs that the late Robert Keane senior showed his ability as a performer, and he could hold an audience spellbound with a terrific version of the fifties classic 'Blue Suede Shoes'.

"I remember Robert in The Bingley Arms when all the Irish lads would go out together. Somebody brought a guitar in and he was sitting beside the fireplace. He didn't have a guitar pick but he played that many songs that the tops of his fingers were pumping blood. He just kept going with Robbie encouraging him, 'dad, play that one and this one'.

"My late dad Johnny would have a go, then me and then Robbie. I know the new owner of The Bingley and he told me when I was over there for New Year's Eve in 2011 that he wanted us back. 'It's never been the same' he told me since we left. A lad called Mike Schofield owned it and he went on to Spain. I think he's only in Spain because of us! When we were out, we were out, we wouldn't be sipping on two pints.

"The wives and girlfriends were with us and that added to the family feeling to it. When we had to get our heads down and train and play, we did that. But we could also enjoy ourselves. It was a home from home and when there are nearly a dozen lads there — including the reserves and youths — and when the manager is Irish, then it helps going into training every day.

"The Irish aspect to the club helped it grow because the big names likes Rio Ferdinand, Danny Mills, Robbie Fowler and Nigel Martyn all loved us and the way we enjoyed life. They began to follow us by not going into town and instead coming for the sing-song with Robbie's dad.

"Over there, they only celebrated St George's Day, so we made sure St Patrick's Day was honoured. We would go in after training at 12.30 or one o'clock. They were good times and even though Robbie was only there for a few years of it, he was in the middle of the craic. He was the heart of the craic there and the heart of the dressing-room."

With Inter — where ex-Valencia coach Hector Cuper had succeeded Tardelli — willing to sell Keane, and O'Leary anxious to sign the striker on a long-term deal, it did not take long for a £12m transfer to be completed in July, 2001.

And Kelly was delighted that Keane was now a teammate at Elland Road. Kelly had played against Keane while the latter was with Wolves and Coventry, and would again face him when he later moved on to Spurs.

"Robbie's a nightmare to mark. Some centre-halves would rather mark a 6'2" centre-forward than mark a player like Robbie. He's on your shoulder and, even though you might have marked him out of the whole game, give him half a chance and he'll bury one. Big centre-halves hate marking him.

"One time when I had come back from injury, I played at left-back and he was out on the right for Coventry. He'd lose you because he's so quick. He's so clever and intelligent.

"He would always do something out of the ordinary. Leeds were playing well when we went down to Spurs just after he joined them. He scored from a half-chance. But he didn't celebrate, that was typical him as he was aware of our fans."

Ahead of the 2001-02 season, Keane was aiming to build on the impressive foundation he had laid at Elland Road during his five and a half months on loan. Those nine league goals left him as the club's joint-third highest scorer for the campaign along with Lee Bowyer, two behind Alan Smith, six adrift of top marksman Mark Viduka and two in front of Ian Harte.

However, the Dubliner's goals-to-games ratio matched Viduka, who played in 34 of the 38 league games, and was ahead of Smith (33 games), Bowyer (38) and Harte (29) while midfielder Kewell could only muster two in his 17 matches. Keane would start the 2001-02 season alongside Viduka with Smith on the bench, and by mid-September O'Leary's side was top of the table, where they would stay — apart from one week — until the first week of November.

However, Keane was finding it harder to get on the scoresheet and in those opening 11 league matches, he netted just twice in 10 starts. Keane's best performances were reserved for the knockout competitions, with a hat-trick in the 6-0 League Cup demolition of Leicester City in October and a goal in each of the opening rounds of the UEFA Cup against

Portugal's Maritimo and Troyes of France.

On November 28, Leeds confirmed that they had agreed to purchase Robbie Fowler from Liverpool for £11m. It was ominous news for Keane. And the following Saturday away to Fulham at Craven Cottage, it was Fowler who partnered Viduka up front with Smith deployed as a midfielder. Keane was not involved. Fowler — now aged 26 and with a career haul of 120 goals for the Anfield club in 236 league appearances — would start all but three of Leeds' remaining 24 league matches.

In the weeks prior to Fowler's arrival at Elland Road, Keane's temperament — rarely an issue for a player frequently at the receiving end of dubious means by opposition defenders — had become somewhat suspect. Referee Dermot Gallagher erred on Keane's side when he pushed David Beckham in the upper body during the 1-1 league draw away to Manchester United. It earned only a yellow card from Gallagher but sparked a pointed post-match rebuke from O'Leary.

"I had a go at him because if you raise your hands you are leaving yourself open to the referee," said O'Leary. "If that had happened in Europe I think he would have taken a walk."

A week later, during the 2-1 home win over Spurs that sent Leeds back to the top of the table, Keane found himself watching the final 17 minutes from the bench and was seen to throw his shin pads off late in proceedings as his frustrations boiled over. Significantly, following Fowler's capture, Keane would be restricted to just four starts and nine runs as a substitute in those remaining 25 matches, although an operation on New Year's Eve to address a niggling ankle complaint kept him out of football for a month.

Kelly, like many other players and Leeds supporters, remains puzzled by O'Leary's decision not to persist with Keane and to limit his starts.

"O'Leary bought him but never really started him. And when he did come into the game, he'd always get him out of the shit. That was typical Robbie. When he was on the bench, Robbie would tell the manager 'any chance of me getting on.'

And the games he did start, he was taken off in."

Leeds' form improved in the weeks after Fowler staked his place in the team and the 3-0 New Year's Day home win over West Ham United sent the team to the summit of the table. What's more, on a night that Leeds tore the Hammers to shreds, the Viduka-Fowler pairing looked lethal while the side's sweet, fluid passing style had the purists purring.

However, a 2-1 FA Cup third-round exit at Cardiff City a few days later and the heavy 3-1 league defeat away to Newcastle United the following week sparked a run of eight games in all domestic matches — plus two in the UEFA Cup — where Leeds failed to win. By the time that goals by Fowler and Harte earned a 2-0 home victory over Ipswich Town on March 6, Leeds were in sixth place — out of title contention and with the safety net of a Champions League spot fast disappearing.

There was a 10-point gap between them and the crucial fourth place — UEFA had confirmed an additional Champions League place for the Premiership — that would secure a route back to the Champions League. Keane would score only three league goals in the 2001-02 season — nine behind Fowler, eight adrift of Viduka and five off Kewell.

"It was a frustrating season, I want to play every game but it's not the way it goes," conceded Keane in mid-May as he reflected on the previous nine months.

"The manager has his own views. We will have to have a chat when I go back. We had a few chats last year."

If the news on the pitch was alarming for Leeds fans, then the unfolding events off it were even more disturbing. In December, 2001, the two-month trial at Hull Crown Court of Leeds stars Lee Bowyer and Jonathan Woodgate on charges related to an assault on 20-year-old student Sarfraz Najeib in January 2000 had concluded. Bowyer was acquitted of all charges while Woodgate was sentenced to 100 hours of community service for affray.

Verdicts on the actions of the players' associates, Neale Caveney and Paul Clifford, were also delivered. Caveney was cleared of assault but found guilty of affray and also received 100 hours of community service while Clifford was found guilty of both assault and affray and received a prison term.

An earlier trial had ended in April 2001 when the judge dismissed the jury over fears that a newspaper article might potentially prejudice its verdicts. Now, the outcome of the second trial had left the club badly shaken. To add a further volatile element to this mix, O'Leary's ghosted book account of the 2000-01 season — that included the time of the incident involving Bowyer and Woodgate — and called 'Leeds United: A Season On Trial', was published in early 2002.

Already rocked by the events of January 2000 and the subsequent trials, the manager's decision to speak publicly about the 12 months went down badly in the dressing-room and Ridsdale was far from pleased.

"It would be fair to say the timing of the book has been anything other than helpful and David knows how I feel," explained Ridsdale, although it was clear that once the trial had concluded and there were no legal issues preventing its publication, O'Leary's wishes were very much overshadowed by the publishers' demands.

By March, Leeds' worsening financial position was now the main focus of attention of Ridsdale and his board that had borrowed massively to recruit Viduka, Keane, Fowler, Rio Ferdinand, Dominic Matteo, Seth Johnson, Dacourt and Bakke since the summer of 1999.

Ridsdale and Leeds had pioneered a new way in the British game to fund the signing of players that saw banks or finance houses advance the transfer fee up front, with repayments — albeit at higher than usual interest rates — spread over the duration of the player's contract. If a player was subsequently sold before his contract expired and there was a shortfall in the money still owed to the bank, an insurance firm — whose premium was paid up front when the deal for the new player was first concluded — coughed up the balance.

Later, the terms of the 'sale and leaseback' system — almost identical to the long-established method that allows people to access car finance — were amended to allow only 50 per cent of the original loan to be repaid within the lifetime of the contract, with the balance paid on its completion.

But with other costs at Leeds United growing substantially, another deal was then thrashed out that would see the loans extended over a 25-year term with annual repayments made every September from season tickets and corporate hospitality sales. All parties were satisfied with this arrangement as the value of Leeds' players continued — in the main — to rise in line with all major clubs, while income from television, tickets and merchandising also moved in an upward direction.

However, failure to qualify for the hugely lucrative Champions League — where Leeds had earned £20m when reaching the semi-finals in 2000-01 — in the 2001-02 and 2002-03 seasons was now hitting home. By June, 2002 Leeds United's net debt had reached £82m and debt repayments were close to £1m per month, while the annual wage bill was now £53m.

O'Leary had been told three months earlier that his best players would be put up for sale during the close season in a bid to clear the debt. That signalled the end of Leeds as a Premier League power and by the end of June O'Leary had departed as manager. Terry Venables was quickly appointed as O'Leary's successor on July 8. Miraculously, the fire-sale of players did not materialise during the pre-season period, with Rio Ferdinand's £29.1m move to Manchester United in late July the only major exit at the club before the start of the new season.

Keane was on the bench as Leeds began the 2002-03 term with a resounding 3-0 home win over Manchester City. Keane would score his last goal for Leeds in the 80th minute having replaced Viduka, who had started up front with Smith. A week later, a 3-1 away success against West Bromwich Albion sent Leeds to the top of the Premier League with Keane replacing Kewell. The 1-0 midweek Elland Road defeat by Sunderland — settled by Jason McAteer's strike — which followed a few days later again saw Keane deployed as a replacement, this time for Nick Barmby.

On the following Saturday, McAteer would be exchanging pleasantries with Roy Keane at the Stadium of Light with the Manchester United skipper sent off for elbowing his international teammate. His namesake from Dublin would, by this time, be a Tottenham Hotspur player having moved on August 30 to White Hart Lane in a £7m deal.

Spurs manager Glenn Hoddle was determined to sign a young, established forward with Les Ferdinand approaching his 36th birthday in December while Steffen Iversen had yet to suggest that he could become a permanent fixture in the attack.

Hoddle's predecessor, George Graham, had broken Tottenham's club record transfer fee of £11m in June, 2000 to snap up Sergiy Rebrov but the Ukraine international didn't shine and, after failing to figure in a single league match between August 2002 and January 2003, was offloaded on loan to Fenerbahce during the mid-season transfer window. Teddy Sheringham, now 36, was still leading the Spurs line and would form the other half of the partnership with Keane.

Back at Elland Road, Leeds' form slumped and they would eventually finish 15th in the league, with the further January sales of Woodgate to Newcastle for £9m, Fowler to Manchester City for £3m and Bowyer to West Ham for a nominal £100,000 weakening Venables' hand.

"The shit hit the fan at Leeds and all the big players had to go," says Gary Kelly bluntly. "Robbie was one of those and when there was a bit of interest from Spurs, he went.

"We played them not too much later and the game was live on Sky Sports. And what did he do but score two crackers against us. He moved at the right time for his own career, because what do you do if you are at a club where there is a group of Irish lads? You play golf or go on the beer!

"I think we were probably happy that we all eventually went our own ways and our wives got us back! Robbie had to go because of the financial problems but it was still a good move to join Spurs."

Chapter 11
Settling down

IF ever the term 'sleeping giant' applied to a club, it was the Tottenham Hotspur of August 2002 that Robbie Keane arrived at, following his £7m transfer from Leeds United.

Steeped in tradition and with a reputation for placing the emphasis on stylish football, Spurs intermittently suggested they might construct a side capable of challenging for their first league title since 1960-61. But these spurts of ambition ended in failure — there was even one season in the old Second Division in 1977-78 to contend with and other occasional flirtations with relegation — and the London club would usually set its sights on winning either of the two cup competitions.

It was a policy that did produce silverware in the three decades that followed the double success of 1961, with further FA Cup wins in 1962, 1967, 1981, 1982 and 1991, League Cup victories in 1971, 1973 and 1999, a European Cup Winners' Cup triumph in 1963 and a brace of UEFA Cup successes in 1972 and 1984. Yet in the decade that preceded Keane's signing, Tottenham's league finishes were distinctly average, with the first ever Premier League campaign in 1992-93 producing an eighth-place and the following seasons yielding 15th, seventh, eighth, 10th, 14th, 11th, 10th, 12th and ninth place.

In short, Spurs were a byword for mid-table anonymity with an average finish of 10.4 per season. Even the well of cup wins had almost run dry, with the 1-0 League Cup final win over Martin O'Neill's Leicester City in 1999 their only trophy since their FA Cup glory at Wembley in 1991. To add to Spurs' woes, north London neighbours Arsenal had emerged as Manchester United's main rivals to the big pots and were planning to build a new 60,000 seater stadium a short distance from their famous Highbury home.

Manager George Graham had ushered in the new era of sporting excellence at Arsenal in the mid-eighties and in May,

2002, Arsene Wenger's side had claimed the club's second league and cup double in four years. This was the Gunners' fourth league crown since 1988-89 and the club's eighth trophy since Graham's side lifted the League Cup in 1987.

Graham's strong association with Arsenal — he had also played in their 1971 double triumph — meant he would never be fully accepted by the Spurs supporters on his appointment at White Hart Lane in October, 1998. And even though he steered the team to League Cup glory less than six months later, the continued under-achievement in the league and a more defensive, direct style of football meant that he bowed out shortly before the end of the 2000-01 season.

Glenn Hoddle took over from Graham and immediately vowed to restore the first-team's emphasis on the passing game that had helped make the gifted Hoddle such an inspirational figure at White Hart Lane in the seventies and eighties. In the summer and early autumn of 2001, Gus Poyet was signed from Chelsea for £2.5m, Christian Ziege arrived from Liverpool for £4m and the late Dean Richards made the £8.1m move from Southampton. While Tottenham's league fortunes had improved to some degree in 2001-02 when they finished ninth (compared to 12th a year earlier), they were still hugely inconsistent and scored too few goals (49 over the league season), with the club's £11m record signing from Dynamo Kiev in May 2000, Sergey Rebrov, weighing in with a measly one goal for the entire campaign of nine starts and 12 appearances from the bench.

The fact that midfielder Poyet finished the season as joint top scorer with 10 goals along with Teddy Sheringham (who netted three of his with penalties) told its own story.

The season also saw Spurs lose the League Cup final 2-1 to Graeme Souness's Blackburn Rovers, who were languishing in the bottom three in the Premier League, and denied Tottenham a return to Europe for only the second time in 10 years. The disappointment of losing to Blackburn at the Millennium Stadium with a below-par display was made all the more unpalatable by virtue of the fact that Spurs had thumped Chelsea 5-1 in the semi-final second leg at White Hart Lane to overcome the 2-1 away defeat.

The setback in Cardiff rocked Hoddle and the club and as that campaign neared its end, Hoddle frantically tried to get rid of Rebrov while he also knew that he badly needed new blood in attack where Sheringham was now 36 years of age and Ferdinand was only a year younger.

While Spurs, Sunderland and Middlesbrough had enquired about signing Keane in July, 2002, none of them tabled an of-fer to the Elland Road club. So as the 2002-03 campaign began on August 17 with Spurs earning a 2-2 draw at Everton, Keane was coming off the bench to complete Leeds' 3-0 home win over Manchester City.

Leeds manager Terry Venables had opted to select Mark Viduka as his first-choice main striker with either Harry Kewell or Alan Smith alternating between attack and midfield as the task demanded. For Keane, it was a real blow to return to the substitutes' bench at club level in the wake of his heroics for Ireland at June's World Cup finals. That Robbie Fowler was out of the first-team squad with an injury that would sideline him until early December only served to make Keane's disap-pointment all the more acute.

Keane's frustrations continued in Leeds' second and third Premier League outings against West Bromwich Albion (3-1 win away) and Sunderland (0-1 defeat at home) when he again had to make-do with roles from the bench. After missing out on the win at The Hawthorns, Keane confronted Venables and demanded a move. A week earlier, the manager had stated that he wanted Keane to stay but was now unsure if he would be able to keep him given Leeds' perilous financial state.

Now Venables' position softened further, saying: "If there is any interest in Robbie I will look at it, and if he doesn't want to be here I would feel the same. If someone wants to come to me and make something possible on the club's terms, it's possible that it could go through. He had a great World Cup and he came back and wants to show what he can do.

"I didn't really expect this after two games but, then again, maybe he would not have said it if there wasn't only a week left to the transfer deadline. But it's running out of time now and I would think at this stage nothing will happen."

Despite the final part of his statement, it was clear that Venables did not see Keane as a first-choice in attack, and with the Leeds board still anxious to eat into the club's massive debt, Hoddle swooped on August 30 to sign Keane for £7m.

It was a move that Keane would have preferred not to make as he was enjoying life in Yorkshire with Ireland teammates Gary Kelly, Ian Harte and Stephen McPhail, but his relationship with Venables was already strained, a factor that would resurface a few years later in the striker's Ireland career.

Hoddle's capture of Keane came as something of a relief to the ex-Spurs midfielder, who had been forced to start the opening game at Goodison Park with Sheringham and Steffen Iversen up front. While Spurs' sparkling early-season form saw them go to the top of the table after four games with wins over Aston Villa, Charlton Athletic and Southampton, Hoddle knew that he needed extra firepower, even though Ferdinand and Sheringham both netted in the 2-1 success over The Saints.

Keane — who was introduced to the home fans prior to kick-off against Southampton and sat in the directors' box for the game — had been told by his new manager that once he was match-fit, he would be leading the attack. That meant the first game after the 10-day break at the start of September for Euro 2004 qualifiers.

Hoddle's summer in search of a proven goal-poacher had proved hugely frustrating and even in the week prior to Keane's arrival, he had tried to snap up Fernando Morientes from Real Madrid for £15m and also spoke to Lazio about taking Argentinian star Hernan Crespo on a cut-price deal. However, Crespo joined Inter Milan before moving to Chelsea 12 months later while Morientes stayed at The Bernabeu.

In early August and during July, Celta Vigo's Benni McCarthy, Michael Ricketts of Bolton Wanderers, Real Mallorca's Albert Luque, Roy Makaay of Deportivo La Coruna, Brescia's Luca Toni and Chelsea's Eidur Gudjohnsen were all touted as potential Hoddle signings. So there was a real sense of expectation among Tottenham fans when Keane signed his four-year deal with a two-year option on August 31, the last day of the new FIFA-imposed transfer window.

"I know I said I didn't really want to leave Leeds but when I came here to talk to Glenn, his long-term plans appealed to me and that is why I am now a Tottenham player," said Keane as he was unveiled by his fifth club in as many years.

"Glenn wants to take the club a long way and hopefully I can help. It was frustrating at Leeds. You want to play football and it would have been nice to play for them. But it was not to be and I am looking forward to playing for Spurs instead. This is a big club and Glenn has great ambitions. I am a striker so hopefully I can bring goals to the club, although I also believe I can make goals.

"I just can't wait to put a jersey on and kick a ball around. Now I cannot wait to play against West Ham here in a couple of weeks' time."

It was clear from Keane's comments that although Spurs' interest in him dated back to early July, the deal to bring him to north London had only got into gear a few days previously. It was equally apparent that he would miss Elland Road.

"It happened very quickly," added Keane. "Yesterday, I got the call on my way into training at Leeds, so yesterday evening I was down here doing a medical. I finished it this morning and then I signed.

"It was obviously a big decision for me as Leeds is a massive club and I enjoyed my time there. The fans were absolutely brilliant to me from day one, even when there was a lot of speculation going on. Last week, they were singing my name.

"I understand their disappointment and I'm disappointed at the way things worked out. A footballer wants to play as many times as he can so I am disappointed to leave them. But that's the way it goes. Sometimes you have to sacrifice a few things in life and I'm here now as a Tottenham player and I'm hoping to play a lot more often if I can.

"You want to play every game and I believe in my case, the more I am played, the more you get out of me. Hopefully that will be the case here. I'm not very good at watching games so hopefully I won't be watching one for a while!"

Hoddle welcomed Keane to Spurs and also suggested that it was now time for the Dubliner to settle down and commit himself to a club for the long-term, after permanent transfer deals in each of the three previous summers.

"We're delighted, we have been in negotiations for a while and Robbie's somebody we wanted for a while," said Hoddle. "We had a list of three top players who we wanted and Robbie was one. He is a quality player and he will bring to us a new dimension. He is a little bit different from what we have got up front already and he is excited about the move. He cannot wait to start.

"I think the length of the contract will help him. He's 22 years of age and, astoundingly, £38m has been spent on him and rightly so as he is a quality player. He's had five clubs which is incredible but I think now is the time to settle down, get some consistency in his life on and off the pitch and I think we can probably see even more from him. And I think that is going to bode well for the club.

"I feel we have got Robbie at a very good time and he has got his best moments to come. He is a bubbly character, he is infectious and he loves the game. The fans will take to him because he is nice to watch. Robbie is a cute player who sees things and he will give us something new. He has got an end product which players like Dennis Bergkamp and Gianfranco Zola have."

After returning from Moscow and the sobering 4-2 defeat by Russia in Ireland's first Euro 2004 group qualifier, Keane did not play in the 3-2 defeat at Fulham, with Hoddle understand-ably keeping faith in the league leaders' attack of Sheringham and Ferdinand. But four days later Keane started alongside Sheringham at Ferdinand's expense in his Spurs debut as Hoddle's side beat West Ham 3-2 at White Hart Lane to go second in the table. While the new boy did not score, he created Sheringham's second-half penalty when taken down by Ian Pearce in the box. It was the first of 20 consecutive league starts for Keane, who began to blossom from his exposure to weekly first-team football and the presence of the wily Sheringham, who was his partner up front for all but a few of these games.

He had to wait until the 2-1 away win at Blackburn Rovers on October 6 to claim his first goal for Spurs, firing past Brad Friedel after only six minutes. After a break for international duty, Keane netted his first White Hart Lane goals for Spurs in the 3-1 victory at Bolton Wanderers' expense and by the turn of the year, Keane had scored six times in the league, including the second goal in the 2-0 victory at Leeds on November 24.

However, Keane's old Achilles' heel of missing his quota of clear-cut chances had not deserted him and he was guilty of terrible finishing in the 2-1 League Cup exit at Championship club Burnley on November 6. Crucially, Keane's ability to instantly consign such performances to history remained intact as his post-match comments proved.

He said: "I know I should have scored but as we all know, football can be like that. I think I should have scored two of them but that's the way it goes. There is no point in worrying about it too much, that is when it starts to affect you. You have to concentrate on things you can change and that's the way I look at it."

A hat-trick at home to Everton in the 4-3 win on January 12 was, however, followed by a barren spell that did not end until he cheekily nicked the opening goal in the 2-1 home win over Birmingham City on April 5. Poignantly for Keane, it was his first game for Spurs following the death of his dad, Robert senior, who passed away on the same night the 22-year-old was in action for the club in the 1-0 away defeat to Bolton Wanderers.

It's a goal that lifelong Spurs fan and journalist Neil Silver — who covered the club for many years in his capacity as a football writer for the Press Association and a number of British national daily and Sunday newspapers — fondly recalls.

"Robbie is a clever footballer and also a cute one," says Silver. "All Tottenham fans love recalling the day at White Hart Lane when he cheekily nicked the ball away from Birmingham keeper Andy Marriott, who failed to notice that Robbie was behind him before rolling the ball inside his penalty area.

"If you are naming your list of recent Tottenham attacking legends, then Robbie Keane would be in there," adds Silver. "Teddy Sheringham and Jurgen Klinsmann would be included also and that's how highly he is regarded by the fans. Robbie's goals-per-game ratio was always good but there was much more to him than this one aspect.

"Right from the start, Robbie enjoyed a great relationship with the supporters and they adored him. They loved his goal celebration with the cartwheel and pistols routine and he really was a fans' favourite. And when Martin Jol made him vice-captain, that was a very popular move."

But there was a lot more to Keane's game than finding the net and indulging in crowd-pleasing celebrations, according to Silver.

"Robbie played in attack but he could control games, which is unusual for a striker. I remember when I was working for the Sunday People covering Spurs against Fulham at Craven Cottage in the early weeks of the 2007-08 season, when Robbie was running the show for Tottenham and giving the home back-four a really terrible time.

"But Martin Jol decided to substitute Robbie and that changed the course of the game. Suddenly, Fulham battled their way back into the match and drew 3-3. I wrote in the following day's paper that Martin Jol might have hammered a significant nail into his own coffin with that decision.

"Robbie was a really influential player during his time at Spurs, particularly during that first six-year spell. And I think the two seasons between 2004 and 2006 when Michael Carrick was at the club, Robbie thrived because he had a clever midfield player who was on the same wavelength as him.

"He really enjoyed it when he had Michael passing the ball to him. That was a great pairing and it was no surprise that Tottenham had two great seasons at that time. Unfortunately they just missed out on getting a Champions League place in 2006 with the last day defeat at West Ham."

When the 2002-03 season ended, Spurs had finished tenth (where else) but Keane had assumed the mantle of leading scorer with 13 goals — one ahead of Sheringham and seven more than Poyet and Simon Davies.

Spurs' season was hardly anything to celebrate — they were hammered 4-0 by Southampton in the FA Cup third round after their League Cup exit at the same stage to Burnley — but Keane's arrival was a definite success and the fans voted him Player of the Year. Now, he, Hoddle and the club planned to make strides in 2003-04.

If Spurs fans were expecting a major revolution in the summer of 2003, they were badly mistaken. As Chelsea's new owner Roman Abramovich embarked upon a £92.9m 10-player spending spree having bought the club in June, Hoddle — now under growing pressure from within the club and from supporters to deliver a noticeable improvement — was relatively quiet in the transfer market. He wasn't the only one however.

Arsenal only spent £4m and Liverpool were equally miserly with a £5m outlay. Manchester United spent £23.9m on Kleberson and Eric Djemba-Djemba but those rare Alex Ferguson transfer errors were more than compensated for by the arrival of a certain Cristiano Ronaldo at Old Trafford from Sporting Lisbon for £12.2m. Hoddle also went to Portugal for his largest single acquisition with £6.25m spent on Porto forward Helder Postiga, who had just helped Jose Mourinho's club defeat Celtic 3-2 in the UEFA Cup final.

Hoddle's emphasis on attack also saw Freddie Kanoute arrive from West Ham for £3.5m and Bobby Zamora signed from

Brighton and Hove Albion for £1.5m. Rebrov was finally offloaded while Sheringham and Ferdinand also left the club. Having started up front with Postiga against Birmingham City on the opening day of the 2003-04 season, Keane's progress hit a frustrating note when an ankle injury picked up in an Ireland-Australia friendly at Lansdowne Road on August 20 ruled him out of the next four league games.

He only returned to the bench on September 20 for the 3-1 home loss to Southampton in Hoddle's final game in charge. Having lost four of their opening six league games and with only one victory to their name, the defeat sent Tottenham plummeting to 18th in the table. Chairman Daniel Levy — citing the club's worst ever Premiership start as evidence — and the board axed the former playing hero the following day.

Ex-manager David Pleat took over in a caretaker capacity. Pleat's appointment was good news for Keane for he was an admirer of the Dubliner's ability and wanted him to remain a key part of his side. And for Pleat's first game in charge, a score-less draw at Manchester City, Keane started in attack beside Kanoute.

A week later in the 3-0 home win against Everton, Keane scored his first league goal of the season although he had to wait until November 23 for his second, when he notched the winner in the 2-1 White Hart Lane success against Aston Villa. Pleat's side was slowly stabilising and gradually dropped anchor in the familiar waters of mid-table, while Keane and Kanoute were establishing a strong partnership.

"When Robbie drops off and plays in that hole like Zola, a Bergkamp or a Hoddle he can be fantastic," said Pleat. "Where the supporters once had David Ginola they now have Robbie Keane. He is a real personality."

Yet Pleat also pinpointed one aspect of the 23-year-old's game that still annoyed many observers. "At times Robbie is so talented that he tends to over-elaborate because he knows he can do things other players cannot. So you have to live with his upside and accept any downsides. He has cleverness."

On December 6, the on-fire Keane grabbed a hat-trick when Spurs romped to a 5-2 win over his old club Wolves — the first time that he had faced them since his move to Coventry City more than four years previously. A stunning volley was the pick of his barrage but, once again, he chose not to celebrate a goal against a former employer.

"I've got mixed emotions because Wolves is a club that means a hell of a lot to me," said Keane. "I have got a lot of friends there. I came over from Ireland at 15 years of age and the people there made me feel very welcome. The fans have always been very good to me and the reception I got from them at the game says it all.

"I wanted to show a bit of respect. Wolves and the fans had a lot of respect for me so I didn't want to rub it in by doing my celebration. I hope they stay up, I really hope so because they are a club that deserves to be in the Premiership with the fans they have."

The result sent Wolves to the bottom of the table and suggested Spurs' form might improve. But four straight defeats and only one goal in the following weeks sent Spurs tumbling back down to 18th by the turn of the year. Tottenham were in real relegation trouble again but a much-improved January and February — including a Keane winning goal in the 1-0 defeat of Leeds at Elland Road and a 2-1 success over Liverpool when Keane was once more on target — eased their plight.

Keane was enjoying his best spell of the campaign and things were going to get even better for the Irishman, even if it initially appeared that the arrival of Jermain Defoe for £6m from West Ham might be a threat to his status. Apart from those early weeks disrupted by injury, Keane would be involved in every single one of his side's league games that season, with only three appearances from the bench.

Yet Pleat could not discover a playing partner for him until Defoe arrived and the duo started to link in attack. But after an initial flurry of goals for both strikers, neither player scored during a dismal run of five defeats in six league games in March and early April. That improved slightly in the final six matches with Defoe grabbing three and Keane weighing in with two including the 90th-minute equaliser from the penalty spot in the 2-2 home league draw against the Gunners in late April.

If the dramatic equaliser against Arsenal restored some pride among Tottenham supporters, it could not camouflage the bigger picture that the noisy neighbours had secured the league crown at White Hart Lane — just as they had done when winning the double in 1971 — in a season that would see 'The Invincibles' remain unbeaten in all 38 league games. Spurs' final league placing of 14th represented a fall of four spots in 12 months.

For Keane, his 14 Premier League strikes made him the club's top scorer for the campaign for the second season running — double the tallies managed by Defoe and Kanoute, although the former had scored 11 league goals for The Hammers prior to his move. Pleat stood down from his role and before the end of the Euro 2004 tournament in Portugal, the club announced that France senior team coach Jacques Santini would be taking over as manager in July.

Santini had played a pivotal role in the success of Lyon in France and guided them to the French league title in 2002 prior to his appointment as France boss for the Euro 2004 campaign. Spurs fans hoped that the 2004-05 season would be one of managerial stability and football achievement. However, Santini lasted only 11 league games as the relationship between him and Sporting Director Frank Arnesen disintegrated.

Before he quit White Hart Lane, Santini had overseen the arrival — with Arnesen carrying out the scouting, sourcing and signing — of Sean Davis from Fulham (£3m), Michael Carrick from West Ham (£3m), Coventry City's Calum Davenport (£1.1m), Pedro Mendes of Porto (£2m), Timothee Atouba from Basel (undisclosed), Rodrigo Defendi from Cruzeiro (£600,000), Heerenveen's Erik Edman (£1.3m), Nourredine Naybet of Deportivo La Coruna (undisclosed), Noe Pamarot from Nice (£1.7m), Edson Silva from PSV Eindhoven (free) and Reto Ziegler from Grasshoppers Zurich (free).

Mendes' signing was part of the deal that took Postiga back to Porto. Leaving the club were Stephen Carr (Newcastle United for £2m) and Gary Doherty (Norwich City, undisclosed) though their fellow Irishman Stephen Kelly would take his first tentative steps in the first-team later that season. The appointment of Santini and the arrival of Dutchman Martin Jol as his assistant had finally seemed to end the lengthy period of uncertainty at the club and Jol's coaching methods met with the players' approval.

However, an ankle injury picked up during the pre-season friendly against Rangers at Ibrox in late July meant Keane was ruled out of the first two league games of 2004-05 before he was named on the bench for the third. That meant Santini chose Defoe and Kanoute in attack and after a reasonably promising first six league matches, Spurs stood fifth in the table.

But after the 2-0 loss at Fulham on October 30, the team was back in the familiar territory of 14th. Keane had fought his way into the attack beside Defoe but just 24 hours before the home clash with Charlton, Santini quit for what he termed personal reasons. Keane — starting on the left side of midfield — and Defoe both scored against their city rivals but Charlton won 3-2. Within a week, Spurs promoted Jol to the first-team manager's post.

Keane and Kanoute were alternating as Defoe's strike partner and by February, they had to share that role with Egyptian loan signing Mido, who arrived from Roma as Arnesen's scouring of Europe continued. When the season finished on May 9 with the uninspiring home draw with Blackburn Rovers, Spurs were ninth and Defoe had finished as the team's top league scorer on 13 goals compared with Keane's 11, Kanoute's seven and Mido's two. Keane had also netted three each in the club's FA and League Cup runs while the forwards' respective league appearances made for interesting reading: Keane (23 starts and 12 sub appearances), Defoe (28 and 7), Kanoute (22 and

10) and Mido (4 and 5). With Defoe clearly Jol's first-choice striker, there was a dilemma for Keane.

Jol wanted him to stay at the club but could not guarantee him a place in the attack — a situation that had seen Celtic, Aston Villa and Everton all linked with the Dubliner during the January, 2005 transfer window. Significantly, Keane had been offered a five-year contract extension by Jol in late 2005 and he was also handed the job of vice-captain to skipper, Ledley King. Clearly, Jol saw a key role for Keane yet there was no denying that the early sparkle between him and Defoe had long since dulled.

Keane was in no rush to sign the new deal as his initial contract did not expire until August 2006 and there was still a lingering doubt at the back of his mind over his status in the first team. When he found himself an unused substitute away to Birmingham City in early April, 2005 in a match that saw Kanoute and Defoe start and Mido sent on as one of the three replacements, Keane stormed off down the St Andrew's tunnel.

His act of petulance — a few months earlier he had stormed down the tunnel when replaced against Middlesbrough — earned him a £10,000 fine, a stint training with the reserves and a rebuke from Arnesen.

"You can be disappointed, it's positive when you are but you must be careful how you show it," said Arnesen. "The competition is good, we have four very good strikers, so we will have to sit and have a talk with Robbie.

"I'm sure he'll train hard and when he's needed he'll be up to it, the team is the most important thing. We don't want to see him go, he's a great player. He wants to play but only the manager Martin Jol can make that decision.

"It's who he thinks will be best on the day. It's not a big deal so long as he stays within the team spirit."

Jol added little to Arnesen's words but his message was clear: "It's not about him, it's about the club. Maybe Robbie Keane was angry but it's not a problem for us, it's his problem. It was difficult enough as it was."

Keane — whose contradictory relationship with Jol had seen him offered a new contract and the vice-captaincy but not a permanent role in the side — was apologetic.

"The manager was okay about it, he told me it was unacceptable," conceded Keane. "It was a heat-of-the-moment thing and something that happens to everyone.

"If I could change it, I would. But that's life. I had my reasons at the time, I was frustrated and was not playing. But it's gone. The manager said what he had to say and I had to swallow my pride and hold my hands up. It was out of character."

The spat involving Keane and the management team had no lasting negative impact on the striker and he started four of the remaining league games and was sprung from the bench in the other three, scoring in the 2-2 draw at Liverpool and the 1-1 home draw with West Bromwich Albion. Tottenham had enjoyed decent cup runs during the season until Newcastle sent them tumbling 1-0 from the FA Cup in the quarter-final at St James' Park. Liverpool ended their interest in the same round of the League Cup at White Hart Lane when the visitors advanced 4-3 on penalties after extra time. Keane netted three goals in each competition.

Spurs' ninth-place finish in the league was an improvement of five places on the previous campaign yet was hardly anything to celebrate. Title-winning Chelsea — now with Jose Mourinho overseeing the spending of the Abramovich fortune — stormed to the championship fully 43 points better off than Tottenham while Arsenal defeated Manchester United 5-4 on penalties following a scoreless 120 minutes to lift the FA Cup at Cardiff's Millennium Stadium.

That match would mark Roy Keane's last appearance at a major final in English football and also Arsene Wenger's most recent trophy success. The bookies would have offered generous odds on such a double as the crowds departed the Welsh capital that evening, just as they would have sniggered at the suggestion that a Spurs revival was starting to stir in north London.

Chapter 12
Staying power

IT was little surprise that Chelsea began the 2005-06 season tipped to retain their league crown.

Jose Mourinho's squad was bolstered by the £35.2m summer capture of three players — including Michael Essien from Lyon for £24.4m. And though Manchester United, Arsenal and even Liverpool were expected to mount serious challenges, Mourinho's ability to succeed at this level and the continued financial backing of Roman Abramovich was widely expected to deliver another title.

At White Hart Lane, though, expectations were less grandiose. Tottenham manager Martin Jol was vigorous in the transfer market at home and abroad throughout the summer, although he was now operating without the assistance of Frank Arnesen, who had been lured to Stamford Bridge.

Spurs were none too happy at the way their capital rivals had gone about securing the Dane's services and a reported compensation deal of £5m was eventually hammered out between the clubs. Jol set about acquiring players who he wanted to slot straight into the side, brought in players who would bolster the squad and also signed others who would be groomed for the first-team in the short to medium-term.

Tom Huddlestone was signed from Derby County (£2.5m), Aaron Lennon arrived from Leeds United for a cut-price £1m, Newcastle United's Jermaine Jenas was captured (£7m), Paul Stalteri (undisclosed) arrived from Werder Bremen, Teemu Tainio (undisclosed) was signed from Auxerre, Edgar Davids (undisclosed) moved from Inter Milan, Lee Young-Pyo (£1.36m) was snapped up from PSV Eindhoven while Grzegorz Rasiak was signed in September from Derby County for £2.25m.

There were no significant exits from the club's first-team ranks and, when added to the acquisitions of Nottingham Forest pair Andy Reid (£3.5m) and Michael Dawson (£4.5m) the previous January, there was no questioning the fact that Jol's panel was significantly strengthened.

The presence of midfielders Huddlestone, Lennon, Jenas and Davids caused a stir among the fans who were well aware of Davids' impressive past and excited by Lennon and Jenas's potential for the future. In attack, Jol now had a settled quartet of Defoe, Keane, Kanoute and Mido from which to choose his first-choice partnership.

Keane's pre-season 12 months earlier had been disrupted by injury but at July's Peace Cup in South Korea prior to the new campaign, he was in sharp form as he finished as the tournament's top marksman on four goals — two of them coming in the final as Spurs defeated Lyon 3-1, for whom Hatem Ben Arfa was on target. Before a competitive ball was kicked, Keane admitted that he would face a battle to get into the team but was determined to do so.

"I'm 25 years of age now and I want to knuckle down, not that I have not before, as we have quality strikers here who are battling to start the season. I'm no different to the other three lads in that. I've come back feeling pretty sharp and I did a good bit of work on my own during the summer."

But Keane's aspirations of starting the new term in Jol's side for the opening game away to Portsmouth on August 13 were dashed by a niggling injury. A week later at White Hart Lane he was forced to sit on the bench with Defoe and Mido preferred up front and Kanoute sent on as a substitute in the 2-0 win over Middlesbrough.

A few days later Kanoute was sold to Seville for £5m, so reducing the competition for Keane. However, Kanoute's exit would prove to be a false dawn for the Dubliner, who would start only one of the first dozen league games. Defoe and Mido were selected for most of those matches and even Rasiak found himself ahead of Keane on occasion. He may have been the club's vice-captain but he could not claim a place in Jol's attack.

Spurs' most impressive and sustained start to the league

marathon in many years did not help Keane's cause, with five wins and just one defeat in their first 11 games leaving Spurs third in the table entering November.

However, the statistics suggested that there was precious little to separate the three forwards, with Defoe and Mido netting three each in that spell and Keane chipping in with two goals. As those early-season statistics suggest, it was not all bad news for Keane. He grabbed a late equaliser with a classy finish at Aston Villa on September 17 and then fired home an 80th-minute winner against Charlton at The Valley two weeks later. However, on both occasions he had started on the bench.

Jol was now in charge at the club for 12 months and while it was too early to make a judgment call on his tenure, there was more substance to the side's performances. They were conceding very few goals (only twice letting in two goals in a game during the opening 14 games) and the new signings over the previous 18 months had made a positive impact. The sometimes gruff Dutchman had also made a tactical call on his attack and it was not great news for Keane, even if the manager was intent on retaining the Dubliner's services.

"We had the same situation last year," stated Jol. "If Robbie and Jermain play with Mido, one has to play on the left. They all come to me and say they want to be in the middle."

This was the longest period since leaving Leeds in August, 2002, that Keane had been omitted week-in, week-out from the Spurs first team.

With Ireland ultimately making a tame exit from the World Cup qualifiers during the same period, this was the biggest challenge he had encountered during his career since his short-lived spell with Inter Milan five years earlier. Keane had played the contract negotiations game expertly and the new deal — on offer for almost a year — remained unsigned, with Keane now wondering if he would quit the club the following summer. After all, he would be allowed under FIFA rules to speak to other clubs on January 1.

By the time West Ham arrived at White Hart Lane on

November 13, Keane was back in the attack beside Mido, with Defoe dropped to the bench for only the second time that season. A week later the Dubliner scored the opening goal in the 2-1 away win at Wigan Athletic.

"I don't think there's a lot to choose between Robbie and Jermain," explained Jol. "I chose Jermain for the first 12 games but when he did not score for a couple of games I thought about Robbie. He is motivated and always trains hard.

"Robbie had waited 12 games, came on and scored that very important goal against Charlton but I still played Jermain. So I thought after last week it was time for Robbie. If you see Jermain in training, his finishing is unbelievable but Robbie is very gifted.

"As a team we have a good spirit and the players respect each other. Jermain has seen that Robbie did not moan and he must be the same."

At last, Keane was higher up the pecking order than the England international. Once more, Keane's in-built self-confidence and willingness to fight for his right to play first-team football combined to mould a formidable weapon in his battle to convince Jol.

At training, Keane always gave his all, and while he was privately enraged that Defoe and Mido were getting the nod every week, he did not vent his inner feelings. In pragmatic terms, Spurs' lofty status in the table meant that Keane could ill-afford to criticise anybody, even if the team's haul of 13 goals in those first 11 games was hardly outstanding.

Jol was concerned by this statistic and the focus was on Defoe to rectify it. Keane's exemplary behaviour at Spurs' Chigwell training ground impressed Jol, who also admired the Dubliner's cheeky persona around the club and in the dressing-room.

Tottenham's former Ireland scout, John Fallon senior, pin-points the vice-captaincy and his determination to hold on to Keane as clear indications of how much the manager rated the striker.

"Martin Jol loved him but that does not surprise me," says Fallon. "When you go into a club as a new manager you are looking to the older heads during the first day at training. Everybody thinks Robbie was 30 when he was still only 25. He was a bubbly guy to have around, people like him and he was always a bit of fun. And he's not a bad singer!

"He would have brought that Irishness with him to Spurs, the ability to have a laugh and be good-humoured which I think every club needs. Every successful team needs good characters and Jol knew that he had one in Robbie."

However, just as Keane returned to the back pages for the right reasons, he found himself making the headlines for a training ground spat with Edgar Davids, whose fiery temperament had seen him trade blows with Dutch and club colleagues in the past.

Davids scored the winner at the JJB Stadium, but the following week during training the two squared up to each other in a physical confrontation just 24 hours ahead of the home date with Sunderland. Jol faced something of a quandary. Should he fine the pair or simply ensure they settled their differences verbally and move on?

Jol and the club's hierarchy opted not to take a heavy hand to the matter and issued an amusing statement: "There was an incident but it's all over and forgotten now."

The Tottenham spokesperson added that Davids had been first to congratulate Keane on making the opening goal in their 3-2 win against the Black Cats. "We see it as a sign of the players' passion and commitment to do well for the club."

Typically with Keane, the incident did not affect his performances on the pitch. Having persuaded his boss that he was worthy of a recall to the side in a late November clash with fierce rivals West Ham, the Irish star would feature in the team's remaining 26 league matches, only two of which he started on the bench. Keane's patience, mental strength and unwavering belief in his own ability had seen him overcome adversity once again.

In contrast, the form of Mido and Defoe tailed off as Keane went on to hit 16 Premier League goals for the season, representing his best ever total in the top flight.

In early January, ahead of the FA Cup third-round tie at Leicester City, Keane gave an upbeat assessment of his form and why he had remained steadfast in his belief that he should stay at Spurs.

"I wasn't ready to move at the start of the season and I was quite happy to stay here," he said. "I could have chucked (a transfer request) in and said I wanted to go but I stuck it out and was determined to do well because I believe this club is going places. There is a great squad here and I want to be part of that.

"This Tottenham team reminds me of the Leeds team when I first signed for them, a young side with great potential. At the moment we have great potential with a lot of young players like Aaron Lennon and Michael Dawson. If we can continue on the road we have been going recently then this team can really go places.

"Potentially, we can do what Leeds did. That was a big squad and we also have some quality players who cannot even get into the 16. Speculation about me will never go away. I can sign a new contract and still the next year if I am not playing in a few games it will be the same thing again.

"Ask any player, no-one wants to be on the bench. Of course there were times when it was frustrating but it was up to me to work hard out on the training pitch and take any chance when I got it. At the moment it seems to be going well. I am happy, I am playing, scoring goals and the team is tremendous at the moment.

"I have been at Tottenham longer than I have been at any other club so of course I feel settled. And if I am not playing I'm not just going to be seeking a move. I was not playing a year and a half ago yet I am still here."

Without stating it, Keane was obviously edging towards signing the contract that had been with his agent for more than a year. At the end of 2005, Spurs were in fourth place in the table — a place that would secure them a first ever appearance in the following season's Champions League (albeit the qualifying round) should they manage to stay there until early May.

Before that, however, there was the trip to take on Leicester City, with many Spurs fans believing that this new-look team could win the FA Cup. League Two Grimsby Town had sent Spurs packing from the League Cup in a 1-0 second-round upset at Blundell Park on an evening when Defoe and Keane misfired badly in attack. And hopes of a knockout competition reprieve at the Walkers Stadium were dashed when the Championship side triumphed 3-2 thanks to an injury-time winner by Mark de Vries.

It was a real blow to Jol and his players and Spurs' league form dipped in the following weeks, with only one victory in the next six outings up to the end of February. Yet, with Arsenal's form equally inconsistent, Spurs were still in fourth place — behind Chelsea, Manchester United and Liverpool — when they defeated Blackburn 3-2 at home on the first weekend of March.

The month could not have brought better news for Keane. Within 24 hours of Ireland's 3-0 friendly win over Sweden on March 1, with Keane wearing the captain's armband for the first time, he finally signed his new contract to keep him at Spurs until the end of the 2009-10 season. "It is something that has been going on for a while," admitted Keane.

"I am just happy that it is now signed and I can look forward to a good future with Tottenham. I am flattered and delighted that the club has given me the opportunity to sign. Making the right decision was important for me and I feel I have certainly done that."

Keane signed off a magnificent week for himself by bagging two of the goals as Mido added the winner against Blackburn. Robbie's opening goal after just nine minutes was a stunning individual effort. He collected Mido's throw-in close to the goal line, lifted the ball over Robbie Savage, repeated the trick on Andy Todd and half-volleyed past Brad Friedel.

"It's one of my favourite goals throughout my career and certainly one of the best goals I've scored since I've been at Spurs," smiled Keane.

Twenty-four hours earlier, the Gunners swamped Fulham 4-0 at Craven Cottage in the first of four successive wins as they battled Spurs for that final Champions League place.

Keane was now a pivotal figure in Spurs' quest to make the historic European breakthrough, and keeping him both fit and in form were among Jol's top priorities. With Chelsea on course to retain their title and Manchester United and Liverpool comfortably claiming the two other automatic Champions League group places for the following September, the north London shoot-out for fourth place had become one of English football's chief talking points.

And with Arsenal on their way to that season's Champions League final in Paris, Spurs knew that they could take advantage of the fixture programme confronting Arsene Wenger's men. But Spurs' league form hit a patchy spell in the first half of April with wins over Manchester City and Everton bookended by defeats to Newcastle United and Manchester United.

However, the 1-1 away draw with Arsenal on April 22 — with Keane giving the visitors a 66th-minute lead before Thierry Henry's late equaliser — meant that maximum points at home to Bolton and away to West Ham in their final two matches would secure Spurs the coveted spot.

Aaron Lennon's goal was enough to defeat Bolton and with Arsenal beating Sunderland and Manchester City, it meant that Super Sunday would live up to its May 7 billing at Upton Park and Highbury, where Wigan Athletic visited in the last ever league game at the famous stadium.

By now, Arsenal had qualified to meet Barcelona in the Champions League final, after beating Villarreal 1-0 on aggregate in the semi-final. And if the stakes were not high enough already, UEFA and the FA confirmed that should Arsene Wenger's club finish fifth in the league but defeat the Catalans at Stade de France on May 17, then Tottenham would relinquish their Champions League slot to the Gunners.

It was a scenario that was too awful to contemplate for Spurs and their supporters. Ahead of the short journey to east London, Keane had again been voted the club's Player of the Year. He received his trophy after the final whistle of the victory over Bolton, even if he had to hobble on to the pitch to claim it because of a worrying ankle problem.

Jol expressed fears that Keane would not be able to play against the Hammers because of the injury. However, the medical staff gave him the all-clear to link up with his teammates at their base in the Marriott Hotel in Canary Wharf on the eve of the game. By early the following morning, Keane's ankle problem had been forgotten as Spurs' doctors tried to deal with an illness that had affected 10 of their players.

Keane, Dawson, Carrick, Huddlestone, Davids, Calum Davenport, Radek Cerny, Lennon, Tainio and Lee Barnard were all stricken by a rampant bug that had symptoms of vomiting and diarrhoea. Initial suspicion fell on food poisoning but that was never proven, with the probable cause being a virus. With key players confined to bed, Jol and club chairman Daniel Levy attempted to persuade the Premier League that the game be postponed for 24 hours.

Suddenly, the odds on Spurs winning the game and claiming fourth place lengthened, even if the home side had one eye firmly on the following weekend's FA Cup final against Liverpool in Cardiff. The powers-that-be ruled that the game should proceed as arranged and Spurs took to the pitch with six of the affected group — Keane, Dawson, Davids, Carrick, Lennon and Tainio — in the team.

When Defoe equalised Carl Fletcher's strike before half-time and news came through that Wigan were leading 2-1, the Spurs fans in the capacity 34,970 attendance began to dream. But their side needed to win to ensure they claimed fourth place as a draw would not suffice if Arsenal won. And as Thierry Henry completed his hat-trick to earn Arsenal a 4-2 win, across the city Yossi Benayoun's 80th-minute strike finally buried Spurs' ambitions.

The sense of deflation around Spurs was palpable and made all the worse by the fact that one of their great rivals, West Ham, had inflicted the mortal blow to the team's European hopes and that the club's chief foes, Arsenal, had benefitted.

In the days that followed, Liverpool defeated the Hammers in the FA Cup final while Barcelona collected the European Cup at Arsenal's expense, but neither event lightened the mood at White Hart Lane. On a personal level, Keane had every right to reflect on his most telling campaign to date for Spurs, with his 16 league goals compared to Mido's 11 and nine for Defoe. He was once again the club's most important forward.

"I have been fortunate enough in that the season went really well for me," said Keane. "It is good when the team is doing well because it makes your job a little bit easier. The thing I try to do each season is to do better than I have done in previous years."

Once the gloom of the final day of the season had lifted, an air of optimism returned to Tottenham during the summer of 2006, ahead of a year Jol and his squad hoped would finally yield the breakthrough into football's elite.

However, the departure of Michael Carrick to Manchester United for £18.6m underlined the fact that Spurs remained vulnerable when one of the 'big four' came knocking on the door with a major offer for one of their players. Jol was also active in the transfer market and snapped up lively Wigan defender Pascal Chimbonda, Fulham midfielder Steed Malbranque and Lens defender Benoit Assou-Ekotto for undisclosed sums, while he also paid Roma £4m to make Mido a permanent fixture at The Lane.

But it was the capture of St Etienne midfielder Didier Zokora and Bayer Leverkusen forward Dimitar Berbatov for £10.9m that really sent a buzz around the club and its supporters. Chelsea and Manchester United had both been linked with defensive midfielder Zokora, while Berbatov had an impressive scoring record in the Bundesliga, netting 91 goals in 201 appearances over five years.

Zokora would depart for Seville three years later without ever really delivering on his previous exploits in France, but Berbatov would settle quickly to become a modern-day Spurs legend. Keane would eventually thrive on the Bulgarian's presence in attack, even if initially he was again sharing the attacking responsibilities with Defoe.

Berbatov was first choice for Jol — a decision based not just on the size of the transfer fee but due to the fact that the Bulgarian's eye for goal, physical strength and ability to hold up the ball made him a natural number nine. Defoe started in the first match of the season — the 2-0 away defeat at Bolton — but Keane was restored to the side a week later, where he remained for five games.

However, the sparkle of the previous season had deserted Spurs and the 3-0 hammering at Liverpool on September 23 meant that the side was now languishing in 18th place in the table with just four points from their opening six games, earned by defeating Sheffield United 2-0 and drawing 0-0 with Fulham at The Lane.

Spurs were struggling badly, with the lack of a central defensive partner for Dawson a real blow as Ledley King struggled with injury. Davids was now being phased out in midfield while Berbatov, Keane and Defoe could only muster six league goals between them in the first 14 matches.

With Ireland, Keane was skipper for the 5-2 hammering by Cyprus in Nicosia, although the subsequent 1-1 home draw against the Czech Republic and his hat-trick in the last ever senior football international played at the old Lansdowne Road — a 5-0 win over San Marino — made up to some degree for the embarrassment against the Cypriots.

A 3-0 away defeat to Arsenal on the first weekend of December saw Keane dropped to the bench for the midweek visit of

Middlesbrough, when he scored the second goal in a 2-1 win. But a knee ligament injury sustained in that match ruled him out of football until mid-January.

Keane's absence had not affected Spurs' league position one iota as the club remained in eighth place. He was restored to the attack for the 2-1 away defeat to Sheffield United on February 10 when the team dropped back to 11th position. It seemed that despite all the advances made over the previous season, Spurs were back in the old mid-table routine.

The three cup competitions — the club was also in the UEFA Cup — offered Spurs a more traditional chance to savour glory, with Jol's side only exiting 2-1 to Chelsea in the FA Cup sixth round after a 3-3 draw at Stamford Bridge.

In the League Cup, Arsenal were once more the party-poopers with a 5-3 aggregate victory at the semi-final stage. In Europe, Spurs won every single one of their one-off ties and group games against Slavia Prague, Besiktas, Bruges, Leverkusen, Dinamo Bucharest and Braga to book a quarter-final showdown against Seville.

Keane scored his fifth goal of the European campaign after only two minutes in Spain but a Kanoute equaliser inspired the home team to a 2-1 first-leg success. A week later back in London, a Malbranque own goal and another Kanoute strike ended Spurs' hopes, despite second-half replies from Defoe and Lennon. In defeat, Keane could still be pleased with his tally in Europe and the fact that he had scored 11 goals in all three competitions to add to his 11 in the Premier League.

That tally of 22 pipped Berbatov's 20 and Defoe's 17, so the Irishman could once more be pleased with his overall contribution. Given their exploits, Keane and Berbatov were jointly awarded the FA Premier League's Player of the Month award for April.

Keane's total of 22 goals in all competitions — the highest ever season tally of his career — was notable in that he scored 15 goals in his last 15 appearances of the season. Despite the hectic schedule in the cups, Spurs' league form improved in late February and March when five consecutive wins pushed the team up to sixth. But the gap to the top four of Manchester United, Chelsea, Liverpool and Arsenal was far too large to bridge, although three victories in the last four outings left Jol's men fifth — eight points adrift of The Gunners.

In the green jersey, Keane and his teammates weathered what they hoped was the worst of their Euro 2008 campaign and prepared for the autumn finale when they would seek the runners-up spot and a play-off.

Back at Spurs in the summer of 2007, Keane prepared for the coming season refreshed by the team's strong finish to the previous term and excited about the fact that he and Berbatov had established a strong partnership. The new season began as the previous one finished, with Jol selecting the Bulgarian and Irishman as his first-choice attack.

By the following May, Keane had enjoyed his most productive ever season in terms of a pairing and Spurs were also back among the silverware. But the man who had brought Keane and Berbatov together would be long gone by the time Spurs lifted the League Cup at Chelsea's expense with a 2-1 success at Wembley on February 24.

Another horrendous start to the Premier League, yielding one win and four draws in the opening 10 games, left Tottenham down in 18th position by October 22. Three days later, Levy and the board axed Jol following the 2-1 home defeat to Spain's Getafe in their opening UEFA Cup group game.

As far as the directors were concerned, their summer investment in Charlton Athletic's Darren Bent (£15.5m), Lens' Adel Taarabt (undisclosed), Auxerre's Younes Kaboul (undisclosed) and Hertha Berlin's Kevin Prince-Boateng (undisclosed) deserved a better return.

With Keane and Berbatov first choice, Bent became first replacement while Defoe began to cut a lonely figure at the club and would make only three league starts (with 16 more appearances from the bench) during a season cut short by injury.

Keane had soundly seen off his rival and was now flourishing despite the dreadful start. While the Irishman and Jol had enjoyed a sometimes feisty relationship, the now 27-year-old forward had seen his game mature during the Dutchman's three years in charge.

There was no doubting that Keane was now a better all-round player, contributed more in a team sense and had harnessed his popularity among his peers to become a leader as the club's vice-captain.

Footballers rarely dwell too long on the departure of a manager unless they find themselves out of favour with his successor. And while the Spurs panel was surprised to learn of Jol's exit, they quickly settled down to life with Juande Ramos, whose appointment within 48 hours gave credence to his later claim that he had turned down the post two months earlier.

Fifty-three-year-old Ramos had won the UEFA Cup in 2006 with Seville after a resounding 4-0 win over Middlesbrough and repeated the feat 12 months later when beating Espanyol on penalties after a 2-2 draw at Hampden Park. En-route to Glasgow, the stylish Spanish side ousted Spurs as they underlined their status as La Liga's third strongest team after Barcelona and Real Madrid.

In addition to their UEFA Cup victories, Ramos guided Seville to the UEFA Super Cup in 2006 when beating Barcelona 3-0, a Champions League place in 2006–07, the Copa del Rey and the Spanish Super Cup. With a handsome annual salary of more than £3.5m, Ramos was expected to deliver a marked improvement in Spurs' results. He tasted success in his first game in charge as Tottenham beat Blackpool 2–0 in the League Cup at White Hart Lane, courtesy of goals from Keane and Chimbonda.

However, three days later Spurs lost their first league match under Ramos, although Keane was on target in the 2-1 home setback to Blackburn. Inconsistency remained the most notable feature of the team's displays and results during the weeks and months that followed. However, Ramos's brief experiment with Bent and Defoe in attack for the 1-1 draw at Middlesbrough on November 3 was quickly abandoned and the Keane-Berbatov pairing was back in vogue for the next game.

Between that point and the end of the season, this partnership would start the vast majority of the side's matches. Sensing the need to bring a trophy to the Lane and realising that a top-four finish may not be realistic, Ramos pinpointed the knockout route to glory. With the side comfortably sitting in midtable, Spurs saw off Manchester City 2-0 with only 10 men to book a semi-final showdown with Arsenal in the League Cup.

On a night to cherish for all Spurs fans, Tottenham routed The Gunners 5-1 in the second leg at White Hart Lane on January 22 for a 6-2 aggregate win. Apart from the fact that the outcome represented Spurs' first north-London derby win in nine years, all that stood between Spurs and a first trophy since the 1999 success in the same competition were 90 minutes, albeit against a formidable Chelsea side.

Keane and Berbatov started up front against John Terry and Ricardo Carvalho in Tottenham's first appearance at the new Wembley. Didier Drogba put Chelsea ahead in the 39th minute but Berbatov's penalty in the 70th minute sent the match into extra-time, where Jonathan Woodgate claimed the 94th-minute winner.

Spurs were ecstatic as the Ramos era was blessed with an early trophy. However, any hopes of progressing in the FA Cup were ended by a 3-1 away defeat to Manchester United at the end of January. UEFA Cup hope petered out in early March against PSV Eindhoven, although Spurs could count themselves slightly unfortunate as a 1-0 first-leg defeat was rescued by the same scoreline in Holland before the team exited 6-5 on penalties.

At least a place in the following season's UEFA Cup was secure. That was just as well, as Tottenham remained lethargic in the league. On January 1 the team was rooted in 12th place, and when the campaign concluded on May 11 with a 2-0 home defeat by Liverpool, Ramos's side had climbed just one position.

For Keane, a first ever winners' medal and another impressive haul of goals over the nine months compensated largely for a hugely disappointing league showing by the team.

The season had also produced a series of milestones for the Dubliner and the club. In December, 2007, he had become the latest Tottenham player to score 100 Premier League goals, while a month later he became the fifteenth Tottenham player to score 100 goals for the club.

By the season's end, Keane was also the first Tottenham player to score more than 10 goals in six consecutive seasons and the first player to win Spurs' Player of the Year award three times. Keane and Berbatov finished with 15 league goals each (Keane had scored three penalties compared to the Bulgarian's one), with Bent and Defoe weighing in with six and four respectively.

In the FA Cup, Keane and Berbatov could not be separated either, with two goals apiece although Keane shaded it two to one in the League Cup. In Europe, Berbatov's five to Keane's total of four meant that the duo netted 23 goals each in all competitions to emphasise their status as one of the league's most lethal combinations.

As Keane walked around White Hart Lane on May 11 to say thanks to the fans, little did he know that it would be his final appearance there as a Tottenham Hotspur player — for now.

Chapter 13
The wilderness years

IT was an era of three Ireland managers, as many failed qualification campaigns, a record-breaking number of international
goals for Robbie Keane and his elevation to the status of
Ireland skipper.

The years between 2002 and 2008 in the green shirt could
hardly be described as mundane for the Tallaght man. But for
all the contrasting elements to Keane's Ireland involvement in
those seasons between the heady heights of Japan and South
Korea in 2002 and the arrival of Giovanni Trapattoni as coach
in May, 2008, the central event of that time for Keane was the
loss of his beloved father Robert.

Having departed for Wolves just days after his 16th birthday
in 1996, Keane had almost seven years of experience of life in
the fast lane when Robert slipped from this life at the young
age of 50. The sudden bereavement of Robert senior on March
24, 2003, would severely test the then 22-year-old. He would
emerge from the sad passing of his father an even stronger
person.

In the wake of Ireland's heroic appearance at the 2002
World Cup finals, it appeared that there was only one immediate course for the senior international side. And that was in a
positive direction, a school of thought emboldened by the easy
3-0 away friendly win over Finland two months later when an
experimental Irish side might have doubled their margin of
victory.

Keane scored in his fourth consecutive game for his country,
with substitutes Colin Healy and debutant Graham Barrett
completing the visitors' account in a match where Dean Kiely
started in goal and Thomas Butler made his debut on the left
flank.

However, by the time Ireland travelled to Moscow in early

September, the flickering embers of the Saipan saga had been stoked. Mick McCarthy declared that Roy Keane would not figure in his future plans while Keane had stated that he hoped to resume his Ireland career but not during McCarthy's tenure.

A number of pundits were now questioning McCarthy's wisdom in ignoring the Manchester United powerhouse, even if the manager's position had been strengthened by a new contract worth more than €500,000 annually and the widespread belief among football fans that he and his team had performed impressively at the tournament.

In the space of little over five weeks, McCarthy's apparently unchallenged status was eroded by back-to-back defeats against Russia and Switzerland in the opening games of the Euro 2004 qualifying campaign.

At the start of previous campaigns, Ireland had often successfully targeted teams who were tired or distracted — or both — in the wake of major tournament appearances. Now it was the turn of Ireland to be ambushed 4-2 by a highly-motivated, sharp, committed and stylish Russia side, themselves eager to bounce back from a very disappointing World Cup campaign that saw them bow out at the group phase.

The omens ahead of the match were unnerving. Ireland fans had been attacked at several locations in the centre of Moscow in the hours before the early evening kick-off, while the atmosphere inside the compact 28,800 capacity Lokomotiv Stadium could be generously described as tense, with elements of the Russian security personnel adopting a highly hostile approach to crowd control both inside and outside the ground.

Within 24 minutes, the Russians were two goals up after efforts by Andrei Karyaka and Vladimir Beschastnykh, by which time Damien Duff had been forced off through injury. Gary Doherty's 69th-minute headed goal gave the Irish hope of salvaging a point but within two minutes Alexander Kerzhakov restored the two goal advantage.

However, Clinton Morrison again offered the visitors a lifeline when turning Steve Finnan's cross home in the 76th minute but Kerzhakov ended Irish resistance two minutes from full-time when his low shot was well saved by Shay Given only for Phil Babb — on the pitch only three minutes — to divert the rebound into his own goal to mark his last appearance in the green shirt on an unfortunate note.

At Sheremetyevo airport the following morning, McCarthy faced a media grilling over his stance on Roy Keane but reiterated that he would not consider the midfielder, whose absence the previous evening had been keenly felt.

The momentum to see a recall for Keane was gathering pace. And when Ireland slumped to a 2-1 home defeat to Switzerland at Lansdowne Road on October 16, the pressure on the FAI to call time on McCarthy's six and a half years in charge became almost unstoppable.

In the immediate aftermath of the game, McCarthy and the FAI both stood firm but subsequent talks between the association, McCarthy and his agent Liam Gaskin saw him depart by mutual consent on November 5. Within a week, FAI general secretary Brendan Menton had also opted to leave the organisation while the Genesis Report — commissioned to investigate the events in Saipan and the World Cup — pinpointed a number of flaws in aspects of the FAI's planning for the tournament but also long-standing structural and administrative deficiencies, for which it recommended changes to elected positions and senior management levels of the organisation.

Ireland's hopes of qualifying for the finals in Portugal in June, 2004, were now hanging by a thread although the appointment of Under-16, youth and Under-20 manager Brian Kerr was met with the broad approval of most of the media. The senior players were also supportive of the Dubliner's arrival in charge, although there was a minority of people within the FAI and in the press who were unsure if Kerr could make the successful transition from underage supremo to senior boss.

A comprehensive 2-0 friendly win over Scotland at Hampden Park in his first match in charge in February 2003 augured well for the new coach ahead of the tricky back-to-back away qualifiers in Georgia and Albania on March 29 and April 2 respectively. Ireland required at least four points from these matches to keep the team's qualification hopes intact.

However, Robbie Keane would not figure in the crucial 2-1 win over the Georgians in Tbilisi as he attended the funeral of his devoted father Robert, who had been such a rock of support and encouragement from his earliest days. That Keane senior passed away while his son was making his comeback for Spurs away to Bolton Wanderers after injury in Sky Sports' Monday Night Football game only added to the poignancy.

Robert had been battling cancer for several years but nobody expected him to die so suddenly and his passing was a massive shock to family and friends. By early Tuesday morning, Keane was back with his family in Tallaght preparing for his dad's funeral on Thursday morning following requiem mass at St Agnes' Church in Crumlin village.

Kerr and the FAI handled the matter with great sensitivity, with the manager telling his striker that he would leave a decision on whether he would play that Saturday in Tbilisi completely up to him. Keane, understandably, decided to remain with his mother and siblings in Dublin while the Irish secured a 2-1 victory.

"He was more like my brother, I'll miss him greatly," said Keane about his dad. "My father was a massive influence on my career as well as being inspirational in every part of my life.

"He fought a very brave and long fight against cancer but always remained in good spirits. It fills me with pride to remember that the last match he saw me play was against Everton when I was lucky enough to score a hat-trick."

That 4-3 win over The Toffees at White Hart Lane on January 12 reflected Keane's swift transition to life in the English capital, where he quickly established a great rapport with Teddy Sheringham following his move from Leeds the previous August for £7m.

At international level, Keane had not scored since the win in Helsinki but informed Kerr that he would link up with the squad in Tirana ahead of the game against Albania the following Wednesday. The decision by Keane — backed by his family — to play in the second leg of the double header was much-appreciated by his teammates and management of Kerr, his assistant Chris Hughton and coach Noel O'Reilly.

Robbie played 67 minutes of the dour scoreless draw before making way for Spurs teammate Gary Doherty. By June, Keane was back in the groove with Ireland, scoring the opening goal in the 2-1 group win over Albania in Dublin on March 7 and then adding the clinching second goal in the 2-0 success over Georgia at home four days later.

The results meant that going into the summer break Ireland's qualification bid was back on track as they sat second in the table on 10 points — two behind the Swiss and three ahead of Russia, who had a game in hand. However, when Russia came to Lansdowne Road on September 6, 2003, Robbie Keane was unable to take his place in the home attack having sustained an ankle injury just three weeks earlier in the 2-1 friendly win over Australia at the same venue.

Although Damien Duff's dazzling run and strike put the Irish ahead against the Russians, Sergei Ignashevich equalised in a 1-1 draw. The outcome was far from a disaster for the Irish, who knew that they could book their place in the finals or at least make the play-offs by beating the Swiss in Basel on October 11.

But even the presence of Keane beside David Connolly in attack was unable to inspire Kerr's side, who produced a muted display. The outstanding Hakan Yakin gave the Swiss a sixth-minute lead and Alexander Frei confirmed their win on the hour mark.

A month later, Keane netted twice in the 3-0 friendly win over Canada in Dublin and when he was again on target in the 2-1 friendly success over Czech Republic at Lansdowne Road in March, 2004, he moved on to 19 senior Ireland goals. He was now level with Don Givens, Tony Cascarino and John Aldridge in the all-time rankings of Irish scorers, one behind

Frank Stapleton and just two adrift of leading marksman Niall Quinn on 21. It was only a matter of time before he smashed through that barrier.

Keane emulated fellow Dubliner Stapleton with a classy winner away to Holland in the Amsterdam friendly date in June and now Quinn, who had grown up only a short distance from both Crumlin and Tallaght in the suburb of Perrystown, was in his sights.

By September, Keane had equalled the milestone by slotting home a second-half penalty in the easy 3-0 World Cup 2006 qualifying win over Cyprus in Dublin that saw Andy Reid cap a fine performance with a stunning goal.

By this stage, Roy Keane was back in the Ireland side having been courted by Kerr throughout 2003 with a view to restoring the inspirational figure to the side. An initial approach had ended in failure on the eve of the Scotland match in February, 2003, with the timing of the player's statement confirming his continued absence doing neither party any favours.

Undeterred, Kerr continued to regularly text Keane and when the pair eventually sat down in Manchester for a chat in early 2004, it was clear that the former captain wanted to add to his 58 senior caps, the last of which had been collected in the 2-1 Lansdowne Road friendly defeat by Nigeria on the eve of the departure for Saipan two years earlier.

Amid great fanfare on April 20, 2004, Kerr confirmed that Keane was in his squad for the following week's away friendly date with Poland in Bydgoszcz. With Kerr rightly receiving kudos for ending the 32-year-old's exile, Keane duly reported for duty on Sunday, April 27, met the media the next day in the squad's Portmarnock Hotel and Golf Links base but was then forced to withdraw from the panel just prior to departure due to a hamstring injury sustained 48 hours earlier in the 1-0 home defeat by Liverpool.

A month later on May 27 in Dublin, Keane finally wore the green jersey once again when playing the entire 90 minutes in the 1-0 friendly success over Romania. He did not, however, feature in either of the two Unity Cup games against Nigeria and Jamaica at The Valley in London, nor the win against the Dutch. The win over Holland and enterprising display against an admittedly poor Cypriot outfit injected belief among the players and media that qualification was within the team's ambit before the side returned to Basel for a crunch qualifier four days later on September 8 and with the following month's trip to Paris to play France looming.

Clinton Morrison's early goal against the Swiss justified the upbeat mood but Hakan Yakin levelled by the 17th minute and the match ended 1-1 in a game that saw the two Keanes start a competitive international together for the first time since the 2-0 victory over Iran in November, 2001. Carried by the twin currents of the raging Celtic Tiger and the optimism generated by the first two group results, 25,000 Irish fans descended on Stade de France on Saturday, October 9 to witness an outstanding Ireland performance in a 0-0 draw that might have yielded all three points had John O'Shea sent his effort a few inches inside rather than outside the post.

However, Shay Given had also been called upon to make several saves in a game that was undoubtedly the highpoint of Kerr's reign. Goal chances had been at a premium against the Swiss and French but the home clash with the Faroe Islands back in Dublin four days later would surely provide the opportunity for Robbie Keane to exceed Quinn's 21-goal career tally.

So a match that would have scarcely attracted a second glance provided the stage for Keane to set a significant record in Irish football history. Fourteen minutes into his 56th cap, he stroked home from the penalty spot after Damien Duff was fouled.

Roy Keane set up Robbie's second goal — and 23rd for Ireland — before the interval. In truth, Robbie should have clocked up the quarter-century by the final whistle given the opportunities that fell his way, but he was well entitled to salute his achievement.

"It's a great feeling, I can't really describe it," he beamed.

"When I was a kid I would play on the streets of Tallaght and dream of playing for my country and scoring goals. To break the record is extra special."

Kerr was thrilled that a player who had graduated from the underage ranks had now eclipsed Quinn's haul from 91 appearances by the age of just 24.

"I think it's a wonderful achievement for him to get the record at such a young age," said Kerr. "It's been inevitable for a while. When he got in the team people said he would break records and I'm sure he will extend the record. I don't see him ending up as a centre-back."

And the watching Quinn gave his former strike partner heartfelt words of praise. "It was a great moment for him, a poignant moment," stated Quinn. "Robbie lost his dad, who was a big influence on his career and he would have been thinking of him. I'm really happy for him."

McCarthy had moved on to become the Sunderland manager in March, 2003. He watched with pride as Keane's hunger for goals and international action combined to see him achieve in six and a half years what had taken Quinn 14 years to clock up.

"How many has he scored in friendlies?" asks McCarthy but not with a hint of criticism. "I'm not being ungracious to him by saying that. Robbie deserves the record because he turns up for every single friendly.

"He's got it as he has turned up and played. There has never been whinging and him saying 'it's a friendly, I don't want to turn up' or 'I'm too big to play in this'. No, Robbie turns up and wants to play and play and score.

"He's got his rewards for it. I know he's had some great winners and scored important goals against Germany and Spain. He gets the big goals but I'm sure his tally has been swelled by turning up for every single game.

"It's the same with your haul of caps going up when you turn up for every single game. I love that about him."

A month later, Keane clocked up his 24th Ireland goal with

the winner in the 1-0 friendly success at home to Croatia as Kerr experimented with a 4-3-3 system that had Liam Miller, Graham Kavanagh and Kevin Kilbane in midfield and Stephen Elliott joining Keane and Duff up front.

At Spurs, he found himself jousting with Freddie Kanoute to be Jermain Defoe's strike partner but as 2005 loomed, Keane could reflect on a year when he and Ireland had both made positive strides.

Another single-goal friendly home win achieved with Andy O'Brien's strike, this time against Portugal in February, kicked-off a year that promised much. But back-to-back away and home draws with Israel in March and June undid the good work achieved the previous autumn. The fact that Ireland surrendered a 1-0 lead in Tel Aviv and a two-goal cushion in Dublin angered fans and prompted probing questions for the first time of the manager.

There were rumblings of discontent among a number of the Ireland players with Kerr's regime and his emphasis on constant team briefings and meetings.

One star even took to using the DVDs on forthcoming opponents as ideal mini-frisbees.

Open hostility had also now broken out between Kerr and elements of the media. Robbie Keane netted against the Israelis in Dublin on June 4 but missed the far-from-compelling 2-0 away win over the Faroes four days later through injury. When the campaign resumed in September, Ireland's destiny was firmly in their own hands, although predicting the likely outcome to a section where the top four teams were within three points of each other was almost impossible.

Many felt that a win away to Cyprus sandwiched by draws with the French and Swiss in Dublin would probably be enough. However, Thierry Henry's legitimate moment of magic in the second half secured France a priceless victory at Lansdowne Road that, added to their 3-0 home win over the Faroes a few days earlier, sent them three points ahead of Ireland. As France won in Dublin, the Swiss and Israelis produced yet another draw (1-1) between the top four.

On October 8, Elliott's early scrambled goal in Nicosia earned Ireland a very fortunate three points against the enterprising Cypriots. The Swiss arrived in Dublin for their October 12 showdown knowing that a point would ensure they at least claimed the runners-up spot and the lottery of the play-offs.

With France hosting Cyprus in Paris, nothing but a win would be good enough for Ireland. Les Bleus duly strolled to a 4-0 defeat of Cyprus while in Dublin the loss of Roy Keane — who sustained a nasty foot injury in the September 18 scoreless league draw with Liverpool at Anfield, his last game for Manchester United — came sharply into focus.

By the end of November, Keane would be history at Old Trafford and shortly after 9.30 in the evening of October 12, Switzerland's ability to claim a 0-0 stalemate meant that Ireland's ambitions of reaching Germany the following summer were also over.

Ireland finished fourth in the table, with Israel only missing out on second spot by virtue of Switzerland's 2-2 away draw in Tel Aviv. France's win in Dublin would prove to be the only decisive result among the top four's encounters, and so gave Raymond Domenech's side the crucial edge to take the automatic route to the tournament, where Kobi Kuhn's Swiss side would join them following a fractious away goals success over Turkey.

In common with most of his colleagues, Robbie Keane had failed to fire in the final three games and he was replaced by Elliott midway through the Switzerland match. Prior to the finale, FAI sources had indicated that Kerr's contract would not be renewed unless the team qualified.

By the end of October, the departure of Kerr was confirmed and the search for a new national senior team manager commenced. Martin O'Neill, David O'Leary, Kevin Keegan, Bryan Robson, Gerard Houllier, Terry Venables and Alex Ferguson — who was deliberating over his Old Trafford future at the time — were all linked with the post, but it was Steve Staunton who was appointed in late January in a set-up where the hugely-experienced Bobby Robson would act as his international adviser.

It was a risky strategy by the FAI, although the presence of Robson — the former England, Barcelona, Porto, PSV Eindhoven, Ipswich Town and Newcastle United manager — went a long way to addressing many people's doubts over the county Louth man's lack of experience in management.

Nobody questioned Staunton's passion for the Ireland job, his outstanding Ireland international career of 102 caps and appearances at three World Cup finals, but many felt that his coaching CV of reserve team boss at Walsall in the third level of the English game left him short of relevant experience.

However, in the aftermath of the sour end to Kerr's era in the hotseat there was a degree of urgency among most people in the game to move on and see if Staunton could harness the undoubted talent that was there. 'Stan' was told by the FAI that his was a four-year project, with qualification for the 2010 World Cup in South Africa the target — not guiding the team to Euro 2008 in Switzerland and Austria.

Roy Keane had retired from international football, as had skipper Kenny Cunningham and Matt Holland. Cunningham had been a popular skipper with the players and a loyal lieutenant for Kerr, so Staunton would have to choose carefully when selecting his successor.

Given, Dunne and O'Shea and right-full Stephen Carr all made most pundits' shortlist, as did Robbie Keane, but the consensus was narrowing on centre-half Dunne or keeper Given to wear the armband.

Ireland's first game of the Staunton era would be at home to Sweden on March 1 and three nights before the match, there were two indications that Keane was Stan's man.

During the FAI international football awards show, Given revealed during his acceptance speech after winning the senior gong that he would not be the new captain. A short time later

Keane beamed a toothy smile and booming 'hello' to the media table — with whom he had a working but hardly warm relationship — as he skipped past.

It was obvious that Keane was the gaffer's choice. It was a bold move by the manager and one that has since proved to be the right one. Undoubtedly, Keane's appointment as vice-captain the previous season at Spurs had influenced Staunton.

But it was Keane's popularity in the Irish camp, the respect that teammates showed him, his commitment to the cause and his willingness to listen to younger players that were the chief reasons for his appointment. And as a player who was never afraid to let colleagues know what he expected of them on the pitch, Keane could be a demanding task master.

So he followed in the illustrious footsteps of a who's who of recent modern Irish football legends when attaching the armband that week, with Liam Brady (1980-90: 13 times), Frank Stapleton (1983-88: 30 times), Mick McCarthy (1986-92: 22 times), Kevin Moran (1988-93: 13 times), Andy Townsend (1992-97: 40 times), Staunton himself (1997-2002: 16 times), Roy Keane (1998-2002: 23 times) and Kenny Cunningham (1998-2005: 32 times) all serving lengthy spells as the manager's voice on the pitch.

Given had no ill-feelings at the time over missing out on the role and six years later believes it was a shrewd move by Stan.

"There was no disappointment from me, not at all," says Given. "For me, he was the automatic choice, to be honest. Obviously, you would love to captain your country but it's not one of those things that you would be arguing over.

"I think Robbie's our talisman and he's recognised in most football nations around the world. And rightly so for the goals he has scored for us and he proved that again in the Euro 2012 campaign.

"Robbie has been a great captain for Ireland and is a great influence around the camp, especially on the younger players due to what he has done for Ireland. That's not just down to the goals he has scored but the importance of them at crucial times in qualifying games and finals. People have got that great respect for him."

John O'Shea has been equally impressed by how Keane has assumed the role of leader despite being a forward. "You see how vocal Robbie is on the pitch," points out O'Shea. "Obviously the general consensus is that over the years centre-forwards are not usually captains, it's normally a centre-half or central midfielder.

"But I can see how Robbie makes the new lads feel right at ease when they are called in. Believe me, when he has to get his points across as captain he does it very, very well. People on the outside looking in probably would not see it as much but when he has to get his message across, he is very, very clear and very concise as to how he wants the team to approach situations.

"Maybe that is an aspect of the team and Robbie that people don't realise. Robbie has been such a prolific scorer and has scored so many important goals for us that he is a massive player for us. His record of scoring goals for Ireland is phenomenal. When his record is analysed when he does stop playing for Ireland, believe me, we will miss him.

"People have always known Robbie as a clever player but when you see him up-close in training and in games it is amazing. The technique he has got to finish goals is fantastic and you can see why he has been a top-class player throughout his career."

O'Shea has twice worn the armband when taking over the role, once from Keane in the 4-0 drubbing of Denmark in Aarhus in August, 2007, and also when Steven Reid was replaced at the interval of the 4-0 home hammering by Holland 12 months earlier.

"It's an amazing feeling. You have come so far, come through the ranks from Under-15 all the way through to get to the pinnacle and become the senior team captain. It's a great feeling and something that you would like to think that you could do again."

Jason McAteer admits to having reservations about Keane's

cocksure personality when the teenage Keane first broke into the senior squad but the pair grew to have a strong friendship. And McAteer feels that Keane simply harnessed that early natural lip when taking over as captain.

"No, I was not surprised by Stan's decision," says McAteer. "Robbie was the glamour boy and he had the experience of playing in the 2002 World Cup and so many qualifiers. He knew what he was talking about and he is quite vocal on the pitch.

"He always has something to say and that goes back to when I first met him. He had too much to say back then but now on the pitch he has something to say."

A crowd of 34,000 turned up at Lansdowne Road for Staunton's first match in charge and left for home more than satisfied at what they had seen.

Against a Swedish side that appeared more concerned at avoiding injury than anything else, the Irish showed a refreshing energy and a strong attacking emphasis with a 4-2-3-1 formation that had Steven Reid and John O'Shea as holding midfielders and debutant Kevin Doyle up front with Elliott, Keane and Duff operating just behind.

Keane marked his new role with an unstoppable volleyed goal from 16 yards after Duff put the home side in front, with substitute Liam Miller firing home a 25-yard beauty for the third on a night when Stephen Ireland also made his senior debut.

"It was a great feeling to lead the team out but we needed to get a good result for the games to come," smiled Keane after the final whistle. "I wore the armband but you need 11 captains out there and that's what we had tonight.

"I'm happy with the job Stan asked me to do and I thought the lads did brilliantly. Stan asked me to play a deeper role and asked the front three to stay high up the pitch. We showed a good team spirit. It would be wrong to say there wasn't a good team spirit under Brian Kerr, but now we are starting off again.

"You could see how well the lads worked as a team and it's

great to start off with a good result."

However, the 1-0 home friendly reversal by Chile in late May — when Staunton deployed a 3-4-3 system with Keane, Doyle and Duff in attack — saw the Irish in a strangely subdued state.

But worse was to follow in Dublin on August 16 when a rampant Holland side cruised to a 4-0 friendly success against an Ireland side that was disorganised, short of ideas and was run ragged by the interval. Staunton had abandoned any previous ideas about experimenting with his side, but the 4-4-2 formation was torn apart and the final score might have stood at seven or eight to the Dutch.

With the opening Euro 2008 qualifier against Germany in Stuttgart only 17 days away, it was no exaggeration to say that the Ireland camp was on the verge of a crisis, even if the absence of Keane, Given, Dunne and Duff against the Dutch was a mitigating factor.

To add to the concern in the Irish camp, Bobby Robson would not be able to work at the Germany game as he suffered his second relapse in the space of five months in his ongoing cancer battle.

Stan was on his own even if he had the strong support of coach Kevin McDonald and Pat Devlin, who had been brought in to liaise with the League of Ireland clubs and take charge of the occasional games involving the Ireland B international side.

However, in the stadium where Ray Houghton had put the ball in the English net 18 years earlier, a disciplined, well-organised and feisty performance by Ireland saw them almost earn a scoreless draw with the Germans, whose winning goal from Lukas Podolski's 56th-minute free-kick took a major deflection off Keane's heel to beat Given.

Keane might have done better with a second-minute header but at least the side had steadied the ship and a defeat away to Germany would not decide the team's qualifying fate. That was the good news. On the flipside, Staunton got himself sent off for arguing with referee Luis Cantalejo and kicking a water bottle away in a temper.

Staunton would now sit out the following month's away trip to Cyprus where Kerr's side had been fortunate to win 1-0 12 months earlier and where the 4-0 victory in 2001 had been very flattering to the Irish.

What unfolded at the GSP Stadium in Nicosia on October 7 remains one of the all-time low points for Irish football as a bedraggled side was humbled 5-2 by the rampant, slick-passing Cypriots whose usual smart approach work was, for once, matched by clinical finishing.

Richard Dunne was sent off 13 minutes from the end for his second bookable offence but trying to pin the blame for the defeat on this factor was wide of the mark. Ireland were a shambles in every department as McDonald and Devlin in the dugout watched on in horror. Staunton sat speechless in the stand and even Keane picked up a rare booking.

While Staunton would be back on the touchline for the home date with the Czech Republic four days later, the manager now had 13 first-choice and squad members missing through injury and suspension. However, just as the players had rallied against the Germans, the team produced a top-class 90 minutes against the Czechs at Lansdowne Road to earn a 1-1 draw, with keeper Wayne Henderson and centre-half Paul McShane excellent in a side that understandably lined out with five in midfield and Keane as a lone striker.

The pressure had been temporarily lifted from Staunton and the easy 5-0 win over San Marino on November 15 in the last ever senior international match played at the old Lansdowne Road further soothed frayed nerves in the upper echelons of the FAI.

Keane marked the occasion with his first ever hat-trick at any level for Ireland, a fitting milestone to herald the famous old arena's imminent demolition to make way for the spanking new Aviva Stadium. But by February 5, 2007, there were renewed calls for Staunton to quit when it took Stephen Ireland's injury-time goal to secure a 2-1 win away to San Marino on a night when all the worst aspects of the Nicosia horror show resurfaced against a side ranked in the bottom handful of football nations on the planet.

In late March, Ireland were making their football debut at Croke Park, which would serve as the home for most of the senior international football and rugby games until the Aviva was opened in August, 2010.

Staunton was now battling to save his job and the original talk just 12 months earlier of building a side to compete in the 2010 World Cup appeared fanciful. The continuing false economic boom and the historic breakthrough of seeing football being played at 'Croker' attracted a near capacity attendance (for competitive football matches it was 76,000) of 72,539 fans for the Saturday, March 24 visit of Wales.

It was by far the largest ever crowd to witness a football match on the island, dwarfing the 53,000 at Lansdowne in 1981 for the 3-2 win over Michel Platini's France and beating the 60,000 that would somehow cram into Windsor Park for Northern Ireland games with England on either side of World War Two.

Stephen Ireland slotted home the game's only goal before the interval to cap his impressive display in an attacking midfield role. But Keane's second yellow card of the campaign ruled him out of the following Wednesday's 1-0 win over Slovakia when Doyle's header separated the sides in a game watched by another remarkably huge attendance of 71,297.

In a tight section, the four consecutive wins breathed life into the belief that this team might yet edge out the Czechs and Slovaks for second place. The hugely experimental teams that figured in the 1-1 friendly draws with Ecuador and Bolivia in Boston and New York in late May did not involve Keane, but he was back in the side as Staunton's men chalked up a stunning 4-0 friendly win over Denmark in Aarhus on August 22.

Keane grabbed a brace of goals and half-time substitute Shane Long added the other two on a night when another interval replacement, Darron Gibson, caught the eye with his aggressive, attacking midfield play. Ahead of the crunch away double header with the Czechs and Slovaks in early September, it was the perfect fillip.

However, the frailties of earlier away matches came back to haunt the Irish in both Bratislava and Prague, where Stephen Ireland's 'Grannygate' saga unfolded in the hours after the 2-2 draw with the Slovaks. Ireland and Doyle scored but the visitors conceded an injury-time equaliser on a night when they did enough to win.

By the following evening, as the squad was settled in Prague, the FAI confirmed that Stephen Ireland had departed for home on compassionate leave to attend the funeral of his grandmother. By the end of the week, it transpired that both of his grandmothers were hale and hearty and that the Manchester City star had returned to his home in the north of England to comfort his partner, who had suffered a miscarriage.

While there was universal sympathy for his girlfriend, there was little or none for the then 21-year-old, whose deception left red faces in the FAI.

Five years later and the saga continues to rumble on, with the gifted player's recent statements on a return to international football a clear indication of the side's current success and his own deep-down realisation that he has handled the issue extremely badly.

Against the background of the unfolding drama surrounding Ireland and his family, Staunton's team needed to avoid defeat against the Czechs. But full-back Marek Jankulovski's 15th-minute goal and Stephen Hunt's dismissal only minutes after replacing the injured O'Shea saw the Irish again hit the now familiar self-destruct button. Only a bizarre combination of results in their remaining three Group D games would see Staunton's men snatch the runners-up spot.

A month later at Croke Park, Germany were held to a scoreless draw by the battling Irish and it seemed that Staunton's job was safe.

Within 72 hours, that scenario changed completely with yet

another rudderless, disjointed 90 minutes against the Cypriots, this time at Croker.

Steve Finnan's powerful drive from the edge of the penalty area in the 90th minute rescued a 1-1 draw for the home team but could not keep Stan in a job.

Keane made a spirited defence of Staunton on the The Late Late Show in the wake of the Cyprus draw and criticised the media for what he believed was their part in fermenting the opposition among many fans — evidenced by booing during that game — to Stan's continued role as manager.

Ireland had finished the 12-game campaign on 17 points, fully 12 behind group winners the Czechs and 10 adrift of Germany. By the time that Ireland completed their fixtures away to Wales on November 17, Don Givens was caretaker boss after the FAI decided to terminate Staunton's contract halfway through its term.

In the half-empty Millennium Stadium in Cardiff, Keane and Doyle netted for Ireland in an entertaining 2-2 draw.

The real action was starting to unfold in the FAI's corridors of power, but a significant meeting had already taken place the previous night at the Ireland squad's plush base at Celtic Manor, where chief executive John Delaney canvassed the views of senior players, including Keane, on who should succeed 'The Gaffer'.

Chapter 14
Dreams come true

IN the innocent mind's eye of millions of young boys, the dream of playing football for your country, scoring goals in the Premier League and signing for the club you support would rank as one of the most popular.

Long before the start of the 2007-08 season, Robbie Keane had fulfilled the first two parts of that treble and the final chapter was about to become a reality.

And as if life was not treating the 27-year-old from Tallaght well enough, there was also the rather important matter of his marriage to Dublin-born model Claudine Palmer in June, 2008. Roy of the Rovers? No, just another chapter in the remarkable rise of Robbie Keane.

He was now one half of Ireland's answer to Posh and Becks, even if the Dubliner chose a far more low-key lifestyle than the former England captain and his ex-pop star wife.

The season just finished at Spurs had proven to be hugely successful for Keane. The appointment of Juande Ramos and capture of the League Cup boded well for the player and the club. The FAI had appointed legendary Italian coach Giovanni Trapattoni as Ireland international manager, Keane would remain skipper and, according to the wily ex-coach of Juventus, Inter Milan, Bayern Munich and Benfica, the striker would be a player around who he wanted to build his side.

It was little surprise, then, that when Keane and his large circle of friends departed for Miami in May for his stag party, he was full of the joys of life. Little did he then realise that his upcoming nuptials would be just the first part of an on and off-pitch double that would see him fulfil another aspect of his childhood ambitions.

Once Keane and Palmer began dating in 2002, the social diarists went into overdrive. For them, a relationship between one of the country's most attractive and popular models and the poster boy of the Ireland football team was manna from heaven.

By the time Claudine was appearing at the Nokia UCD Students' fashion show at The Point in Dublin in March, 2004, the romance was flourishing. However, this was the first time that Keane had turned up for one of her public assignments. And Ms Palmer's attire of skimpy underwear and stockings on the catwalk did not appear to ruffle her new boyfriend, who looked on with pride. Given his girlfriend's frequent lingerie shoots in the years that would follow, it was just as well.

By July that year, Claudine — who would graduate from college with a double first class honours degree in economics and finance — was among the favourites to win the 2004 Miss Ireland contest at Dublin's Citywest Hotel. The previous year's winner, Rosanna Davison, had gone on to become Miss World but, as it happened, county Donegal's Natasha Nic Gairbheith surprised those present to claim the title and become the first ever fluent Irish speaker to triumph in the competition.

If Claudine was disappointed at the outcome, she failed to show it and her modelling career continued apace as she graced many advertising and marketing campaigns and established a high profile in the media.

While Claudine's career was based in Dublin, she gradually started to work in London and the relationship with Keane blossomed, leading to their engagement in October, 2006 and wedding on June 7, 2008 in St Alphonsus and Columba Church in the south Dublin suburb of Ballybrack.

From there, the bridal party made their way to the Ritz Carlton Hotel on the famous Powerscourt Estate in county Wicklow for a reception. As ever with Keane, the occasion would be centred on family, with his sisters Natasha and Amy two of the five bridesmaids; his older brother Graham the chief groomsman to best man, ex-Wolves keeper and long-standing friend Matt Murray. Keane's niece and nephew, Tasha and Craig, acted as ring-bearers. Reflecting their love of music, singer Mary Black joined the Dublin Gospel Choir for a rendition of

'Happy Day' in the church.

Each blessed with striking good looks, the 27-year-old groom and his bride, two years younger, cut a handsome dash as they emerged from the beautiful 150-year-old church. Even the venue in the parish of Ballybrack and Killiney seemed to appropriately sum up the happy couple's respective backgrounds.

For Claudine, Killiney was not too far removed from her upbringing in middle-class Malahide on Dublin's coastal northside, with Ballybrack resonant of parts of her new husband's Tallaght. On the eve of the wedding, Keane was far from pleased to discover that members of the media were enjoying a drink at the bar of the Ritz Carlton where he was staying, forgetting that public figures who enjoy the limelight in their day jobs will find themselves the focus of such attention on major occasions in their lives.

However, having tied the knot, Mr and Mrs Keane were the perfect smiling couple for the phalanx of photographers after the ceremony finished. And the fact that the pair had turned down a substantial six-figure offer to sell the exclusive picture rights of their wedding also went down well with the public.

A who's who of Keane's Ireland and Spurs teammates, ex-players and their wives and partners whooped it up for two days at the luxury hotel with Damien Duff, Shay Given, Gary Breen, Gary Kelly, Jonathan Woodgate, Michael Carrick, Ian Harte, Jermaine Jenas, Ledley King and Jamie Redknapp among the long list of sporting guests. Models Rosanna Davison and Pippa O'Connor, with her future husband Brian Ormond, were also present.

At Powerscourt, a band was hired to entertain the guests but Redknapp was on the money when predicting that the groom might try to help them out.

"I suspect by the end of the evening Robbie will be up on stage singing an Irish song," joked the Sky Sports pundit.

And as Kathryn Rogers reported in the Irish Daily Star on the following Monday, Keane did not let the opportunity pass without taking the microphone for an impromptu karaoke session. "Romantic Robbie took to the stage to sing the moving Garth Brooks song 'If Tomorrow Never Comes' for his new wife," Rogers revealed.

"The gesture followed his moving speech in the ballroom of the Ritz Carlton Hotel where he paid tribute to his stunning bride, Claudine Palmer. However, Robbie also didn't forget his humble origins and he also thanked Crumlin United Football Club for putting him where he is today. He invited several people from his club in Crumlin and 'he thanked them specifically during his speech which was nice' said one guest. 'He also went around all the tables afterwards and thanked everyone individually for coming to their wedding'.

"Guests dined on prawns for starters, Tipperary roast beef and potato gratin with roast vegetables as the main course and molten chocolate fondant and vanilla ice cream for dessert.

"They were surrounded by €20,000 worth of white flower displays from Mad Flowers in Dublin. After the dinner, guests were also treated to spectacular fireworks and a water-and-light display that lit up the grounds of the hotel against the backdrop of the Sugarloaf Mountain.

"After the display, guests were ushered into a marquee which was transformed into a slick garden nightclub decorated with sparkling chandeliers and fairy light. Each table featured a bowl of blue and pink M&Ms on the table with each sweet printed with the names 'Robbie and Claudine' and the date of their wedding.

"The bride wore a crystal-encrusted white silk satin dress by Lebanese fashion designer Elie Saab which is believed to have cost €15,000. She needed the help of two of her five brides-maids to carry the train of her veil during the entire reception. 'The veil stretched the entire length of the church aisle,' revealed a guest.

"The wedding was organised by Peregrine Armstrong Jones who had also planned David and Victoria Beckham's 1999 marriage in Luttrellstown Castle on the outskirts of Dublin."

Keane's attraction to Palmer and subsequent strong relationship leading to their marriage was no surprise to Derek Daniels — who owns Assets' modelling agency in Dublin. Daniels has known the Malahide woman from her first fledgling steps as a model where her personality always shone in what is a business that can be riddled with unpleasant rivalries and petty jealousies.

"Claudine is one of the most pleasant models I ever had the pleasure to work with," says Daniels. "From my very first meeting with her I could tell that she is a really nice person. There were no airs and graces about Claudine and that's the way she has remained.

"Claudine is really glamorous and that's one thing that really strikes you from the first time you meet her. From a professional point of view, Claudine was really dedicated to her work and had a great attitude. And while she has a great social life and likes to party, there's so much more to her as a person.

"And she possesses a lovely laid-back manner. There are some people in the business who are really competitive and that stands out from day one. That's the case with Claudine. It's also great to see that she's so close to her mum Joan. They are like sisters and are almost joined at the hip!

"I don't know Robbie too well but as a couple they have been very happy. And their wedding was one of the best I have ever attended. One thing I do remember very well that day was the fact that Robbie made time to speak to everybody and he went around every table.

"And while some models set out from the start to marry a footballer or rugby player that was not the case with Claudine. They are a couple with their own successful careers."

Four years later and now based in Los Angeles, Claudine's future career probably lies in the USA although she continues to fulfil occasional contracts in Ireland and the United Kingdom.

"I know that Claudine will do well in the USA and she will also continue to work here when her availability allows it."

After honeymooning for a fortnight in Sardinia, the Keanes returned to London, where Robbie was due to report for pre-season training at Spurs in the first week of July. But the first cogs in the transfer machine were beginning to turn in a process that would take Keane to Liverpool Football Club, the team he had worshipped as a cheeky kid.

Liverpool had finished fourth in the Premier League in May, 2008, 11 points behind champions Manchester United. And manager Rafa Benitez was told by his American owners that there was cash to spend on players to finally end the wait for a 19th league title that had by this stage stretched to 18 years.

Why Benitez signed Keane remains one of the still unresolved aspects to Keane's short stay on Merseyside given the fact that the team's attacking system did not always suit the Dubliner and the manager was happy to allow Keane return to White Hart Lane only six months later.

Was Benitez following the orders of joint chairmen Tom Hicks and George Gillett as many people believe when he began his pursuit of the forward in late June? Initially, this theory does not appear to hold much substance for early reports from Anfield clearly indicated that Benitez was making the running on the matter with Tottenham steadfast in their unwillingness to sell one of their most prized assets.

Would a manager who is lukewarm to a possible transfer target pursue the matter with the same diligence as Benitez applied to the Keane chase in June and July 2008? After all, Liverpool already had Fernando Torres up front and were seeking a player to complement the Spanish star rather than a striker who would transform their attack.

Torres had just fired Spain to the Euro 2008 title with an exquisite winning goal in the 1-0 final victory over Germany in Vienna. He also scored 33 goals (including 24 in the league) in all competitions in 2007-08, his first campaign at Anfield. There was no disputing that the Reds required extra firepower, with Andrei Voronin and Peter Crouch contributing only five league goals each in 2007-08, Ryan Babel four and Dirk Kuyt on target just three times.

Yet, surely Benitez — who had guided Liverpool to the

Champions League in 2005, the FA Cup 12 months later before being beaten by AC Milan in the 2007 European Cup final — would be strong enough to dictate transfer policy at the club.

Tottenham boss Juande Ramos was well aware that for his team to progress he needed to keep Keane and Dimitar Berbatov at the club or, failing this, to retain at least one of the pair who had scored a total of 46 goals in all competitions between them the previous season.

But Keane barely had the suntan lotion packed away when Benítez made his first offer for him that proposed a cash plus Peter Crouch deal. Benitez knew that Spurs were keen to land Crouch and felt that if he persisted, then Tottenham would start negotiating. Crouch had been valued at £12m by Liverpool but Keane would cost £20m.

Liverpool were also cranking up their campaign to sign Aston Villa midfielder Gareth Barry who had expressed a desire to move to Anfield. The lure of Champions League football — as long as Liverpool surmounted the qualifying round in late August — was a powerful magnet for both players.

By mid-July, with pre-season training now in full swing at all the Premier League clubs and squads preparing to embark upon local friendlies prior to the now customary overseas tours, Benitez remained frustrated at the lack of progress in signing Keane and Barry. But his increasingly public declarations on both players were a source of much annoyance at Villa Park and White Hart Lane.

"Keane is one of the names on our list and we are still working with other names," said Benítez, who ruled out any prospect of signing Spain striker David Villa from Valencia. "We were in contact with Tottenham and we will see now. Keane is clearly a player that has game intelligence.

"We are looking for players who can fit into our systems and improve the team. We're looking for players with the right quality and I think we'll find some in the next few days, although not necessarily the names that everybody knows."

By this stage, Peter Crouch had departed for Portsmouth in a deal worth a total of £11m, handing Benitez extra scope to conclude cash-only agreements with Spurs and Villa. But Spurs were digging in over Keane and Berbatov and on July 21 decided to lodge a formal complaint with the Premier League over Liverpool and Manchester United's pursuit of their strikers.

"The behaviour of both clubs has been disgraceful," declared Spurs chairman Daniel Levy. "We told both clubs very early on that we had no interest in selling Robbie or Dimitar, respectively, and that they should refrain from pursuing the player.

"Both clubs arrogantly chose to ignore this request and we now have evidence that both clubs have systematically been working to prise the players away from us, outside of Premier League rules of conduct.

"Benitez made comments in respect of Robbie recently and we made an official complaint to the Premier League about the conduct of Liverpool earlier this week. I have absolutely no wish to sell either player and to date we have not accepted any offer for either."

But as is so often the case with the transfer of big name stars, the public protestations proved to be a minor diversion and a week later on July 28 the clubs agreed a transfer fee of £20.3m for Keane, with £1.3m of the deal based on future performance compensation. Within 24 hours, Keane's personal terms were thrashed out and he put pen to paper on a four-year contract.

"I've been a Liverpool fan all my life, going back to when I was a kid growing up in Dublin, and I always had a Liverpool shirt on my back," beamed Keane when introduced to the media at the club's Melwood training ground. "So to be here now as a Liverpool player is incredible and I couldn't be happier."

While Tottenham withdrew their official complaint against Liverpool after the club made a donation to the Tottenham Hotspur Foundation and apologised for their behaviour prior to the deal, Levy remained unhappy with the events of the previous six weeks and claimed that his club had been forced into transferring the player due to Liverpool's interference.

"I'm not disappointed (by) his comments because you have to understand that as a club they have to look after themselves and I appreciate that," added Keane, who had been instructed to submit a transfer request by the Tottenham chairman before the deal could proceed.

"It was a tough situation when Liverpool came in for me because everything was great for me at Tottenham and I've got a relationship with everyone there, from the players to the staff, the chairman and everyone else. I've got strong feelings for the club and that will never change but it was no secret that I'm a Liverpool fan and that I always wanted to play for Liverpool.

"John Barnes, Ian Rush and John Aldridge were my heroes as a kid and I'm ambitious to have my name alongside theirs and hopefully I can achieve that. At the age I'm at now, the opportunity came along and it was too good an opportunity to let it pass. I think that if I didn't come to Liverpool I'd probably have regretted it for the rest of my life."

Benitez appeared chuffed with his big-name acquisition and his body language once more suggested that the deal to purchase Keane was initiated by him and not those above him at the club.

"I am sure defenders in the Premier League will be worried about facing Keane and Torres next season," stated Benitez.

"Managers will try to do different things to stop them but that's where Steven Gerrard, Ryan Babel and Dirk Kuyt will be so important for us because they cannot cope with them all. If you want to be at the top of the table fighting for trophies, you need good players and big names.

"When you know you are very close, sometimes you need a little more quality, more experience, because last season we had a lot of draws that maybe with more experience we could have won.

"That's one of the reasons we are looking for players with quality who are settled down in the Premier League. We can play 4-4-2 with Keane and Torres or someone, or 4-2-3-1 and

Keane can play on the right or on the left or as a second striker. It won't be a problem.

"It will be important for Torres in his second season to have another striker who can score goals, like Kuyt, Gerrard or Babel and now Keane," added Benítez who intriguingly stated that he felt that Keane's purchase was less of a risk than his £20m outlay to Atletico Madrid 12 months previously for Torres.

"Everybody knew that Torres was a good player but he needed to settle down in the Premier League. Keane is someone we know has already settled down. He's already playing well so maybe it is easier for him to adapt to our team and the things that we want to do."

Ahead of Keane's first appearance in the red shirt in the pre-season friendly against Rangers at Ibrox on August 2, Torres gave a hugely upbeat assessment of his new strike partner.

"Robbie really wanted to come to us and I think he is going to add an enormous amount to the team with his hard work, goals and experience," stated Torres.

"He will bring the level of the team up a notch and I'm sure he is going to be very important this season. He had a proven record and he has great mobility and versatility. He can play wide or a bit behind the striker. I think it is very good for the team to have a player who can get in between the opposition's midfield and defence and score goals. He is quick and clever and I think he will really help us."

Liverpool strolled to a 4-0 victory over Rangers and then defeated Valerenga 4-1 in Norway three days later to ease the pressure on Benitez, whose attack had been goal-shy in earlier warm-up games.

Benitez started Keane and Torres in attack in both matches and although the new signing failed to score, he set up Xabi Alonso for the opener in Norway with a neat pass. However, the relationship between the coach and the club's owners, Hicks and Gillett, had now moved centre stage with strong speculation that the latter pair were stalling on providing the money needed to fund the £18m signing of Barry.

Matters on the pitch were also far from smooth and it required a Pepe Reina penalty save to earn the team a 0-0 draw in their Champions League qualifying round first leg tie at Standard Liege, with Gerrard replacing Keane midway through the second half. Within days, stories emerged from Anfield that Benitez was now willing to walk away from the club if the Barry deal was not completed.

Torres' 83rd minute goal gave Liverpool an opening day Premier League win at Sunderland with the Spaniard and Irishman once more named together up front, though Keane was replaced by Nabil El Zhar 13 minutes from time. A week later, Keane and Torres were again asked to lead the attack but it was Keane's old Spurs colleague Mido who gave Middlesbrough a 70th minute lead, only for late goals by Emanuel Pogatetz (own goal) and Gerrard to earn the home side all three points.

Keane failed to muster an attempt on goal although his sluggish performance was no worse than many of his teammates. Benitez had handed the famous Liverpool number seven jersey to Keane, the shirt worn with so much success by Kevin Keegan, Kenny Dalglish and Peter Beardsley in previous eras and there was no indication that the Dubliner was going to be omitted from the team despite his slow start to life on Merseyside.

So Torres and Keane started in the return clash with Liege on August 27 when it took a Kuyt goal two minutes from the end of extra time to ensure the club's name featured in the group stage draw with Reina again the hero with two outstanding saves to ensure a less than impressive 1-0 aggregate win. Benefitting from their status as top seeds, Liverpool were drawn against PSV Eindhoven, Marseilles and Atletico Madrid.

As the clock ticked down to the summer transfer window deadline, Keane's old teammate Berbatov finally completed his £30.75m move to Manchester United but at Anfield, Benitez waved the white flag in his attempt to land Barry from Villa.

Apart from missing one match through injury, Torres partnered Keane in attack for the opening six league encounters that yielded that solitary opening day strike for Torres until the Spaniard grabbed both in the 2-0 victory at Everton at the end of September.

That win was the side's second significant scalp of the campaign following the earlier 2-1 home success at the expense of Manchester United. However, Keane was finding it hard to settle and found himself substituted in four of those half dozen games and for the following week's 3-2 away win at Manchester City he found himself on the bench as the manager changed his formation to include an extra midfielder in Javier Mascherano.

There was no need to panic on the Irishman's part for he returned to the side following the 10-day international break for the 3-2 Anfield defeat of Wigan Athletic as Torres was ruled out through injury. Crucially, he retained his place for the next match, the 1-0 away victory at Chelsea, that sent Liverpool to the top of the table for the first time that season.

However, he was left on the bench for the midweek home win against Portsmouth when Gerrard played in an advanced role just behind lone striker Kuyt. The result meant that Benitez's side started November as league leaders but Keane had yet to open his account for his new club in the Premier League.

The Champions League proved a happier hunting ground for Keane and he registered his first goal for Liverpool on October 1 in the 3-1 win against PSV at Anfield and quickly followed that up by scoring the opener in the 1–1 draw with Atletico three weeks later.

Liverpool's impressive start to the campaign came to a halt at Spurs on November 1, with Roman Pavlyuchenko's injury-time strike earning all three points for the home team. Keane once again was named in the first eleven, this time as a lone forward, and set up Kuyt's third-minute goal before being substituted.

He was roundly booed by a substantial percentage of the home support but by no means the majority. Keane was again frustrated at failing to find the net but he could console

Robbie made a major impact at an early stage for Wolves, a fact illustrated by his stunning debut against Norwich (*above*) when, at the age of 17, he scored twice; (*below*) with manager Gordon Strachan after joining Coventry

Keane was snapped up by Inter in 2000 *(inset)* but didn't get much time to showcase his talents and before long he was on his way back to England

Robbie Keane arrived to add further firepower to David O'Leary's Leeds United during a time of unprecedented spending at Elland Road

Such was the strength of Leeds' squad, however, openings were limited, though his talent was recognised with a Player of the Month award in 2001

Robbie enjoyed his best football during his first spell at Spurs between 2002 and 2008, when he was made club captain and scored over 100 goals

Although it was like a dream come true when he arrived at Anfield, his short spell at Liverpool never quite scaled the heights that Robbie was hoping for

Robbie joined Celtic on-loan at a difficult time for the Parkhead club, but he more than played his part by scoring an impressive 16 goals in 19 matches

Robbie and his beautiful wife Claudine enjoyed a fairytale wedding in 2008

himself with the fact that his summer move now looked like an even wiser decision. The reversal may have allowed Chelsea go top, but his former club Spurs was languishing second from bottom after a truly terrible start to the new season that had prompted Ramos's exit a week earlier and the swift appointment of Harry Redknapp.

Little did Keane realise, but events at White Hart Lane would soon impact on him once more. A few days later Keane was replaced in the 1-1 home draw with Atletico without scoring but finally, on Saturday, November 8 at Anfield, Keane claimed his first Premier League goal for Liverpool. In fact, he was twice on target in the first period to send the team on their way to a 3-0 win over West Brom. The home fans acclaimed their summer signing with a celebration that was genuinely warm in its affection.

"The goals have been a long time coming but deep down I knew they would," said Keane. "I might have worried about it when I was younger but not now."

Surely now Keane would add to his tally but although he started the next three league matches, he failed to score. After not being involved in two league outings, Keane did make a timely impact on December 21 with his team's goal in the 1-1 draw at Arsenal that kept them on the summit.

On St Stephen's Day, he netted twice in the 3-0 home success against Bolton and with Torres still injured, there was added pressure on Keane to deliver. The FA Cup failed to provide Keane with any respite and he was replaced during the away win at Preston North End in the third round.

By the time Everton visited their near neighbours on the final Sunday in January, the rumours about Keane rejoining Tottenham had gathered momentum. Keane's absence from the side for that day's FA Cup tie only fanned the speculation.

Redknapp had steadied the listing Spurs ship since his arrival in late October and wanted Keane to come back and lead his attack where Bent was struggling to score and summer recruit Puvlyuchenko was taking time to settle. So while two Torres goals assured Liverpool of a crucial 2-0 Anfield victory against Chelsea on Sunday, February 1, Keane was in the process of finalising his move back to north London ahead of the following night's transfer deadline.

When the £12m deal (potentially rising to £16m with add-on clauses) did go through shortly before the window's closure, Redknapp was happy to give his assessment of Keane on Sky Sports News.

"The chairman Daniel Levy has dealt with it and has done excellently," said Redknapp, who had also snapped up Pascal Chimbonda from Sunderland and Jermain Defoe from Portsmouth just 12 months after signing him for Pompey.

"We've brought back three ex-Tottenham players and for me they are all excellent players. And they are players the chairman did not want to lose in the first place, he fought hard to keep and has now fought harder to bring back. I'm well pleased with what he has done.

"I think Robbie Keane is a fantastic player and I think he will make a massive impact. He's not only a good player, it's his enthusiasm for the game, his character in the dressing room and around the place. He is a boy who wants to win at whatever he does.

"I think that rubs off on people and I think you need people like that in your club and I think he will bring so much to us. Robbie is full of energy and every time he puts a shirt on he gives everything he has got. He's got fantastic ability and that's why he is such a great player in my opinion."

The debate on why Keane failed to make the expected impact at Liverpool continues to this day and his former Ireland coach Mick McCarthy is unsure if the original transfer deal was wholeheartedly supported by Benitez.

"It suits Robbie if there is just one centre-forward and he is allowed to roam about," argues McCarthy. "It didn't work out because he was not the manager's signing, was he? I'm only reading it as an outsider. It never seemed destined to succeed right from the start. Whether that's true or not, I don't know.

"It was strange that he went there, was such a good player and was then out the door in months. Afterwards when you hear he was not Rafa's signing it was always going to end in tears, wasn't it? It's strange, because he fits the modern game more than most other strikers as you play one up front and he drops in. It suits him."

This latter point is one that Giovanni Trapattoni has frequently alluded to when describing the role that hands Keane most opportunity to display his wares. And Ray Houghton — who enjoyed five successful years at Liverpool from 1987 to 1992 — echoes his former teammate's viewpoint.

"I was surprised that it didn't work out because I felt he would do well at Liverpool. It was his style of play and (I thought) that he would appeal to Liverpool fans with his approach," explains Houghton.

"But we were unsure at the time as to who brought Robbie in. Was it the board or was it the manager? And if it wasn't the manager and he doesn't have to play you as he has other players, it doesn't half knock your confidence. And I think that was the key factor with Robbie.

"I think his confidence was dented and maybe he felt that because the manager was not going to play him in every game that he had to perform to a very high level in the matches he was involved in to be outstanding. So I think there was too much pressure put on him and it was the right club at the wrong time.

"I think he went there when the wrong manager was in charge. If he had gone to Anfield under Kenny Dalglish, I think Kenny would have got more out of him. Craig Bellamy went there the first time and it did not quite work out. If a manager is not encouraging you and you are not getting any feedback from him, it does knock your confidence and it does not matter who you are."

Keane started 16 of Liverpool's 23 league games and came on as a substitute in three more up to the time of his exit while he netted seven goals in 28 appearances in all competitions.

So there is a body of opinion that believes Keane should have stuck it out longer on Merseyside, especially as the club was mounting a title challenge to holders Manchester United, had comfortably qualified for the last 16 of the Champions League and looked odds-on to take a top-four finish and so make the following season's Champions League.

"Only the player can make that decision," reasons Houghton as to whether Keane should have opted to battle for his place at Liverpool rather than beat a hasty retreat to Tottenham, who were back in mid-table and out of both the FA and UEFA Cups.

They had booked their place in the League Cup final against Manchester United — but Keane could not play as he was cup-tied.

"I remember when I was at Liverpool and I had my best season in 1991-92, won club Player of the Year and also got into the top six for PFA Player of the Year. I left because I felt the manager did not treat me particularly well," adds Houghton.

"I went for a new contract and he was saying that I had been his most consistent player. Then he offered me a pittance. You must make a decision, do you stick it out while hoping he might go or think 'what's best for me in the long term' and go and play in somebody else's first team?

"That was when I made the decision to go to Aston Villa because I did not like what Graeme Souness was doing. So maybe Robbie felt that if I sit here I might not be playing and I am wasting my career. It's a tough one."

Keane agreed a four-year deal with Redknapp and for the Ireland skipper there must have been a real sense of déjà vu: Spurs were anchored in 14th place in the Premier League table, there was a misfiring big-name striker in Russian Pavlyuchenko (who had arrived from Spartak Moscow for £14m five months earlier).

The recent changing of the managerial guard with Redknapp's appointment meant that Keane would be playing for his sixth boss at the club in just seven years. Redknapp quickly appointed Keane as team captain in succession to Ledley King who continued to be plagued by injury.

"I just felt with Robbie coming in there would be a new impetus with him as captain," explained Redknapp. "He can give an awful lot. He is a big personality and we are a quiet team. If Robbie has something to say, he is going to say it. He is a leader and has the personality to be a captain of Tottenham."

Always one capable of focusing on the future rather than dwelling on the past, Keane spoke of his reasons for leaving Liverpool.

"I'm delighted to be back at a club I have very strong feelings for, having previously spent six wonderful years here," said Keane. "Coming back to Spurs was an easy decision to make because this is my home. Firstly in respect of the club but also my house is in the area and everything is set up for me to walk right back into.

"It's funny how football works sometimes and situations turn around very quickly. It would have been difficult for me to have gone anywhere else while a club I have such strong feelings for has this fight on its hands.

"It was a difficult time for me at Liverpool but there's no point in dwelling on it. Now I have the chance to work with a fantastic manager in Harry Redknapp who has done a great job since he came in, so I am lucky to be getting this exciting opportunity."

Defoe's untimely acquisition of a foot injury during training at the end of January had played its part in persuading Redknapp to sign Keane and it was a shrewd move with Defoe only involved during the final weeks of the season.

In contrast, Keane started each of his team's remaining 14 league matches although he was forced to sit in the Wembley stands on March 1 when Spurs lost 4-1 on penalties to Manchester United after a goalless League Cup final.

Keane's second coming for Spurs began on February 8 with a fiercely-contested scoreless north London derby at home to Arsenal but he was back in the groove with the first goal in the

4-0 hammering of Middlesbrough at White Hart Lane in early March. A few days later, he grabbed a last-minute equaliser at Sunderland as Spurs slowly improved their league status.

Redknapp rotated Bent and Pavlyuchenko to partner Keane but Defoe and Keane was the preferred pairing for the last three outings of the season, against Everton, Manchester City and, amusingly, Liverpool — a game that saw Keane score and receive a positive reception from The Kop in a 3-1 defeat.

Keane's short-lived stint on Merseyside had not gone unnoticed in the advertising and marketing world, where Virgin Trains cashed in to announce that they could get passengers 'A Liverpool to London return faster than Robbie Keane'.

But Keane appeared happy to be back on familiar turf and further goals followed against Blackburn and Manchester City, leaving him with five Premier strikes for Spurs (two from spot kicks) when the season concluded at Anfield.

Following his departure from Liverpool in early February, Benitez's men finished only four points behind Alex Ferguson's side in the title race, decimated Real Madrid 5-0 on aggregate in the second round of the European Cup (winning 4-0 in the second leg at home) and then lost 7-5 to Chelsea in the quarter-finals after an extraordinary second leg at Stamford Bridge that ended 4-4.

Long before the season ended, Keane dismissed suggestions that he would accept a medal if Liverpool did win the title.

"It would mean nothing at all to me now, my brother is a Liverpool fan so I'd probably give it to him," quipped Keane. "The way I look at it is that a medal means something when you are a part of the squad and involved in winning a trophy. When you are in and out of the squad and not involved in games, there are times when you don't feel part of it."

As far as the now 29-year-old was concerned, Liverpool belonged to the past and he was ready to help Tottenham to future glory under Redknapp. So when he reported back for pre-season training in early July, the Dubliner was buzzing in anticipation of the year ahead.

Redknapp's decision to sign the towering figure of Crouch from Portsmouth for £11m in the same month — a year after £1m more had taken him to Pompey from Liverpool — suggested that Tottenham might take a more direct route to goal.

But the boss remained intent on choosing Keane and Defoe as his first-choice attack to reflect the quality of the squad that was now brimful of players blessed with pace, good touch, great technique and a range of passing ability.

In their first game of the 2009-10 season, Liverpool were beaten 2-1 at The Lane with two defenders, Benoit Assou-Ekotto and Sebastian Bassong, notching the goals. Keane and Defoe spearheaded the attack while midfield boasted a maturing Aaron Lennon, the physical presence of Wilson Palacios, the silken skills of Luka Modric and, by season's end, the burgeoning talents of Gareth Bale, when chosen at left-wing.

Keane and Defoe each scored in the 5-1 away drubbing of Hull City and 2-1 wins over West Ham and Birmingham City left Tottenham second to leaders Chelsea on goal difference heading into the international break in early September.

On the resumption of club action, Spurs entertained Manchester United at White Hart Lane but lost this crucial test 3-1 and then crashed 3-0 away to Chelsea eight days later. The early optimism had been replaced by a pragmatic acceptance that this side was still very much a work in progress and it was not helped by an injury which sidelined Modric for several months.

But Keane then netted four goals for the first time in his senior career when Spurs demolished newly-promoted Burnley 5-0 at home at the end of September. Redknapp was mainly persisting with Keane and Defoe up front and the partnership that had failed to sparkle in a previous era was now producing results even if the loss of key games against the big guns — notably Arsenal (0-3 away) on October 31 — stopped the team from mounting a credible league title challenge.

Despite that defeat, Spurs were third by the end of November, although Keane missed the 9-1 demolition of Wigan Athletic at White Hart Lane on November 22 through injury when Defoe notched five.

Of greater concern to Keane was the growing influence of Crouch in first-team selections after the England star took advantage of Defoe and Keane's short-term injuries to stake his claim for inclusion.

But as the season entered the festive period, Keane found himself with far greater worries than holding down his place in the side. Now, his very future at White Hart Lane was in doubt. Given the time of year, Spurs players had assumed that they would be able to indulge in a traditional footballers' Christmas party.

But Redknapp — alarmed at the growing number of instances when such bashes had become front page news — banned any such gathering. However, under the guise of a golfing break in Dublin, Keane and 15 of his teammates took the one-hour flight to his home town for 24 hours of R&R.

It was only after the surprise 1-0 home defeat by Wolves a week later that the furious manager learned of the non-sporting aspect of the break that included several hours in Copper Face Jacks nightclub. By Friday, December 18, and despite the 3-0 midweek defeat of Manchester City, Redknapp was on a war-footing with the majority of his first-team squad and confirmed that they would face an uncomfortable grilling at the club's training ground the following Monday after the trip to Blackburn.

As team captain, Keane's role in the escapade came under additional scrutiny. Reports from White Hart Lane indicated that Keane might be allowed to leave the club during the following month's transfer window with all those involved facing possible fines of two weeks' wages, the maximum allowed under an agreement between the PFA and the Premier League.

Before the Wolves game, Redknapp had spoken of his disapproval of footballers' Christmas parties and said that his players would "never take the liberty" of holding one without his permission. Now the manager had been made to look silly by those same players.

"I am not happy and it will be dealt with, and dealt with severely, on Monday," declared Redknapp about the Dublin trip. "I was shocked when I heard about it. I didn't have a clue they were going and they were told not to do it. They didn't ask my permission and they will have to take the consequences of that, which they will do.

"Other teams let their players have parties. I just didn't want my players having one. I don't see why parties should happen in today's football — they're more trouble than they're worth. Most people can go out, get drunk, fall over and be stupid but as a footballer you can't do that.

"People are always waiting to catch you out by taking your photo or whatever. I don't sympathise with players. Being sensible is part and parcel of being a footballer and you're well paid for it. I'm a football manager — I wouldn't go out and get drunk, falling around and pulling some old slag. I'm not that stupid. Even if you wanted to do it, somebody would catch you out. Having said that, Tiger Woods didn't do too badly!"

For the following afternoon's 2-0 win at Ewood Park, Keane found himself on the bench and although he started against Fulham on December 26 and Hull City on January 16, he was back among the substitutes for his side's final three games of the month against Liverpool, Fulham and Birmingham City with Defoe and Crouch up front.

Tellingly, Keane had not scored since November 7 and had only netted in three of the 20 Premier League matches he had been involved in. The rumour-mill about Keane's future had moved into overdrive, with Celtic favoured to take him on loan. A huge chunk of his £60,000 weekly wages would have to be funded by Spurs, due to the SPL club's strict salary policy that limited players' pay packets to £25,000 per week.

Again, Keane's agitation at not playing weekly football meant that he would almost certainly opt for a move — even to a lower level of the game — if it addressed his hatred of keeping the bench warm. And so it transpired with Celtic and Spurs confirming Keane's temporary move to Parkhead four hours before the midnight transfer deadline on February 1.

More than 2,000 Celtic fans turned up outside the main entrance at Celtic Park to welcome Keane to the club with Keane's role as Ireland captain adding to the attraction for the supporters. For manager Tony Mowbray, it was a last throw of the dice in the title race with champions Rangers holding a 10-point lead at the top of the SPL table.

The Celts had started as favourites to regain the crown they had allowed slip from their grasp the previous spring with a poor run-in and led their city rivals until mid-December when a 2-1 away defeat to Hearts put Rangers on top of the pile. A 1-1 home draw with the Gers on January 3 and the 2-1 Park-head defeat by Hibernian later that month had placed massive pressure on Mowbray and his misfiring side.

In contrast, Rangers had won nine and drawn just two of their 11 league matches to the end of January. In a bid to address his side's goalscoring problems, Mowbray had already added Diomansy Kamara from Fulham on loan and Morten Rasmussen from Brondby during the January transfer window.

A few hours prior to the Keane deal being completed, Australia international Scott McDonald made the £3.5m move to Middlesbrough while another striker, Chris Killen, also made the same Riverside trip earlier in the month.

"The club is massive and as a Celtic fan I did not have to ask much about it," said Keane. "I always wanted to play for Celtic and it works for all parties. I did not want to come here when I was 34 and struggling. I still feel I am in my prime and hope I can help the club."

By Redknapp's hectic player trading standards, January had been quiet with only defender Younes Kaboul brought back from Portsmouth for £5m and no other major midfield or attacking permanent arrivals other than the loan agreement to take Monaco's Eidur Gudjohnsen until the end of the season.

"He is a Celtic man so it's a dream come true for him," said Redknapp. "Robbie needs to play. He's too good a player not to be starting here regularly. He wants to play all the time.

"It's been difficult to guarantee Robbie a starting place at the moment. He's not a happy man when he's not playing regularly. He's a great trainer and a great man about the place."

Celtic chief executive Peter Lawwell confirmed that the club's previous manager Gordon Strachan had sought to sign Keane.

"We've been pretty persistent in the last few windows in terms of keeping in touch with what he was wanting to do," explained Lawwell. "Thankfully, today, we were able to do a deal. We've known for a while that Robbie is a Celtic supporter and he's a great connection with the club and our supporters.

"Up until today, things were not looking very great at all. Things changed this afternoon and we were able to put a deal in place very quickly.

"His situation at Spurs was made, I think, pretty plain to him. He always knew we were very, very keen to get him," added Lawwell, who suggested that Celtic might seek to make the agreement permanent during the summer but refused to comment on how the club was funding the loan contract.

As had been the case at Liverpool, Keane inherited the number seven shirt and, like Anfield, quickly discovered the number's rich heritage having been the jersey of two of Celtic's greatest ever players, Jimmy Johnstone and Henrik Larsson. So no pressure then on the Dubliner.

Asking Keane to single-handedly inspire Celtic to the title was unrealistic, even if Celtic had a game in hand on the Ibrox outfit and 16 league games were left. After all, Celtic had been inconsistent for several months. Mowbray had undertaken the task of transforming Strachan's old squad into a new panel but using 37 players in 38 league games between August and May was extravagant by any measure.

Keane's registration had reached the SFA offices in time for him to make his Celtic debut the following evening at Kilmarnock where victory would cut Rangers' lead to seven points and place a degree of pressure on the champions ahead of the Glasgow derby at Ibrox at the end of the month.

But on a night when Celtic played poorly and Keane missed

three good chances to score, Killie emerged with maximum spoils thanks to Chris Maguire's goal.

Keane opened his Celtic account five days later in the 4-2 Scottish Cup fifth round win at Dunfermline Athletic and then chalked up his first league goal the following weekend in the 4-4 draw with Aberdeen at Pittodrie. Keane then grabbed the only goal of the home game with Dundee United and claimed both in the 2-0 away success at Falkirk.

Significantly, however, Celtic lost 1-0 to Rangers — thanks to Maurice Edu's 90th-minute goal — in a game sandwiched between those victories to restore Rangers' 10-point lead with a game in hand. With 11 games to go, the league title race was effectively over.

However, the Scottish Cup remained a realistic route to glory and Keane's 18-minute second-half hat-trick at Kilmarnock on March 13 put Mowbray's men into the last four. By now, Keane was almost scoring for fun although a truly awful performance on March 24 that saw Celtic lose 4-0 at relegation-threatened St Mirren ended Mowbray's time at the helm.

Reserve team boss Neil Lennon was placed in charge as caretaker manager and Celtic went on to win their last eight league games — including a 2-1 home win against Rangers — although Walter Smith's men had secured the title with three games to spare two weeks previously.

Keane would finish the campaign as the team's leading league scorer with 12 goals, compared to 10 each for Marc-Antoine Fortune, Scott McDonald and Georgios Samaras and seven for Aiden McGeady.

As if to add further insult to Celtic's season, they lost 2-0 to First Division Ross County in the Scottish Cup semi-final with Keane as ineffective as the rest of his teammates.

Keane could reflect with a degree of pride on his 12 goals in 16 league games and four goals in three cup ties, but it could hardly be termed a success given the empty trophy cabinet come the end of May.

Chapter 15
Rocky road to Poland

BETWEEN May 1980 and November 2002, only three men occupied the role as the manager of the senior Ireland international football team.

In the early hours of October 24, 2007, the FAI started the process of seeking its third coach to take charge of the nation's fortunes in just 24 months.

Eoin Hand, Jack Charlton and Mick McCarthy had been at the helm for a combined period of almost 23 years. In contrast, Brian Kerr lasted 31 months while Steve Staunton remained in the post for just 20 months. Staunton's reign was ended by a poor Euro 2008 qualifying campaign, particularly the away defeat to Cyprus, home draw against the same opposition and hugely fortunate 2-1 away win in San Marino.

With Under-21 manager Don Givens asked to take over as caretaker boss for the final qualifier away to Wales in November that ended 2-2, the FAI set to its task of recruiting a new manager. In the weeks that followed, Graeme Souness, David O'Leary, Paul Jewell, Glenn Hoddle, Gerard Houllier, Terry Venables, Sam Allardyce, Roy Hodgson, Kevin Keegan, Liam Brady and Kenny Dalglish were all linked with the vacancy.

On the eve of the game in Cardiff on November 17, FAI chief executive John Delaney led a small delegation of senior association figures to meet the international squad's most experienced stars. Among the players to attend were Shay Given, Kevin Kilbane, Lee Carsley and Robbie Keane.

The FAI correctly believed that it was proper to gauge the feelings of the players, who had undoubtedly given their backing to both Kerr and Staunton following their respective appointments but whose performances had dipped at critical times over the previous five years.

In the wake of the flak it had received for its appointment of Staunton, the FAI hierarchy established a three-man committee of respected English coach Don Howe, Ireland legend Ray Houghton and former national team record goalscorer and Under-21 manager Givens to speak to prospective candidates and then return to the FAI board with their recommendation for the post.

While the ultimate decision would still have to be formally ratified by the board under FAI rules, there was no escaping the fact that this trio would be hugely influential in determining the new man, even if there was a degree of confusion as to what input other people in the FAI could have in the weeks ahead.

Initially, the FAI aimed to have Staunton's successor in place before the World Cup qualifying group fixtures meeting in Sofia on January 16. By this stage Houllier and Venables were the two favourites while Dalglish remained firm in the betting.

However, by the first week of February a new figure emerged to overtake all other contenders on the rails with a late surge. The man was Red Bull Salzburg coach Giovanni Trapattoni, whose CV as a club boss since the mid-seventies was impeccable.

Six Serie A titles with Juventus had been followed by one title each at Inter Milan, Bayern Munich, Benfica and Salzburg while he also boasted victories in all three major European cup competitions. If there was one blot on his career copybook, then it was his disappointing record with Italy at the 2002 World Cup finals and Euro 2004, when the Italians were beaten in the second round by co-hosts South Korea and failed to emerge from their group in Portugal.

From their first meeting with Trapattoni at his then home in Salzburg, the FAI's three wise men of Howe, Houghton and Givens were immediately struck by the Italian's hunger for success, enthusiasm and, noticeably, desire to rectify those fruitless weeks spent in Japan and South Korea and later Portugal. This last factor would be a recurring theme in Trapattoni's press conferences.

By February 12, the FAI and Trapattoni had reached an agreement on a two-year contract worth €2m per annum to the Italian, who would celebrate his 69th birthday a few weeks later on St Patrick's Day.

Liam Brady and Italy's 1982 World Cup-winning star Marco Tardelli would later be appointed as assistant managers, with Alan Kelly named as goalkeeping coach and Fausto Rossi confirmed as fitness guru to complete the coaching set-up that would cost in the region of €3m annually.

Wealthy Irish businessman Denis O'Brien's offer to meet 50 per cent of the cost was accepted by the association and Trap announced that he would take up his new role on May 1 when the Austrian league season ended.

"This is the time in a year when football managers receive offers and this is what has happened to me," stated Trapattoni when the deal was concluded. "In the last two weeks I received offers from various clubs and about 10 days ago representatives of the Football Association of Ireland approached me. I found their offer very interesting. I am very comfortable here in Salzburg. We won the Austrian title last year and we have a great chance to win the title again this year.

"Leaving the title as a farewell present to my Bulls is now my number one aim. But the opportunity to manage the Irish team will give me a lot more time to spend with my family. Yesterday my lawyers in Milan and representatives of the FAI came to an agreement and I accepted their offer."

Givens had again taken charge of senior team affairs for the 1-0 friendly defeat to Brazil at Croke Park on February 6, with Keane wondering if this would be his last game as skipper. However, Keane's fears were allayed on April 8 when Brady and Tardelli unveiled Trapattoni's preliminary squad of 40 players at the FAI's Abbotstown headquarters — the panel being later whittled down to a more manageable number from which he intended to work with during the end-of-season games and training camp.

And Brady soon confirmed that Keane would retain the armband. "I thought I might get that question today so I rang Giovanni. Robbie is captain and will stay as captain — he has a lot of personality and experience," said Brady, who added that the new coach was keen to see Stephen Ireland back on international duty.

"Giovanni has already been in touch with Manchester City boss Sven-Goran Eriksson and had a chat with him about Stephen Ireland," added Brady. "I know Sven would like him to come back because international football can help you as a player.

"I'm very optimistic it will be sorted out — I haven't heard that he doesn't want to be in the squad so we will be speaking to him and he will definitely be in the 28 for the summer unless he says he doesn't want to be. If there are any issues to be resolved, we're happy to speak with him."

Now it was a case of waiting for Trapattoni to work his notice at Salzburg — where he failed to retain the league title — ahead of his first press conference in Dublin's RDS Main Hall on May 13, where he would name his first squad for the friendlies against Serbia and Colombia at the end of that month and the five-day training camp on Portugal's Algarve that would precede them.

The trip to the plush Oceanico resort at Estrela da Luz, close to Praia da Luz, was clashing directly with Keane's stag celebrations in Miami. In contrast to the fate that would await other players who opted to fulfil personal engagements rather than report on international duty, Keane was excused attendance in Portugal, although he had planned the journey to the USA prior to confirmation of details of the camp. He could also point out that he was due back in Dublin three days before the date with the Serbs at Croke Park.

West Brom keeper Dean Kiely — who quit the Ireland squad in the spring of 2003 — accepted Trap's offer to return to the panel, as did Steve Finnan, but Andy O'Brien and Ireland refused to make concrete commitments and were deemed to have opted out. Trap would soon discover that he had inherited his own low-grade version of Saipan in the shape of Ireland.

Training matches against local Algarve opposition was followed by the 1-1 draw with Serbia at Croke Park, with substitute Andy Keogh's last-gasp wonder volley securing a debut draw for Trap. Given Tardelli's celebrations as the ball found the net, it might have been another World Cup-winning strike.

Five nights later at London's Craven Cottage, Keane's early goal gave Ireland a fortuitous 1-0 win against the Colombians, who dominated much of the friendly in a game that significantly saw Glenn Whelan play his second full 90 minutes for Trapattoni. The Italian's team was beginning to take shape.

Keane was again on target in the Oslo mud and rain in mid-August when Ireland drew 1-1 with Norway in the final warm-up match ahead of the 2010 World Cup qualifying campaign.

By now, Keane had celebrated his marriage to Claudine Palmer in June and become a Liverpool player in a £21.3m transfer from Spurs at the end of July. Prior to the encounter in the Ullevaal Stadium, Keane issued a stark analysis of Ireland's failings since their appearance at the 2002 World Cup finals. Beside him, Trapattoni nodded his head as if to indicate that he understood both the translation of Keane's words by Manuela Spinelli and his captain's sentiments.

"I don't think there were any excuses before from the players — it just hasn't been good enough," argued Keane. "It's as simple as that. As a player you must take the responsibility, both individually and as a team."

As Keane struggled to adapt to his new Anfield surroundings, Ireland opened their campaign to reach South Africa with a solid 2-1 win — Kevin Doyle and Whelan on target — over Georgia on September 6 in the German city of Mainz. Georgia and Russia had engaged in a short, bloody war in the latter part of August over the disputed region of South Ossetia that made the hosting of an international sports fixture in the Georgian capital impossible at that time.

The squad then travelled to Podgorica where, the following Wednesday, Ireland claimed a crucial scoreless draw against Montenegro in the baking heat of the early Balkan evening. The results were encouraging but it was the early morning dispute between Trapattoni and midfielder Andy Reid over the terms of the players' curfew after the Georgia victory that had the greater immediate impact.

While Reid was selected for the squad for the following month's 1-0 Croke Park win over Cyprus — Keane again on target — he was dropped for the November Dublin friendly against Poland.

Trap cited the fact that Reid — then playing fairly regularly for Sunderland in the Premier League — was not suited to the type of disciplined midfielder that the Italian wanted, although it was clear that the argument in Wiesbaden was also central to his decision.

Keane was forced by a shoulder injury to withdraw from the 3-2 defeat by Poland — watched by a staggering attendance of 60,000 at Croker with up to 25,000 Polish fans present — and by the time he was back at the home of the Gaelic Athletic Association for the February 11 visit of Georgia, the skipper was again wearing the colours of Spurs.

The Georgians had every right to feel aggrieved by FIFA's earlier diktat on the earlier fixture venue with Ireland, but this time their beef was with Finnish referee Jouni Hyytia. Ireland conceded a defensively dreadful goal after only 45 seconds as right-full Stephen Kelly hesitated to allow Alexander Iashvili to nip in and beat Shay Given.

The well-organised visitors — managed by former Valencia and Inter Milan coach Hector Cuper — set out to frustrate the subdued home side that increased the tempo in the second period yet looked short of attacking ideas. Their prayers would be answered by Hyytia.

Eighteen minutes from full-time, Kevin Doyle's pass to Keane, who was flagged in an offside position by the referee's assistant, touched the shoulder of Ucha Lobjanidze. Hyytia pointed to the spot and Keane converted. A hugely lucky break for the home side, who then netted the winner six minutes later as Aiden McGeady's corner was directed by Keane's shoulder to the net.

"I don't know whether the penalty cost us the three points but for sure, it cost us one point, minimum," declared Cuper. "The penalty penalised us very much. The situation was strange and vague, nobody understood the reason. The players are all very angry. We did not deserve to lose."

The spot-kick had engineered an escape route for the Irish and left them joint top of Group Eight alongside Italy, with the back-to-back games with Bulgaria and the Italians looming at the end of March and beginning of April. Keane was the side's attacking talisman with four goals from as many outings, with the disappointment of his brief Liverpool stay not affecting him in the green shirt.

Ireland were second best for long stretches against Bulgaria in Dublin and the visitors deserved their 1-1 draw despite Richard Dunne's first-half opener. Now, it was imperative not to lose to Italy in Bari four days later if Ireland were to keep their hopes alive of making the top two.

The Italian media had been intrigued by Trapattoni's decision to take on the Ireland job 12 months earlier and now that he was back on home soil for a competitive international, he became the focus of attention for the hosts' journalists, photographers and cameramen. And how Trap lapped it up as he upstaged Azzurri coach Marcello Lippi with whom, judging by the body language between them, he enjoyed a formal yet somewhat cool relationship.

Lippi was already unpopular with local fans less than pleased by his continued decision to ignore Bari's own enfant terrible Antonio Cassano, who was enjoying a productive season in the Sampdoria attack. Thousands of supporters whistled at Lippi when he appeared from the tunnel before the game. In contrast, the majority cheered Trapattoni.

Ireland's luck once again looked good when Giampaolo Pazzini was sent off after only three minutes when catching John O'Shea in the face with his arm. The decision looked slightly harsh but eight minutes later Vincenzo Iaquinta put Italy ahead. Now, Trap deployed all his years of experience by replacing Andy Keogh with the towering Caleb Folan in the 22nd minute with Kevin Doyle switching to Keogh's right-wing place.

As the game ebbed and flowed and Folan's bulk caused Italy real problems, Ireland began to enjoy periods of possession but looked short of that final piece of inspiration in the Italian penalty area. But the introduction of Darron Gibson for Keith Andrews in the 55th minute and Noel Hunt's replacement of Kevin Doyle seven minutes later helped the Irish step up another gear.

And three minutes from the end, Given's long clearance floated from well outside his area was flicked on by Folan with Keane applying a close-range finish just before Noel Hunt could make contact with his left boot. Keane and Hunt both raced away to claim the credit for earning Ireland a point and it took several television replays to confirm that the skipper was the one to be awarded the goal.

Seconds later, Keane squandered a glorious opportunity to claim all three points when he stabbed the ball wide from close range. The Irish thoroughly deserved their point but an away victory would have been unfair on Lippi's men.

Two weeks before the end of the league season, Keane and Claudine were celebrating the birth of their son Robert Ronan junior on May 10 at Dublin's Holles Street Hospital.

"We are delighted with the arrival of Robert Ronan Keane, he weighed in at a healthy 7lb 5oz," said Claudine. "We are all thrilled with Robbie junior who has been named after his father and my brother Ronan, who is his godfather. I was fortunate enough to have had a natural, healthy delivery and both myself and my family would like to thank Dr Peter Boylan and the staff at Holles Street Hospital, Dublin, for their encouragement and support throughout."

Keane was present for the delivery of his son having dashed back to Dublin the previous evening from Liverpool following the 0-0 league draw with Everton. To ensure Keane did not run the risk of picking up an injury, he would sit out the

1-1 friendly draw with Nigeria at Craven Cottage on May 29 ahead of the away qualifier against Bulgaria in Sofia on June 6.

Sean St Ledger's debut in London so impressed Trapattoni that he was handed his first competitive start against the Bulgarians as Richard Dunne's partner, allowing O'Shea to switch to right-full. The Irish then served up a classy opening half hour in Sofia with Dunne heading them into an early lead from Stephen Hunt's corner.

But prior to the interval, the Bulgarians exploited a slight gap between St Ledger and Kevin Kilbane to level through Dimitar Telkiyski. The visitors were well worth their point to leave them well-placed to at least claim the runners-up spot and a play-off in November.

The FAI's decision — based chiefly on the massive cost of hiring Croke Park — to decamp to Limerick's Thomond Park for August and September friendlies with Australia and South Africa yielded a 3-0 defeat and 1-0 victory, but two hugely disappointing official attendances of 19,428 and 11,300 witnessed the first ever senior football internationals staged on Shannonside.

Critically, however, Trapattoni's side defeated Cyprus 2-1 in Nicosia in the qualifier played between those games, with Keane heading the 83rd-minute winner from Damien Duff's perfect cross. Kevin Doyle had put the Irish ahead only for Marios Elia to level on the half-hour mark in a game that saw the home side denied at least one strong penalty claim.

The odds were once more favouring the Boys in Green. Now, Ireland were closing in on second place in the group and they could even finish top if they defeated Italy and Montenegro at home in their final two matches on October 10 and 14 and the Italians failed to beat Cyprus in Parma on the second of those dates.

And for 120 glorious seconds at Croke Park on Saturday, October 10 that dream grew legs in the final minutes of the game. Earlier in the evening, Bulgaria's 4-1 drubbing by Cyprus guaranteed Ireland second place and the home fans in the 70,640 attendance went into mental orbit when Whelan fired home a wonderful opening goal.

In a highly entertaining encounter, Mauro Camoranesi levelled by half time only for St Ledger to head what appeared to be an 87th-minute winner. Amid the tumultuous uproar in the stands and behind Shay Given's goal on the seated Hill 16, the Ireland defence switched off mentally to allow Alberto Gilardino to plunder a 90th-minute equaliser and so secure Lippi's men their tickets to South Africa.

A deathly silence descended on the stadium with delirium giving way to despondency as it became clear that the following Wednesday's game at home to Montenegro — that finished scoreless — was now completely meaningless. The good fortune that had benignly assisted the Irish earlier in the group stage was now evaporating rapidly.

In late August, FIFA had decided that the draw for the four play-off ties would be dictated by its rankings, pushing Ireland into the non-seeded section instead of the games being determined by an open unseeded draw.

At the time of that decision, it was noted that both France and Germany's ambitions of automatically qualifying for South Africa were far from certain. Could football's greatest show on earth afford to lose one or two of these powerful nations? The Germans subsequently comfortably nailed down their place in the finals with a strong finish to their group, but the French ended up second and so entered the play-off draw on October 19 as one of the seeded sides along with Portugal, Russia and Greece.

The unseeded pot included Ireland, Ukraine, Bosnia-Herzegovina and Slovenia. Unless they were matched with Greece, Ireland were guaranteed a tough two-legged affair on November 14 and 18 and when the draw was made in Zurich, they found themselves pitted against Raymond Domenech's France. The 1998 World Cup winners and 2006 runners-up would enjoy home advantage for the second leg.

At a heaving Croke Park in front of 74,103 fans, Nicolas

Anelka's goal — that owed much to the unfortunate deflection it took off St Ledger's boot — gave France a victory that they just about deserved on a night when Les Bleus played in patches but the home side fell some way short of their best.

It was going to require a superhuman collective effort in Stade de France four days later to prevent France from going to the finals. Against the odds, the views of the vast majority of pundits and the evidence of the opening 90 minutes in Dublin, Ireland dug out one of their best ever performances away from home.

Resolute defending, sweet passing in midfield and a real edge to the attack of Keane and Doyle — suitably aided by wingers Duff and Liam Lawrence — saw the visitors take a grip of the game early on. And in the 33rd minute a sweeping move down the left flank involving the rare sight of the overlapping Kilbane and Duff, saw the latter pull the ball back from the endline for Keane to majestically sweep home past Hugo Lloris for the goal that levelled the tie.

Now the French were beginning to sweat and their confident swagger of Dublin disappeared. O'Shea and Duff almost grabbed a second goal before Keane did beat Lloris in the dying minutes only to run out of space and concede a goal kick.

The game now entered extra-time, when one of sport's most brazen instances of cheating on the big occasion became a global talking point.

A minute before the interval of extra-time, Bacary Sagna's free kick was allowed to travel deep inside the Ireland penalty area where Thierry Henry — who had evaded the attentions of substitute Paul McShane at the far post — controlled the ball with his left arm not once but twice before squaring it across the goalmouth past Given for William Gallas to tap into an empty net.

As the ball crossed the line, Given was already on his feet to lead the Irish protests to Swedish referee Martin Hansson. The bemused official — who was unable to spot the blatant cheating by Henry — was persuaded to consult with his assistant

Stefan Wittberg, but he too had noticed no infringement.

Ireland were clearly winded by the incident and they failed to mount an assault on the French rearguard capable of claiming the goal that would have sent them through on the away goals rule.

At the end of the game, Henry sickeningly walked from one Irish player to another to offer his condolences. The image of the former Arsenal star embracing Dunne — who somehow retained his composure — is an image that will live long in the memories of Irish fans.

By the following day, the FAI — spearheaded by a statement by Keane — was asking the French Football Federation to agree to a one-off replay of the tie. FAI officers and senior officials also implored FIFA to order another game. The chances of either body agreeing to such a move were virtually non-existent and when Trapattoni flew home to Italy less than 24 hours later it signalled his belief that the matter was now closed.

A subsequent prickly meeting between FAI personnel and senior FIFA bosses, including president Sepp Blatter, had seen the possibility raised of Ireland becoming an additional side — team 33 — at the finals in South Africa.

The FAI denied that they had sought this but Blatter stated it at a press conference a few days later in Cape Town. Henry's acceptance that he did handle the ball might have served his own purposes but his words rang hollow for the players, management, FAI and Irish fans.

Those who believe in good and bad karma could only look on with glee the following summer when the French campaign erupted into open warfare between players, management and the federation. Keane could only wonder if he would ever again grace a major finals, although his goal in Paris brought his total in the green jersey to an impressive 41 in 96 games. At the age of 29, it was now clear that he would break the 50-goal barrier unless a major injury intervened.

Given preceded Keane in the Ireland senior set-up by two years, but their international careers have become intertwined since Keane made his first appearance under Mick McCarthy against the Czech Republic in March, 1998 in the city of Olomouc.

When the Czechs earned a 1-1 friendly draw in the Aviva Stadium on February 29, 2012, Given was winning his 121st Ireland cap while Keane was collecting his 115th, extending their records as the nation's most feted goalkeeper and outfield player respectively.

"Robbie's had an amazing career and the amount of goals he has scored over his career for a small country like ourselves is phenomenal," says Given. "To be up among the great scorers of all time is amazing. Sometimes he does not get the credit he deserves.

"Robbie's a clever player and is always that way in and around the box. His movement is excellent and when he gets into one-versus-one situations he's deadly. He's a thinker, looks at the keeper and while other forwards panic, once Robbie gets into that position he has great composure.

"When he gets into the nitty-gritty of scoring goals he's excellent and that's why he's got so many. He uses his head to assess a situation and passes the ball into corners. Looking at his goals, you can see that they have been all types but one thing he always has is loads of composure and he knows how to weigh up his options in a split second."

There's another aspect to Keane's play that Given does not think receives enough exposure.

"Robbie is just hungry to win and whatever it takes for the team to win like dropping into midfield to get the ball back, then that's what he will do.

"He hates losing, like we all do, and Robbie is a prime example of that. And when there is a five-a-side game going on, he even hates losing in training. That rubs off on the players around him."

Gary Kelly played alongside Keane for Ireland for five years and in the Leeds United shirt for 18 months. He has watched as his friend's thirst for goals shows no sign of abating.

"There is not an Ireland game that he plays in that you don't think he could fail to score in," says Kelly.

"The scoring record he holds will keep on getting better and it will continue that way until he loses the appetite and I don't see that happening.

"Robbie can make scoring look so easy and some of his goals have been simply brilliant. And he never looks like missing penalties. If he gets a half-chance, you know that he can put it away. And now the way he drops into midfield, he has almost created his own new role. He's an out-and-out centre-forward but he drops back into midfield.

"He causes havoc as he can play out on the left, out on the right or down the middle, while he also tracks back. We're blessed to have him. At the moment we have a good number of strikers but Robbie is still the one who has that happy knack of putting the ball in the net."

The emotions of November 2009's events in Paris were still raw when, on February 22, 2010, Trapattoni named his squad for the prestige friendly with Brazil at the Emirates Stadium in London on March 2.

The Italian took the opportunity to give first senior call-ups to Wigan Athletic midfielder James McCarthy, Portsmouth's versatile defender Marc Wilson and Manchester City left-back Greg Cunningham. Ireland lost 2-0 to a Brazil side containing Robinho, Kaka, Lucio, Maicon, Adriano, Ramires and Michel Bastos and used substitutes Daniel Alves and Luisao.

McCarthy looked calm and comfortable on the ball during his 21 minutes on the pitch although Cunningham and Wilson did not feature. Both would rectify that in May during the RDS friendlies with World Cup-bound Paraguay and Algeria that yielded 2-1 and 3-0 wins respectively, with Keane scoring twice against the North Africans.

However, a near fatal injury suffered by Shane Duffy in the training match against the Ireland amateur team at Malahide United's Gannon Park four days before the Paraguay encounter overshadowed the get-together. In an accidental clash with

Ireland amateur keeper Adrian Walsh, the blood supply to Duffy's liver was cut off and it required emergency surgery at Dublin's Mater Private Hospital by specialist Gerry McEntee, the former Meath Gaelic football star, to prevent a tragedy to the 18 year-old.

Thankfully, the Derryman made a full recovery. Cynics suggested that Keane's decision to play in both RDS matches was simply to ensure he would chalk up his century of senior caps against Argentina in the first ever international football match at the new 50,000 all-seater Aviva Stadium on August 11.

However, the team captain could point to a strong previous record on turning up for such games as evidenced by the fact that he was now about to reach the milestone that only Given (now on 103 appearances) and Steve Staunton (who retired on 102 caps) had conquered.

"I still have that buzz and enthusiasm for the game and I always want to play for my country," declared a proud Keane on the eve of the match where he would be accompanied by 15 month-old son Robert as mascot. "You've all known for many years, I've never pulled out of squads for any reason. But I love playing for my country, I love coming back, and I don't think that will ever change.

"It's hard to believe, though, it'll be my 100th cap. For years I didn't think about how many I might win. I know I'm very fortunate to have reached 100 caps but hopefully there will be a few more to come after. So I'm really looking forward to the occasion, particularly as my little lad is going to be the mascot.

"I've played a lot of games now as captain and I feel I've grown into the role. I really enjoy it. As for me, I feel great. As you get older you look after yourself even more, so I certainly feel really good. I'm looking forward to the new season as it's probably the best I've felt for a while."

Starting the new season with 43 international goals, there was also the possibility that he could smash through the totals achieved by legendary English forwards Bobby Charlton (49), Gary Lineker (48) and Jimmy Greaves (44) having long since eclipsed the 30-goal mark of Scotland's Denis Law and Kenny Dalglish and the 28 tallied by Wales' Ian Rush.

"Every Irish fan keeps mentioning that record to me and of course it would great to beat it. I certainly feel I've a few more goals and caps left in me so it would be a great achievement.

"But more than that I want to help us qualify for the European Championship. If you look at the games we've been involved in, we've come very close on occasion but we've made mistakes or we just didn't have that bit of luck we needed.

"I certainly feel we should have been involved in more tournaments than we have recently."

However, the historic night at Lansdowne Road would have to take place without Trapattoni, who had been brought to hospital in the early hours of the previous day suffering from a stomach illness and underwent minor surgery on the day of the game.

Angel di Maria, offside when he received the ball, won the game for Argentina with a subtle first-half lob over Given.

After making a full recovery from his ailment, Trapattoni returned to Italy within a few days and began to prepare for the real business of seeking to qualify for the Euro 2012 finals in Poland and Ukraine.

Ireland were in a qualifying section containing Russia, Slovakia, Macedonia, Armenia and Andorra. On the first Friday of September, a hugely disciplined Ireland display in Yerevan earned Trap's men a 1-0 win in their opening fixture.

Substitute Keith Fahey marked his competitive debut with the priceless 77th-minute strike. Four days later, Kilbane, Keane and Doyle were all on target to secure a 3-1 home win against Andorra. Next up was the first of the pivotal double-headers against Russia in Dublin and away to the Slovaks in Zilina.

Keane was experiencing by far his most demoralising spell at Tottenham, where the arrival of Rafael van der Vaart from Real Madrid for £8m in late August allowed Harry Redknapp to make the defining alteration to his midfield and attack. No longer would he seek to play with two out-and-out strikers. Instead, van der Vaart would operate just behind Peter Crouch, Jermain Defoe, Roman Pavlyuchenko or Keane. By the time the Russians arrived in Dublin for the October 8 clash, Keane had started only one league match — the 3-1 win at Wolves — and been used as a substitute in three more without finding the net.

But it was not just Keane who looked out of sorts as Ireland were outplayed by the fluid Russians as the visitors raced into a 3-0 lead. Trap's policy of sticking with his 4-4-2 system was brilliantly exploited by Dick Advocaat's side who strolled through the Irish midfield almost with ease.

The introduction of Shane Long for Lawrence instigated a recovery in the final quarter and the Tipperary man's goal and Keane's successful spot-kick almost saw Ireland claim an undeserved draw.

Indeed, Keane might have been awarded a second penalty just before full-time when he appeared to be fouled but Dutch referee Kevin Blom was not interested. Now the hard work in Armenia had been undone and there was the daunting task of travelling to Slovakia who had already shocked Russia 1-0 in Moscow.

However, the Slovaks were subdued on their own patch in Zilina and St Ledger's close-range finish, after Fahey's free-kick dropped to him, gave the visitors the lead. But by half-time, Slovakia had levelled and they held out for a draw when Keane chalked up a rare miss from the penalty spot after McGeady was fouled.

Long and Doyle were handed the chance to start in the following month's 2-1 friendly home defeat by Norway as Keane cried off with an ankle injury. The problem only compounded Keane's woes, as his opportunities at White Hart Lane were still few and far between. His goal off the bench in the 4-1 League Cup third round extra-time defeat by Arsenal at White Hart Lane only added to his frustrations.

Even in the Champions League group stage Keane found

himself a peripheral figure, failing to start any of the six group stage games and only used as a substitute in three. He was chosen by Redknapp to play with Van der Vaart for the 2-0 away defeat at Manchester United on October 30 in what would prove to be his last ever start for Spurs.

Keane's last two appearances for the club he had served with such distinction since 2002 would be as a substitute against Chelsea in December and Everton in January prior to his loan move to West Ham.

The short hop from north London to the east end should have offered Keane a new lease of life, even if he was switching from a club chasing a place in the top four and further European Cup glory to one rooted to the bottom of the table. Hammers boss Avram Grant reckoned Keane's goals could be vital in the remaining three months of the season and when the Dubliner cracked home the second in the 3-1 win away to Blackpool on February 2 on his debut, it appeared that the former Israel coach could be proved correct.

But Keane picked up a slight calf problem that night at Bloomfield Road and hobbled off during the 1-0 home defeat by Birmingham City four days later. This setback ruled Keane out of the opening 3-0 Carling Nations Cup win over Wales 48 hours later and he didn't return to action for The Hammers until April 2, when he was used from the bench in the 4-2 home defeat to Manchester United.

Fortunately for Ireland, he had been cleared by his club to play for his country in the previous week's Euro qualifier against Macedonia in Dublin when McGeady's early goal was followed up by Keane's 21st-minute strike to earn Trap's side a nervous 2-1 victory against an enterprising away team.

Having clocked up his 46th Ireland goal, he was excused playing against Uruguay in the friendly that followed a few days later. Back at Upton Park, the side was in a tailspin of despair and although Keane would be involved in seven of the team's last eight games — only starting three — they slumped to a horrendous finale. Seven defeats and one draw plunged the club into the Championship, seven points from safety and six behind fellow drop zone residents, Blackpool and Birmingham.

Two goals was scarcely a haul for Keane to be shouting about but the team's failure to stay up was rooted in long-term problems rather than recent events. Had West Ham survived, Keane might have made his role at the Boleyn Ground permanent. Instead, he was returning to an uncertain future at Spurs.

Again, Keane brushed off any cobwebs from his league form when linking up with the Ireland squad prior to the four end-of-season matches that included the key away qualifier with Macedonia, the concluding Carling Cup games against Northern Ireland and Scotland and the attractive friendly date with Italy in the Belgian city of Liege.

Results on the pitch proved to be hugely significant and the skipper's vocal intervention off it illustrated a new-found maturity in that role.

The Ireland squad assembled in Dublin on Sunday and Monday, May 22 and 23, prior to the Carling Nations Cup against Northern Ireland on the Tuesday night at the Aviva Stadium.

When Trapattoni addressed the media at lunchtime on Monday, he was seething with anger over the absence of a number of players and what he believed was the lack of respect some of this group had shown to the rest of the squad by failing to contact him.

In Trap's sights was Anthony Stokes, whose decision to withdraw due to tiredness infuriated the Ireland manager, while Darron Gibson's text message to inform him of a groin problem prompted laughter at the press conference.

But the coach's greatest ire was directed at Wigan Athletic's James McCarthy and Marc Wilson of Stoke City, especially as he named Wilson in his side for the Northern Ireland game but only discovered on the day of the match that the defender would not be reporting due to injury.

Trap let it be known that he was very unhappy about the lack of communication from these players and vowed to ensure it never happened again.

On the following Friday ahead of the Scotland game, Keane vented his own anger at those who had not turned up or whose reasons suggested a less than committed attitude.

"It frustrates everybody but what can you do about it?" stated Keane.

"I don't know the answer. I would never do it but if people don't want to play for Ireland, don't declare yourself to play for Ireland. It's simple. I have never once pulled out of a squad for any reason apart from being injured.

"I am a proud Irishman. As a kid growing up it was always a dream to play for my country. I still have that same hunger and enthusiasm that I had when I first had the opportunity. That will never change for me."

The verbal attack on colleagues was by far Keane's most enlightening press conference since taking over as captain. Keane privately worried subsequently if he had been too harsh with his words but the look on Trap's face suggested he had nothing to fear from that quarter.

The 5-0 rout of a very poor Northern Ireland side at the Aviva on May 24, with Keane scoring twice, meant that Ireland needed only a draw in the following Sunday's showdown with the Scots to lift the trophy.

Keane was now on 48 international goals and he added number 49 with a powerful low left-foot shot that deceived Allan McGregor in the Tartan goal for the winner. At the final whistle, Keane was presented with the trophy — Ireland's first such success since Jack Charlton's side claimed the Iceland Triangular Tournament against the hosts and Czechoslovakia in 1986.

The sceptics poured scorn on the success but Trapattoni immediately sought to harness the added confidence that the two wins and the flavour of success had added to the mix.

Nobody was under any misapprehension about the following Saturday's task in Skopje, where Mick McCarthy's side had slumped to a 3-2 defeat in 1997 and then conceded an injury-time goal in a 1-1 draw in 1999 that prevented automatic qualification for Euro 2000. Throw in Jason McAteer's Kung Fu kick and red card in 1997 and it's clear that the southern Balkans were a place of grim memories for the Irish.

Naturally, there was plenty of pre-match talk of those events from the late nineties, even though it was only Given (reserve keeper on both occasions), Keane (played in the second encounter), goalkeeping coach Alan Kelly (started both games) and Kevin Kilbane (unused substitute in 1999) who remained in the current set-up.

Keane's priority, as outlined at the pre-match press conference, was to ensure Ireland claimed the three points. Hitting the 50-goal mark and so edging past Bobby Charlton's international goal record for these islands was very much an afterthought. But the skipper need not have worried about letting personal ambition stymie the greater team requirements. By half time, Keane had scored twice — the first with a deflected shot and the second a neat finish following a dreadful defensive error.

Goals 50 and 51 left Ireland in a strong position ahead of the decisive finale to Group B that would resume with the home date against Slovakia on September 2 and trip to Moscow four days later. Before that, a much-changed Ireland team — with Keane absent — defeated the Italians 2-0 with goals by Keith Andrews and Simon Cox. In terms of personal pride, the win meant so much to Trapattoni and Tardelli but it also emphasised that the manager's system worked and he now had strength in depth.

In August, Keane was back as captain for the turgid scoreless friendly with Croatia in Dublin before an official attendance of 20,149. On the eve of the following month's clash with Slovakia, Trap announced that Shane Long would replace Doyle in attack but on the morning of the match at the Aviva, Long reported a calf complaint that ruled him out and prompted the recall of Doyle.

Keane's 110th senior cap was marked by a poor home display

when the visitors' passing style once more created plenty of midfield headaches for the hosts in the 0-0 draw.

Now, Ireland needed to avoid defeat in the Luzhniki Stadium in Moscow to keep their bid for a top-two finish on course. In an unchanged Ireland side, Keane spent large tracts of the match dropping into midfield to help out his struggling central pairing of Andrews and Whelan. If the match in Paris two years earlier had been a victory for Irish style, then these scoreless 90 minutes in Moscow represented a triumph for gritty determination.

The Irish somehow kept the Russians at bay, most noticeably with Dunne's goal-line block from Igor Semshov and Given's late save from Konstantin Zyryanov. Dunne's commitment to the cause — that included him receiving stitches for a face injury when he careered on to the running track — prompted Paul McGrath to describe his performance as the best ever by an Ireland centre-half. As ever, the Tallaght man deflected the praise in his modest manner.

As the Irish party waited to board their flight back to Dublin, news came through from Zilina that the Slovaks had been dismantled 4-0 by Armenia, leaving Slovakia out of the qualifying race. However, Armenia now moved up to third in the table, one point behind Ireland and three points behind Russia with two games to play.

Ireland would take on Andorra away on October 7 with Armenia travelling to Dublin four days later. One player not at the departure gate for Dublin on that remarkable night in Moscow was Keane, who was flying in the opposite direction after joining Los Angeles Galaxy on the August 31 deadline from Spurs in a £3.5m transfer. It was a move that only served to enforce the Keanes' image as Ireland's answer to Posh and Becks.

The first indications that the wealthy Californian club — managed by ex-USA coach Bruce Arena — were set to snap up Keane came from a report on the ESPN website by former Reading, Newcastle United, Portsmouth and West Ham goalkeeper Shaka Hislop on the evening of Friday, August 12.

Clarifying either the club or Keane's intentions were difficult given the eight-hour time difference between London and Dublin and the west coast of the United States. Arena would only confirm that "we are always looking to improve our squad and have contacted or been contacted by a host of players during the current transfer window. As soon as we have something confirmed in regards to any potential player acquisitions, we will be sure to alert everyone."

With the MLS transfer window closing on Sunday evening and Galaxy needing to offload one of their three 'designated' players to sign Keane, the club furiously set about selling Colombia's former Aston Villa forward Juan Pablo Angel, who eventually moved to Chivas USA. The path was now clear for Keane to travel the 5,437 miles to his new home and the deal was confirmed by Monday as he joined Beckham and Landon Donovan as their third designated player.

"I am delighted to be joining the LA Galaxy," gushed Keane, who along with Claudine, was welcomed by hundreds of Galaxy fans on his arrival at the city's international airport.

"I have always wanted to come and play in the MLS so it's the perfect combination for me and a dream come true. My family and I have already been made to feel very welcome in telephone calls from Tim Leiweke and Bruce Arena at the club.

"Also, when David Beckham came and trained at Spurs recently he couldn't speak highly enough about the Galaxy, their fans and the league in general, so I can't wait to get started."

Arena gave his verdict on his high-profile signing: "Robbie Keane will be a great addition to our club. I have followed his career and have always respected his ability as a competitor and a goalscorer.

"I believe that he brings qualities in and around the penalty area that we have been lacking. Hopefully, he will be another piece of the puzzle in our quest for the Supporters' Shield and an MLS Cup championship as well the CONCACAF Champions League."

A torrential storm on the east coast of the USA forced the postponement of Galaxy's crucial game at the end of August away to New York Red Bulls where Keane would have faced the home side's Thierry Henry. That chance for revenge would have to wait for another day.

Life at the Home Depot Center Stadium was something of a drop in football status for Keane, now aged 31, but he, Claudine and son Robert quickly adapted to their new surroundings, soaking up the sun and enjoying a lifestyle of shades and shorts.

The only concern from an Ireland viewpoint was the inherent risk of Keane suffering from jetlag prior to games. He arrived in Barcelona prior to the match in Andorra via Madrid and showed no ill-effects from his journey to lead the Ireland attack with Doyle.

The Wolves forward opened the scoring in the seventh minute from close range, with McGeady's drive that took a massive deflection off Ildefons Lima securing the points in the 20th minute.

With Russia winning in Zilina, it meant Advocaat's men only required a win over Andorra in their final match to top the group. That disappointment for Ireland was tempered by the fact that a draw at home to Armenia in Dublin 72 hours later would be enough to claim the play-off.

Keane, however, would not feature against Armenia as an adductor muscle injury sustained in the Pyrenees flared up the following day to eventually rule him out of the Armenia game.

In the wake of the victory in Andorra, Trapattoni voiced a rare criticism of his captain when it emerged that Keane had played on through the entire match with the problem despite noticing it early on. Initial reports confirmed that the injury now left him doubtful for the following month's play-offs.

"Sure, I said this to him after the game," stated Trapattoni when asked if he had spoken to Keane about the matter.

"If it was a knock I am not afraid but he made it worse. I said to him that he should have said about the injury immediately and maybe should have gone off. It should be so immediately with muscular problems. Never put into question the muscular problems.

"He was a doubt before the game with it. You can never play 90 minutes with this injury. But sometimes it's just the eagerness, the willingness to play."

Keane departed for Los Angeles where Galaxy's medical crew started work on the condition.

"We'll know more in 10 days, I've got to get another scan and hopefully it settles down and isn't as bad as it was when I had the first scan done immediately after the game, when there was a lot of bleeding," explained Keane. "I'll go back to the club and see. It's a four-to-six week injury and it will be touch and go."

However, Keane denied that a two and a half hour coach journey from Andorra to Barcelona and then a flight of a similar duration back to Dublin in the middle of the night had affected the injury.

"That's not true - it was just one of those things. I actually did it during Kevin's goal. The adrenaline gets you through but straight after the game, I knew that it was a tear.

"Of course, I would take injections but this is different. It's a muscle injury and not just pain. It's a grade-two tear, grade three is the worst. It's disappointing and I'll do my best to get back. The medical facilities are very, very good in LA and hopefully the doctors over there will get me back."

A tense but optimistic home following arrived at The Aviva in expectant mood. And by half time, it was clear that the football gods – absent in Paris – were now hovering above the Aviva Stadium. For after 26 minutes, Armenia keeper Roman Berezovsky was sent off by Spanish referee Eduardo Gonzalez for handling Cox's lob outside his penalty area.

And it was easy to sympathise with the Armenians for Cox had controlled the ball with his right arm, there was some doubt as to whether Berezovsky struck the ball with his arm while it could be also argued that he had not denied Cox a clear goal scoring opportunity.

Ireland, as they had previously found against Russia and Slovakia in Dublin, struggled to assert themselves against the neat, passing game preferred by Armenia and even after the harsh dismissal of Berezovsky, they only took the lead through Valeri Aleksanyan's bizarre 42nd minute own goal when the right full turned Duff's low cross into his own net under no pressure.

When Dunne chested home McGeady's cross for the second goal, the party started in the stands but a quick response from Henrikh Mkhitaryan made the home fans sweat until the final whistle. The country was heading for its seventh ever tournament play-off with only one previous success to take succour from.

With Doyle ruled out of the first leg through suspension, it was crucial to have Keane available although the draw that twinned Ireland with Estonia went a long way to suggesting that Ireland would be back at a major finals in the summer of 2012. The Estonians, appearing at this stage of a qualifying campaign for the first time, were the easiest potential opponents with Turkey, Montenegro and Bosnia-Herzegovina the other unseeded nations.

Ireland had secured a top seeding for the play-off draw due to a combination of their own efforts and the results from other qualifiers that formed UEFA's up to date coefficient rankings, so avoiding Portugal, Croatia and Czech Republic.

Thanks to intense work by the medical staff at Galaxy, Keane linked up with the Ireland sqaud in Dublin prior to their departure to Tallinn for the first leg on November 11. With Shane Long ruled out of both games with a chipped tibia, Trapattoni handed Jon Walters his first ever competitive start beside Keane with Cox on the bench.

On a poor surface, Ireland took time to settle but once Keith Andrews headed the opening goal in the 12th minute it was hard to see anything but an away win. When Andrei Stepanov was sent off in the 35th minute for a foul on Keane the outcome was surely nailed on.

Walters added Ireland's second with his first goal for his country with Keane the unselfish provider with a deft chipped cross. The skipper claimed the third with his 52nd international goal in the 71st minute when he pounced on the rebound from an Andrews' free-kick. Keane was leading the home rearguard a merry dance and Raio Piiroja became the second Estonian to be red-carded as he handled the ball to deny Keane a clear run on goal. Two minutes from the end, a foul on substitute Stephen Hunt gave Keane the chance to make it 4-0 from the penalty spot. The goals meant that he had now scored for Ireland in 14 consecutive seasons.

"The cat is in the sack," mused Trapattoni after the game, "but the sack is not closed, there are still 90 minutes to go and the cat is still dangerous, it's a wild cat."

For all of the Italian's niceties to Estonia, the tie was dead and Ireland would be back at the European Championship finals for the first time in 24 years.

A rare full house of 51,151 fans celebrated with the players, management, backroom staff and FAI in Dublin on the following Tuesday night. Konstantin Vassilijev cancelled out Stephen Ward's first-half opener with a long-range effort that left Given slightly red-faced. But that one small blemish could not stop the party that lasted long into the night and early morning across a country that badly needed a source of joy in an era of austerity and emigration.

"We were ever so unlucky not to reach the last World Cup and I think we have progressed since then and we deserve to be in the Euro 2012 finals," said Keane. "You need a bit of luck in football and we have had that along the way but full credit to the lads, we fully deserve to be there.

"We will go there with a lot of confidence and if you look at the history of Irish teams at major finals, we have always been a hard team to beat and always upset a few people. So I am sure we can go over there and make an impact. Now that I am older than 10 years ago, you appreciate it more as there probably won't be too many more."

Reflecting on his own personal tally of seven goals in the campaign, Keane was thrilled with his input.

"I scored seven in the last qualifiers and I have scored seven in this one and all you can do is to try and match your previous number of goals."

Trapattoni had withdrawn Keane on the hour mark with a view to Galaxy's MLS Cup final against Houston Dynamos the following Sunday in Los Angeles, but also to allow the Irish fans pay their own loud tribute to the skipper.

Back in California the next weekend, Keane and Beckham set up Donovan's winning goal to see LA Galaxy crowned the kings of American football. This was only Keane's second club success so it meant much to him although by January 12, 2012 he was back in English football after signing a six-week loan agreement with Aston Villa.

Keane insisted the move — the notion of which he had dismissed just two months earlier — was not a precursor for a swift summer return to the Premier League. But Villa boss Alex McLeish was soon seeking avenues to make Keane's switch permanent before the January 31 transfer window deadline, as the lively forward stunned his old club Wolves with two outstanding goals at Molineux to earn Villa a 3-2 league victory.

Villa's form was beginning to concern McLeish and Keane found himself with little supply of the ball during his other six games, although he did score in the 2-1 defeat at Newcastle United on February 5. Keane was present at Villa Park a week later when his great friend Richard Dunne sustained a horrendous broken collarbone in the 1-0 league defeat by Manchester City.

Dunne's absence until the end of April and Keane's departure for Los Angeles following the scoreless draw at Wigan on February 25 combined to deepen the club's woes.

En-route to the Galaxy, Keane started against the Czech Republic at The Aviva Stadium on February 29, captaining his country for the 50th time but not adding to his 53 senior international goals. Keane made way for Walters 19 minutes from full-time but the biggest roar of the night was reserved for James McClean's entrance in the 79th minute for McGeady.

Fourteen years earlier Keane's cheeky, loveable attitude on the pitch had wowed the Irish football public in a friendly against Argentina. McClean did not have as much time to impress those present but many in the crowd believed they were witnessing the first small steps of what should be a long and successful career in the green jersey.

A few weeks short of his 32nd birthday, Keane has indicated that he will continue to play for his country, with the 2014 World Cup qualifying campaign beginning in September 2012 with the trek to Kazakhstan.

"I am in no doubt that Robbie can continue to play on for Ireland," believes Given. "He showed and proved to lots of people while at Aston Villa — including himself — that he still has got lots of football in him.

"Robbie is similar to myself that he grew up playing football. It's something that we would be lost without. He's the same and I have always said that you are a long time retired so he has plenty more years left in him."

While Keane's rapturous reception from the fans as he walked from the pitch during the 1-1 draw with Estonia reflected his status in the eyes of the majority of Ireland supporters, there remains a rump who have failed to warm to the striker and his outstanding achievements for Ireland. It's a stance that amazes most people in the game.

"I don't understand why certain fans get on his back, I have no idea whatsoever," says Jason McAteer. "But football is like that, it's a fickle industry. I have always believed that Robbie gives his all.

"When Kevin Doyle came into the team I thought he was lazy and that Robbie was doing his running. Doyle has gradually come on and realised that he has got to work harder. He has learned off Robbie and he works tremendously hard now and takes a bit of the load off Robbie.

"Robbie's got a great attitude off the pitch, I have never seen him get into trouble or make the front pages of the papers. He's a real professional and I don't know why these people want to have a go at him. Sometimes you become a better player when you are not playing because people suddenly realise that you are alright and that 'we could do with him and his goals now'," adds McAteer, who has one reservation about Keane's future.

"I think he's got a part to play in the next World Cup campaign. Some players play through a campaign and then decide 'enough is enough'. If I was the manager I might not see Robbie as the number one striker for the 2014 qualifiers, but I would certainly have him around the place. There is a time and a place for Robbie Keane to come on.

"I just think the way that football is going and with the way he plays his game, I'm not sure if he has another campaign in him. He does a lot of running.

"But as I say, he may only convince the doubters when he finally hangs up his boots. Then they might look back at all those goals he scored and admit they were wrong."

Ten years ago, the world got its first prolonged look at Robbie Keane as he scored three crucial goals while Ireland progressed to the last 16 of the World Cup finals.

Few would bet against the man from Tallaght repeating that feat when Giovanni Trapattoni's side seeks to carve its own history in Poland and Ukraine in the summer of 2012.

Career record
Professional club level

ROBBIE KEANE – CLUB APPEARANCES AND GOALS

Season	Club	League Apps	Goals
1997-98	Wolves	38	11
1998-99	Wolves	33	11
1999-00	Wolves	2	2
1999-00	Coventry City	31	12
2000-01	Inter Milan	6	0
2000-01	Leeds United	18	9
2001-02	Leeds United	25	3
2002-03	Leeds United	3	1
2002-03	Tottenham Hotspur	29	13
2003-04	Tottenham Hotspur	34	14
2004-05	Tottenham Hotspur	35	11
2005-06	Tottenham Hotspur	36	16
2006-07	Tottenham Hotspur	27	11
2007-08	Tottenham Hotspur	36	15
2008-09	Liverpool	19	5
2008-09	Tottenham Hotspur	14	5
2009-10	Tottenham Hotspur	20	6
2009-10	Celtic	16	12
2010-11	Tottenham Hotspur	7	0
2010-11	West Ham United	9	2
2011	Los Angeles Galaxy	8	3
2011-12	Aston Villa	6	3
2012	Los Angeles Galaxy	8	3
CAREER TOTALS		**460**	**168**

HAT-TRICKS

(4) Tottenham v Burnley	Prem League	26/9/09
(3) Tottenham v Leicester City	League Cup	9/10/01
(3) Tottenham v Everton	Prem League	12/1/03
(3) Tottenham v Wolves	Prem League	6/12/03
(3) Celtic v Kilmarnock	Scottish Cup	13/3/10

FA Cup		League Cup		Eur./Conc.		Total	
Apps	Goals	Apps	Goals	Apps	Goals	Apps	Goals
3	0	4	0	0	0	45	11
2	2	4	3	0	0	39	16
0	0	1	0	0	0	3	2
3	0	0	0	0	0	34	12
3	2	0	0	5	1	14	3
2	0	0	0	0	0	20	9
0	0	2	3	6	3	33	9
0	0	0	0	0	0	3	1
1	0	2	0	0	0	32	13
3	1	4	1	0	0	41	16
6	3	4	3	0	0	45	17
1	0	1	0	0	0	38	16
5	5	3	1	9	5	44	22
3	2	5	2	10	4	54	23
1	0	1	0	7	2	28	7
0	0	0	0	0	0	14	5
1	1	3	2	0	0	24	9
3	4	0	0	0	0	19	16
0	0	1	1	5	0	13	1
1	0	0	0	0	0	10	2
0	0	0	0	3	1	11	4
1	0	0	0	0	0	7	3
0	0	0	0	2	0	10	3
39	**20**	**35**	**16**	**47**	**16**	**581**	**220**

RED CARDS

v Bolton Wanderers	Premier League	25/2/07
v Birmingham City	Premier League	2/12/07

(Robbie scored two goals in each of those matches)

LEADING ALL-TIME PREMIER LEAGUE GOALSCORERS

Pos	Player	Goals
1	Alan Shearer	260
2	Andy Cole	189
3	Thierry Henry	176
4	Robbie Fowler	163
5	Frank Lampard	150
T6	Les Ferdinand	149
T6	Michael Owen	149
8	Teddy Sheringham	147
9	Wayne Rooney	143
10	Jimmy-Floyd Hasselbaink	128
11	*Robbie Keane*	126

(He is 15 goals ahead of the next highest current players, Jermaine Defoe and Emile Heskey. Only 22 players have scored at least 100 Premier League goals).

LEADING ALL-TIME TOTTENHAM HOTSPUR GOALSCORERS

Pos	Player	Goals
1	Jimmy Greaves	266
2	Bobby Smith	208
3	Martin Chivers	174
4	Cliff Jones	159
5	George Hunt	138
6	Len Duquemin	134
7	Alan Gilzean	133
8	Teddy Sheringham	124
9	*Robbie Keane*	122
10	Jermaine Defoe	116

Career record
Senior international

Cap	Opponent	Date	Status
1 (sub)	Czech Republic	25/03/98	Friendly
2	Argentina	22/04/98	Friendly
3	Mexico	23/05/98	Friendly
4	Croatia	05/09/98	ECQ
5	Malta	14/10/98	ECQ
6	Paraguay	10/02/99	Friendly
7 (sub)	Sweden	28/04/99	Friendly
8	Northern Ireland	29/05/99	Friendly
9	Macedonia	09/06/99	ECQ
10	Yugoslavia	01/09/99	ECQ
11	Malta	08/09/99	ECQ
12	Macedonia	09/10/99	ECQ
13	Turkey	13/11/99	ECQP
14	Czech Republic	23/02/00	Friendly
15	Greece	26/04/00	Friendly
16	Scotland	30/05/00	Friendly
17	Mexico	04/06/00	US Cup
18 (sub)	South Africa	11/06/00	US Cup
19	Holland	02/09/00	WCQ
20	Portugal	07/10/00	WCQ
21	Estonia	11/10/00	WCQ
22	Finland	15/11/00	Friendly
23	Cyprus	24/03/01	WCQ
24	Andorra	28/03/01	WCQ
25	Portugal	02/06/01	WCQ
26	Croatia	15/08/01	Friendly
27	Holland	01/09/01	WCQ
28	Iran	10/11/01	WCP
29	Iran	15/11/01	WCP
30	Russia	13/02/02	Friendly
31	Denmark	27/03/02	Friendly
32	U.S.A.	17/04/02	Friendly
33	Nigeria	16/05/02	Friendly
34	Cameroon	01/06/02	WCF
35	Germany	05/06/02	WCF

Venue	Result		Goals	Mins.
Olomouc	Lost	1-2		45
Lansdowne Road	Lost	0-2		90
Lansdowne Road	Drew	0-0		90
Lansdowne Road	Won	2-0		62
Lansdowne Road	Won	5-0	2	83
Lansdowne Road	Won	2-0		65
Lansdowne Road	Won	2-0		11
Lansdowne Road	Lost	0-1		56
Lansdowne Road	Won	1-0		67
Lansdowne Road	Won	2-1	1	90
Valletta	Won	3-2	1	90
Skopje	Drew	1-1		64
Lansdowne Road	Drew	1-1	1	90
Lansdowne Road	Won	3-2	1	90 (rep)
Lansdowne Road	Lost	0-1		90
Lansdowne Road	Lost	1-2		90
Chicago	Drew	2-2		45
New Jersey	Won	2-1		45
Amsterdam	Drew	2-2	1	90
Lisbon	Drew	1-1		84
Lansdowne Road	Won	2-0		88
Lansdowne Road	Won	3-0		90 (rep)
Nicosia	Won	4-0		89
Barcelona	Won	3-0		90
Lansdowne Road	Drew	1-1		61
Lansdowne Road	Drew	2-2		52
Lansdowne Road	Drew	1-1		59
Lansdowne Road	Won	2-0	1	90
Tehran	Lost	0-1		76
Lansdowne Road	Won	2-0	1	71
Lansdowne Road	Won	3-0	1	76
Lansdowne Road	Won	2-1		83
Lansdowne Road	Lost	1-2		61
Niigata	Drew	1-1		90
Ibaraki	Drew	1-1	1	90

Cap	Opponent	Date	Status
36	Saudi Arabia	11/06/02	WCF
37	Spain	16/06/02	WCF
38	Finland	21/08/02	Friendly
39	Russia	07/09/02	ECQ
40	Switzerland	16/10/02	ECQ
41	Albania	02/04/03	ECQ
42	Norway	30/04/03	Friendly
43	Albania	07/06/03	ECQ
44	Georgia	11/06/03	ECQ
45	Australia	19/08/03	Friendly
46	Switzerland	11/10/03	ECQ
47	Canada	18/11/03	Friendly
48	Brazil	18/02/04	Friendly
49	Czech Republic	31/03/04	Friendly
50	Romania	27/05/04	Friendly
51	Nigeria	29/05/04	Unity Cup
52	Holland	05/06/04	Friendly
53	Cyprus	04/09/04	WCQ
54	Switzerland	08/09/04	WCQ
55	France	09/10/04	WCQ
56	Faroe Islands	13/10/04	WCQ
57	Croatia	16/11/04	Friendly
58	Portugal	09/02/05	Friendly
59	Israel	26/03/05	WCQ
60	China	29/03/05	Friendly
61	Israel	04/06/05	WCQ
62	France	07/09/05	WCQ
63	Cyprus	08/10/05	WCQ
64	Switzerland	12/10/05	WCQ
65 (capt)	Sweden	01/03/06	Friendly
66 (capt)	Chile	24/05/06	Friendly
67 (capt)	Germany	02/09/06	ECQ
68 (capt)	Cyprus	07/10/06	ECQ
69 (capt)	Czech Republic	11/10/06	ECQ
70 (capt)	San Marino	15/11/06	ECQ

Venue	Result		Goals	Mins.
Yokohama	Won	3-0	1	90
Suwon	Drew	1-1	1 (pen.)	120
Helsinki	Won	3-0	1	84
Moscow	Lost	2-4		90
Lansdowne Road	Lost	1-2		90
Tirana	Drew	0-0		67
Lansdowne Road	Won	1-0		90 (rep)
Lansdowne Road	Won	2-1	1	90
Lansdowne Road	Won	2-0	1	90
Lansdowne Road	Won	2-1		45
Basle	Lost	0-2		90
Lansdowne Road	Won	3-0	2	90
Lansdowne Road	Drew	0-0		90
Lansdowne Road	Won	2-1	1	90
Lansdowne Road	Won	1-0		90
London	Lost	0-3		84
Amsterdam	Won	1-0	1	90
Lansdowne Road	Won	3-0	1	90
Basle	Drew	1-1		90
Paris	Drew	0-0		90
Lansdowne Road	Won	2-0	2 (1 pen.)	90
Lansdowne Road	Won	1-0	1	90 (rep)
Lansdowne Road	Won	1-0		83
Tel Aviv	Drew	1-1		90
Lansdowne Road	Won	1-0		62
Lansdowne Road	Drew	2-2	1	26
Lansdowne Road	Lost	0-1		90
Nicosia	Won	1-0		88
Lansdowne Road	Drew	0-0		68
Lansdowne Road	Won	3-0	1	90
Lansdowne Road	Lost	0-1		90
Stuttgart	Lost	0-1		90
Nicosia	Lost	2-5		90
Lansdowne Road	Drew	1-1		90
Lansdowne Road	Won	5-0	3 (1 pen.)	90

Cap	Opponent	Date	Status
71 (capt)	San Marino	07/02/07	ECQ
72 (capt)	Wales	24/03/07	ECQ
73 (capt)	Denmark	22/08/07	Friendly
74 (capt)	Slovakia	08/09/07	ECQ
75 (capt)	Czech Republic	12/09/07	ECQ
76 (capt)	Germany	13/10/07	ECQ
77 (capt)	Cyprus	17/10/07	ECQ
78 (capt)	Wales	17/11/07	ECQ
79 (capt)	Brazil	06/02/08	Friendly
80 (capt)	Serbia	24/05/08	Friendly
81 (capt)	Colombia	29/05/08	Friendly
82 (capt)	Norway	20/08/08	Friendly
83 (capt)	Georgia	06/09/08	WCQ
84 (capt)	Montenegro	10/09/08	WCQ
85 (capt)	Cyprus	15/10/08	WCQ
86 (capt)	Georgia	11/02/09	WCQ
87 (capt)	Bulgaria	28/03/09	WCQ
88 (capt)	Italy	01/04/09	WCQ
89 (capt)	Nigeria	29/05/09	Friendly
90 (capt)	Bulgaria	06/06/09	WCQ
91 (capt)	Australia	12/08/09	Friendly
92 (capt)	Cyprus	05/09/09	WCQ
93 (capt)	Italy	10/10/09	WCQ
94	Montenegro	14/10/09	WCQ
95 (capt)	France	14/11/09	WCP
96 (capt)	France	18/11/09	WCP
97 (capt)	Brazil	02/03/10	Friendly
98 (capt)	Paraguay	25/05/10	Friendly
99 (capt)	Algeria	28/05/10	Friendly
100 (capt)	Argentina	11/08/10	Friendly
101 (capt)	Armenia	03/09/10	ECQ
102 (capt)	Andorra	07/09/10	ECQ
103 (capt)	Russia	08/10/10	ECQ
104 (capt)	Slovakia	12/10/10	ECQ
105 (capt)	Macedonia	26/03/11	ECQ

Venue	Result		Goals	Mins.
Serravalle	Won	2-1		90
Croke Park	Won	1-0		89
Aarhus	Won	4-0	2	56
Bratislava	Drew	2-2		90
Prague	Lost	0-1		90
Croke Park	Drew	0-0		90
Croke Park	Drew	1-1		90
Cardiff	Drew	2-2	1	90
Croke Park	Lost	0-1		90
Croke Park	Drew	1-1		69
London	Won	1-0	1	90
Oslo	Drew	1-1	1	90
Mainz	Won	2-1		90
Podgorica	Drew	0-0		90
Croke Park	Won	1-0	1	90
Croke Park	Won	2-1	2 (1 pen.)	90
Croke Park	Drew	1-1		90
Bari	Drew	1-1	1	90
London	Drew	1-1	1	45
Sofia	Drew	1-1		74
Thomond Park	Lost	0-3		90
Nicosia	Won	2-1	1	90
Croke Park	Drew	2-2		90
Croke Park	Drew	0-0		90
Croke Park	Lost	0-1		90
Paris	Drew	1-1	1 (pen.)	120
London	Lost	0-2		90
R.D.S.	Won	2-1		63
R.D.S.	Won	3-0	2 (1 pen.)	90
Aviva Stadium	Lost	0-1		90
Yerevan	Won	1-0		83
Aviva Stadium	Won	3-1	1	90
Aviva Stadium	Lost	2-3	1 (pen.)	90
Zilina	Drew	1-1		90
Aviva Stadium	Won	2-1	1	87

Cap	Opponent	Date	Status
106 (capt)	Northern Ireland	24/05/11	Carling Cup
107 (capt)	Scotland	29/05/11	Carling Cup
108 (capt)	Macedonia	04/06/11	ECQ
109 (capt)	Croatia	10/08/11	Friendly
110 (capt)	Slovakia	02/09/11	ECQ
111 (capt)	Russia	06/09/11	ECQ
112 (capt)	Andorra	07/10/11	ECQ
113 (capt)	Estonia	11/11/11	ECQP
114 (capt)	Estonia	15/11/11	ECQP
115 (capt)	Czech Republic	28/02/12	Friendly

ANALYSIS OF CAPS

1-9	Wolves	9 caps
10-18	Coventry City	9 caps
19-22	Inter Milan	4 caps
23-38	Leeds United	16 caps
39-81, 86-96 and 100-104	Tottenham Hotspur	59 caps
82-85	Liverpool	4 caps
97-99	Celtic	3 caps
105-108	West Ham United	4 caps
109-115	Los Angeles Galaxy	7 caps

World Cup	34 caps	15 goals
European Championship	35 caps	18 goals
Other Tournaments	5 caps	3 goals
Friendly Matches	41 caps	17 goals
TOTAL	**115 caps**	**53 goals**

Venue	Result		Goals	Mins.
Aviva Stadium	Won	5-0	2 (1 pen.)	62
Aviva Stadium	Won	1-0	1	83
Skopje	Won	2-0	2	90
Aviva Stadium	Drew	0-0		90
Aviva Stadium	Drew	0-0		90
Moscow	Drew	0-0		90
Andorra la Velle	Won	2-0		90
Tallinn	Won	4-0	2 (1 pen.)	90
Aviva Stadium	Drew	1-1		67
Aviva Stadium	Drew	1-1		71

MOST CAPS FOR REPUBLIC OF IRELAND

Pos	Player	Caps
1	Shay Given	121
2	*Robbie Keane*	115
3	Kevin Kilbane	110
4	Steve Staunton	102
5	Damien Duff	95
6	Niall Quinn	91
7	Tony Cascarino	88
8	Paul McGrath	83
9	Packie Bonner	80
10	John O'Shea	75

MOST GOALS SCORED FOR REPUBLIC OF IRELAND

Pos	Player	Goals
1	*Robbie Keane*	53
2	Niall Quinn	21
3	Frank Stapleton	20
T4	John Aldridge	19
T4	Tony Cascarino	19
T4	Don Givens	19
7	Noel Cantwell	14
8	Gerry Daly	13
9	Jimmy Dunne	12
10	Ian Harte	11
11	Kevin Doyle	10

LIST OF EUROPEAN PLAYERS WHO HAVE SCORED AT LEAST 50 INTERNATIONAL GOALS

Pos	Player	Country	Goals
1	Ferenc Puskas	Hungary	84
2	Sandor Kocsis	Hungary	75
3	Gerd Muller	West Germany	68
4	Miroslav Klose	Germany	63
5	Imre Schlosser	Hungary	59
T6	Jan Koller	Czech Republic	55
T6	Joachim Streich	East Germany	55
8	*Robbie Keane*	Republic of Ireland	53
T9	Poul Nielsen	Denmark	52
T9	Jon Dahl Tomasson	Denmark	52
T11	Thierry Henry	France	51
T11	Hakan Sukur	Turkey	51
T11	Lajos Tichy	Hungary	51
T11	David Villa	Spain	51